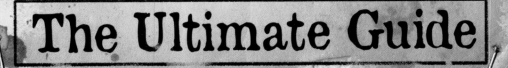

The Ultimate Guide

Five Nights at Freddy's™

UNDER OFFICIAL INQUIRY

THE OFFICIAL, ULTIMATE GUIDE TO THE BESTSELLING VIDEO GAME SERIES.

T0021156

Photo credits: Photos ©: 4 torn paper and throughout: nevermoregraphix/
DeviantArt; 10 graph paper and throughout: rawen713/DeviantArt; 25
bottom: picsfive/Fotolia; 92 bottom left: Marco Govel/Shutterstock;
92 bottom right: Billion Photos/Shutterstock; 144 map: Courtesy Utah
Department of Transportation; 149 wiring diagram: Wire_man/Fotolia; 149
bottom: samiramay/Fotolia; 158 top: Africa Studio/Fotolia; 158 screws:
Andrii Ridnyi/Dreamstime; 159 bottom left: beerlogoff/Fotolia; 159 bottom
right: Africa Studio/Fotolia.

ISBN 978-1-338-76768-1

10 9 8 7 6 5 4   22 23 24 25

Printed in the U.S.A.   40

First printing 2021

Book design by Cheung Tai

Table of Contents

Chapter 1: *Five Nights at Freddy's*. 4

Chapter 2: *Five Nights at Freddy's 2* 14

Chapter 3: *Five Nights at Freddy's 3* 28

Chapter 4: *Five Nights at Freddy's 4* 44

Chapter 5: *Sister Location*. 56

Chapter 6: *Freddy Fazbear's Pizzeria Simulator*. . 72

Chapter 7: *Ultimate Custom Night* 94

Chapter 8: *Help Wanted*. 114

Chapter 9: *The Curse of Dreadbear*. 144

Chapter 10: *Special Delivery*. 164

Chapter 11: The Books. 178

Chapter 12: Fazbear Frights 190

Chapter 13: Fazbear Entertainment Archives. . 228

Chapter 14: Animatronics Inventory 262

Chapter 1

FIVE NIGHTS AT FREDDY'S

It's the game that launched a million screams.

Five Nights at Freddy's (FNAF) is a point-and-click horror survival game that was founded on a simple enough premise: Last one week working as a night guard in a pizzeria populated by homicidal animatronics. But what evolved from this concept quickly consumed gamers the world over.

Fast-forward a bit and (thanks in part to FNAF's startling jump scares) hilarious/terrifying Let's Plays dominated video-sharing sites, fueling the public's curiosity and resulting in billions of views. Still, gamers soon realized there was more to FNAF than just deadly animatronics.

Lurking in the darkened corners of Freddy Fazbear's Pizza are the threads of a disturbing mystery. This mystery—hidden throughout the game in posters that change, hallucinations, and even the mysterious fifth animatronic—has kept fans playing and replaying that first game since it was released in August of 2014.

So, what's all the hype about? We're glad you asked.

The Freddy Scoop

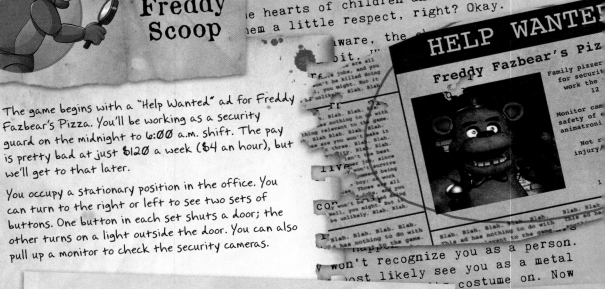

The game begins with a "Help Wanted" ad for Freddy Fazbear's Pizza. You'll be working as a security guard on the midnight to 6:00 a.m. shift. The pay is pretty bad at just $120 a week ($4 an hour), but we'll get to that later.

You occupy a stationary position in the office. You can turn to the right or left to see two sets of buttons. One button in each set shuts a door; the other turns on a light outside the door. You can also pull up a monitor to check the security cameras.

Once you land in the office, the phone starts ringing.

THINGS WE LEARN FROM PHONE GUY

1. Phone Guy apparently worked in the same office, but he's on his last week. If you die (dun dun duuuuuuun!), "a missing persons report will be filed within ninety days—or as soon as property and premises have been thoroughly cleaned and bleached and the carpets have been replaced." Yep. That sounds like a completely normal thing to say.

2. "If I were forced to sing those same stupid songs for twenty years, and I never got a bath . . ." Why haven't these animatronics been cleaned? Wait—how does one clean an animatronic?

3. The animatronics' servos lock up if they get turned off for too long. The animatronics used to be allowed to walk around during the day, but that was before "The Bite of '87." Apparently someone had a daytime run-in with an animatronic and lost his or her frontal lobe, but survived.

4. Since the animatronics will see you as a metal endoskeleton without its costume on✱ they'll try to stuff you into a Freddy Fazbear suit. Yikes. So let's avoid that death.

5. You should only close the doors "if absolutely necessary." As Phone Guy says, "Gotta conserve power."

✱ Phone Guy's endoskeleton explanation doesn't add up. Bonnie often enters the Backstage, sees the costume-less endoskeleton sitting on the table, and never tries to stuff a costume on it.

Gameplay and Strategy

Without using the doors or lights or checking the cameras, power depletes by about 1 percent every 10 seconds. The in-game clock takes 86 to 90 seconds to pass one "hour," which means you'll lose roughly 9 percent power every hour even if you do nothing.

Using one of your actions—checking the cameras, closing the doors, turning on the lights—adds one bar each to the power indicator, up to four. One action (doesn't matter what it is) drains about 1 percent every 5 seconds, using two actions drains 1 percent every 3 seconds, and using three actions drains 1 percent every 2.5 seconds. To keep this straight, we made you a handy-dandy table.

YOU CAN MAKE FIVE POWER BARS APPEAR BY CLOSING BOTH DOORS, TURNING ON A LIGHT, AND FLIPPING OPEN THE SECURITY CAMERAS QUICKLY. BUT THE FIFTH BAR ONLY APPEARS FOR A SECOND, SINCE YOU CAN'T HAVE THE LIGHT ON AND SECURITY CAMERAS OPEN AT THE SAME TIME.

BWANANANANANANA
MATH MAN!

Number of power bars	Average time it takes to drain 1%	Power drained per hour
1	9.6 seconds	9%
2	4.8 seconds	18%
3	3.2 seconds	27%
4	2.4 seconds	36%

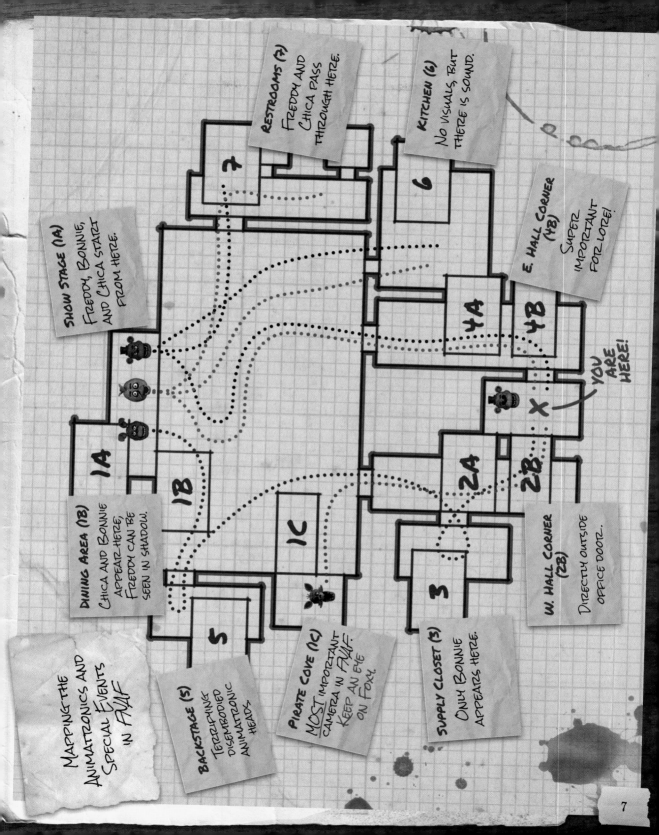

RESTROOMS (7)
FREDDY AND CHICA PASS THROUGH HERE.

KITCHEN (6)
NO VISUALS, BUT THERE IS SOUND.

E. HALL CORNER (4B)
SUPER IMPORTANT FOR LORE!

SHOW STAGE (1A)
FREDDY, BONNIE, AND CHICA START FROM HERE.

YOU ARE HERE!

DINING AREA (1B)
CHICA AND BONNIE APPEAR HERE; FREDDY CAN BE SEEN IN SHADOW.

W. HALL CORNER (2B)
DIRECTLY OUTSIDE OFFICE DOOR.

MAPPING THE ANIMATRONICS AND SPECIAL EVENTS IN FNAF

BACKSTAGE (5)
TERRIFYING DISEMBODIED ANIMATRONIC HEADS.

PIRATE COVE (1C)
MOST IMPORTANT CAMERA IN FNAF. KEEP AN EYE ON FOXY.

SUPPLY CLOSET (3)
ONLY BONNIE APPEARS HERE.

7

ANIMATRONICS:

♦ **BONNIE** is usually the first animatronic to move, and he moves much faster than Freddy or Chica, disabling the most cameras, too. Bonnie is the only character who appears in Backstage, Supply Closet, and West Hall Corner.

♦ **CHICA** sticks to the right (east) side of the restaurant. Chica and Freddy are the only animatronics who enter the Kitchen. You can't see them, but you can hear the clanging of pots and pans. Chica's cupcake disappears when she leaves the Show Stage, although a duplicate cupcake can be seen sitting on your desk in the office.

> BONNIE AND CHICA WILL MAKE A RASPY GROANING NOISE IF THEY ENTER THE OFFICE WHEN THE MONITOR IS OPEN.

♦ **FOXY** starts at Pirate Cove, behind the curtain. As the night goes on, he peeks out more until he is entirely revealed. The next time you check the monitor, he's gone. He'll attack from the left in a matter of seconds unless you close the door in time. After an unsuccessful attack, Foxy returns to Pirate Cove to begin the cycle again. Every time he's blocked by the door, he drains the player's power: 1 percent the first time, then an additional 5 percent every time thereafter.

♦ **FREDDY** sticks to the shadows and can be hard to spot on the monitor, so look for his glowing silver eyes. Watching Freddy on the cameras will slow his movements. Freddy doesn't move until Night 3, unless you run out of power.

Codes, Glitches, and Secrets

♦ Hold down C, D, and + to skip a night.

♦ Click on the poster in the office to honk Freddy's nose.

♦ Try changing the date on your computer to October 31 and booting up the game.

GOING ON A BEAR HUNT

In the West Hall Corner (camera 2B) is a poster of Freddy, which has a very small chance of changing. The poster becomes a close-up of Freddy's face, but his fur is golden, and there aren't any eyes in the mask. Once the poster changes, drop the monitor and an empty animatronic suit, "Golden Freddy," will appear in the office, alongside flashes of IT'S ME. Seeing him will cause the game to crash, but you can avoid this by bringing up the monitor again quickly.

You can also trigger Golden Freddy by inputting 1/9/8/7 on the custom night. You won't see the scene of the empty animatronic suit in the office, though.

♦ **SHOW STAGE (1A):** This secret screen can only be found in the game files.

♦ **W. HALL CORNER (2B):** Poster changes to an image of Freddy ripping his head apart.

♦ **BACKSTAGE (5):** All the parts in Backstage turn toward the camera, including the endoskeleton.

Lore and Theories

LOCAL NEWS

Local pizzeria said to close by year's end.

After a long struggle to stay in business after the tragedy that took place there many years ago, Freddy Fazbear's Pizza has announced that it will close by year's end.
Despite a year-long search for a buyer, companies seem unwilling to be associated with the company.
"These characters will live on. In the hearts of kids- these characters will live on." - CEO

FAN THEORIES: THE MISSING CHILDREN

If you really want to dig into the story of the game, keep an eye on the E. Hall Corner, where the Rules for Safety will change to a series of newspaper clippings that reveal the horrific secrets lurking at the heart of the game:

♦ Kids Vanish at Local Pizzeria—Bodies Not Found

♦ Five Children Now Reported Missing. Suspect Convicted.

♦ Local Pizzeria Threatened with Shutdown over Sanitation.

♦ Local Pizzeria Said to Close by Year's End.

allowed to
ut then there
I-It's amazing that the human
without the frontal lobe,

ing your safety, the only
ou as a night watchman here,
th fact that these characters,
pen to see you after hours
n't recognize you as a person.
likely see you as a metal
without its costume on. Now
ainst the rules here at
ar's Pizza, they'll probably
lly stuff you inside
bear suit. Um, now, that
ad if the suits themselves
with crossbeams, wires, and
ices, especially around the
you could imagine how
head forcefully pressed inside

MISSING CHILDREN

Kids vanish at local pizzeria – bodies not found

Two local children were reportedly lured into a back room during the late hours of operation at Freddy Fazbear's Pizza on the night of June 26th. While video surveillance identified the man responsible, the children themselves were never found and are presumed dead. Police think that the suspect dressed as a company mascot to earn the children's trust.

LOCAL NEWS

Local pizzeria threatened with shutdown over sanitation.

Local pizzeria Freddy Fazbear's Pizza has been threatened again with shutdown by the health department over reports of foul odor coming from the much-loved animal mascots.
Police were contacted when parents reportedly noticed what appeared to be blood and mucus around the eyes and mouths of the mascots. One parent likened them to "reanimated carcasses."

Five children were apparently lured to a back room by someone who wore a mascot costume to gain the kids' trust. A suspect was arrested and charged, but the bodies of the children were never found and they were presumed dead. Shortly thereafter, customers complained of odors and reported seeing blood and mucus around the eyes and mouths of the animatronics, implying that the bodies of the children were stuffed inside Freddy and his friends. This matches Phone Guy's words from Night 1—if you were to be stuffed inside a suit, "the only parts of you that would likely see the light of day again would be your eyeballs and teeth, when they pop out the front of the mask."

One thing seems certain—the animatronics themselves have been possessed by the spirits of the dead children, looking for revenge.

ANOTHER RARE SCREEN IN E. HALL (4A) SHOWS THE POSTERS REPLACED WITH IMAGES OF CRYING CHILDREN.

ONE TRAGEDY OF MANY?

In the years since the original game, it's been established that the Freddy Fazbear's Pizza where *FNAF* takes place is just one of many franchise locations, and its horrific murders were far from an outlier. Fans have instead directed their efforts toward identifying why this location was special, and when its murders may have occurred in the timeline.

MISSING CHILDREN

Five children now reported missing. Suspect convicted.

Five children are now linked to the incident at Freddy Fazbear's Pizza, where a man dressed as a cartoon mascot lured them into a back room. While the suspect has been charged, the bodies themselves were never found. Freddy Fazbear's Pizza has been fighting an uphill battle ever since to convince families to return to the pizzeria. "It's a tragedy."

FAN THEORIES: LINGERING QUESTIONS

THE BITE OF '87

Phone Guy mentioned "The Bite of '87," in which someone was attacked by an animatronic and lost their frontal lobe. This event is why the animatronics' movements are restricted during the day. But questions still remain around which animatronic committed the bite, whether an employee or a child was bitten, and what connection (if any) this bite has to the events of *FNAF4*.

WHY IS FOXY OUT OF ORDER?

FNAF is the first time we meet Foxy, and while Pirate Cove may be "Out of Order," it's clear that Foxy, well, *isn't*. Other games and stories depict Foxy in various states of repair or disrepair for fans to speculate over. Some point to *Help Wanted*, where you ultimately repair him—while dodging his sharp hook and jerky movements—as evidence that Foxy is definitely unsafe for kids. Still others look to the *Foxy Go! Go! Go!* mini game in *FNAF2* (see page 23). Was an OUT OF ORDER sign and a functional animatronic the perfect way to lure kids to an isolated area? Or was Foxy decommissioned because, per the gameplay around Withered Foxy in *FNAF2*, he isn't fooled by a person in an animatronic suit?

IT'S ME

Another mystery that's kept the fandom talking. In *FNAF* it appears in various hallucinations on the Pirate's Cove OUT OF ORDER sign, the East Hall walls, with Golden Freddy's appearance, and in-game flashes as early as Night 1. To make it even more confusing, it seems to be used by different characters . . .

♦ Teaser images for *FNAF4* ask, "Was it me?" implying that the phrase could be tied to one of the animatronic bites.

♦ *The Curse of Dreadbear* features an Easter egg that turns the whole prize screen purple, complete with a banner that says, "IT'S ME," alluding to William Afton.

♦ In *The Silver Eyes* novel, "IT'S ME" is connected to the souls of the missing children inside the animatronics, when the ghost of Michael tells Carlton it is him inside the animatronic.

IT'S ME

Power left: 66%
Usage:

IT'S ME

MIKE SCHMIDT

When you receive your paycheck at the close of Night 5, you'll learn that your name is Mike Schmidt. Many have speculated that Mike isn't just some security guard off the street. In *FNAF*, playing through to Night 7 gets Mike fired for tampering with the animatronics' AI (referring to custom night), which could imply that Mike has knowledge of the animatronics. Fans have also pointed out that he shares a first name with Mike from *FNAF4* (who seems to be "Michael Afton"), and "Mike," the owner of the Survival Logbook.

	0123
	DATE 11-13-XX
PAY TO THE ORDER OF Mike Schmidt	$ 120.50
One Hundred twenty dollars and 50/100	DOLLARS
MEMO employee of the month	Fazbear Entertainment
⑆000045678000 0000⑈ ⑆0000	

Chapter 2

FIVE NIGHTS AT FREDDY'S 2

The terror continues in *Five Nights at Freddy's 2* (*FNAF2*), a game that pushed many players to the limit in terms of . . . multitasking? Yes, there is a *lot* here to manage, and that's putting it mildly. Eleven animatronics roam the floor, looking to kill you or crash your game if you stare at them long enough—not to mention the other four animatronics that are apparently just there to populate your nightmares. Plus there's a frighteningly long list of to-dos: Keep the music box wound, keep the vents clear, strobe that flashlight in Foxy's direction . . . More animatronics now have a set of unique instructions (similar to Foxy from *FNAF*), so there are plenty of details to juggle.

Also new to *FNAF2* are the "death mini games" that are triggered with jump scares. Each mini game has a creepiness factor off the charts and has spawned a flurry of theories about the rapidly expanding mystery at the heart of Freddy Fazbear's Pizza.

The game is also chock-full of new revelations from Phone Guy, like the two additional Freddy's locations, one of which he calls "Fredbear's Family Diner," the seeming origins of the franchise. But we're getting ahead of ourselves. Let's start with Night 1.

HELP WANTED

Grand Re-Opening!!!

Vintage pizzeria
given new life!

Come be a part of the
new face of Freddy
Fazbear's Pizza!

What could go wrong?

$100.50 a week!
To apply call:
1-555-FAZ-FAZBEAR

WE MEET AGAIN . . . PHONE GUY

Sounds like Phone Guy is still alive, so this game likely takes place before the events of the last one. That, or Phone Guy is immortal. Once again, you're working as a security guard on the midnight to 6:00 a.m. shift for Freddy Fazbear's Pizza, but the layout of the place is completely different. . . and there are no doors. Because why would a security office need doors?

Uh, hello? Hello,
welcome to your n
and improved Fred
I'm here to talk
things you can e
first week here
down this new an

Uh, now, I want
may have heard
know. Uh, some
negative impres
that old restau
for quite a wh
you, Fazbear E
to family fun
They've spent
new animatron
advanced mobil
walk around d
neat? -clears
they're all t
database, so
mile away. H
to guard you.

Uh, now that being said, no m

HERE'S WHAT PHONE GUY REVEALS:

1. Something very bad happened at the "old location," so Fazbear Entertainment spent a lot of money on their new animatronics, including facial recognition systems that interface with criminal databases.

2. The animatronics weren't programmed with a proper "night mode," so they wander around looking for people. As a temporary solution, a music box has been placed in the Prize Corner. Its music should keep *one* of the animatronics at bay.

3. You've been supplied with an empty Freddy Fazbear head to wear as a mask. When you wear it, any animatronic that comes into the office will see you, think you're one of them, and wander back out again.

4. This Freddy head won't work on Foxy, unfortunately, but shining your flashlight on him should make him go away.

5. The building lights will never run out of power, but the flashlight will.

6. Old animatronics are sitting creepily in the back room, but they're now used for spare parts. (These *look* like the animatronics from *FNAF*, but they're not exactly the same. Check the animatronics inventory for specifics.)

As we've come to expect from *FNAF*, things tend to unravel quickly. On Night 4, we learn the restaurant is being investigated and may need to close temporarily, as someone seems to have tampered with the animatronics' facial recognition systems. On Night 5, the restaurant is put on lockdown, with no one allowed in or out— especially prior employees.

END-OF-NIGHT HALLUCINATIONS

When you first boot up the game, as well as at the end of Nights 2, 3, and 4, you'll experience a nightmare. In it, you're wearing the Freddy Fazbear head and can only see a peek of what looks like the empty dining area from *FNAF*.

The first time, you'll see Bonnie and Chica on either side of you and hear unseen children laughing. The game will then crash, and code saying "err" will appear in the upper left corner of the screen. Night 2 features a repeat of this nightmare, but now Bonnie and Chica are looking at you. On Night 3, Bonnie and Chica appear angrier than before, and Golden Freddy stands right in front of you. The fourth and final time, Golden Freddy has disappeared, but Bonnie and Chica remain. The Puppet blocks your view no matter which way you look.

When the game crashes on Nights 2 through 4, a different code appears in the upper left corner of the screen: "it's me."

NIGHT 6

After completing Night 5, Jeremy Fitzgerald (you) receives a paycheck for $100.50. This amount probably would have felt more significant in 1987. In any case, making it this far brings up a menu option for a sixth night. Phone Guy will tell you that the restaurant is being closed down after one final event scheduled for tomorrow—a birthday party.

Your reward for making it through an extra night? An overtime paycheck for a measly $20.10.

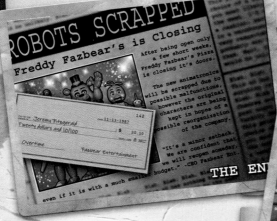

CUSTOM NIGHT

As in the first game, surviving the first six nights unlocks a custom night that allows you to change the AI settings of each animatronic. New this time around is a series of ten pre-set difficulties. For nine of them, beating the night unlocks a collectible toy for the office desk; beating the 10/20 mode, or "Golden Freddy" challenge, earns you a star.

So, aside from some desk swag, what reward do you get for surviving a custom night? Nothing more than a termination notice, made out to—who the heck is Fritz Smith? Looks like Jeremy *did* get switched over to the day shift after Night 6.

Interestingly, they fire Fritz for the same reasons they fire Mike from *FNAF*: "Odor" and "Tampering with animatronics."

Character AI Settings

Game Mode		Freddy	Bonnie	Chica	Foxy	BB	Toy Freddy	Toy Bonnie	Toy Chica	Mangle	Golden Freddy
	20/20/20/20	20	20	20	20	0	0	0	0	0	0
	New & Shiny	0	0	0	0	10	10	10	10	10	0
	Double Trouble	0	20	0	5	0	0	20	0	0	0
	Night of Misfits	0	0	0	0	20	0	0	0	20	10
	Foxy Foxy	0	0	0	20	0	0	0	0	20	10
	Ladies Night	0	0	20	0	0	0	0	20	20	0
	Freddy's Circus	20	0	0	10	10	20	0	0	0	0
	Cupcake Challenge	5	5	5	5	5	5	5	5	5	10
	Fazbear Fever	10	10	10	10	10	10	10	10	10	10
	Golden Freddy	20	20	20	20	20	20	20	20	20	20

Gameplay and Strategy

ANIMATRONICS

♦ Once **BALLOON BOY** starts moving, he'll call out "Hello?" and "Hi!" or giggle. The fourth time you hear him, expect Balloon Boy in the Left Vent. If he enters the office, he'll disable the flashlight and vent lights. Don the Freddy head to get rid of him.

♦ **THE PUPPET** (aka the Marionette) is in the gift box in the Prize Corner (11). If the music runs out, you can still wind the music box so long as the Puppet still appears in the camera shot. If he's gone, you're toast.

♦ **MANGLE** can appear in the Office Hallway, but he won't enter from here. When Mangle is in the Right Vent, don the Freddy head. You'll hear static as she approaches. If he gets in the office, she'll stay until ending your game. Mangle is extremely active! He leaves Kid's Cove right at midnight on Night 2.

♦ **TOY BONNIE** is usually among the first animatronics to move, while **TOY FREDDY** is among the least active. All the toy animatronics including **TOY CHICA** are less active on later nights. Wearing the Freddy head will keep them out of the office.

♦ **WITHERED BONNIE** can enter from the Office Hallway or Left Vent, and he cannot be seen in the Left Vent blind spot. Very active starting Night 3.

♦ **WITHERED CHICA** cannot be seen in the Right Vent's blind spot. She'll move directly from the Right Vent (6) to the office.

♦ **WITHERED FOXY** can be scared off with the flashlight. The Freddy head has no effect on him.

♦ **WITHERED FREDDY** starts moving on Night 2. He's more active on Night 3.

SECRET ANIMATRONICS

GOLDEN FREDDY

Unlike *FNAF*, nothing specific triggers Golden Freddy. He is active on Night 6 and in the custom night—randomly appearing in the Office Hallway as a ghostly head, or in the Office itself as a crumpled animatronic suit. Quickly equip the Freddy mask to prevent Golden Freddy's attack.

RWQFSFASXC AND SHADOW FREDDY

A shadow version of Freddy occasionally appears in the Parts/Service Room. An animatronic known as RWQFSFASXC, or Shadow Bonnie, can occasionally be seen standing on the left side of the office. Looking at RWQFSFASXC for too long will cause your game to crash.

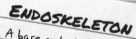

ENDOSKELETON

A bare endoskeleton can be seen in the Prize Corner and Left Vent, though it never attacks the player. There are some interesting fan theories about which animatronic this endoskeleton belongs to.

JJ

An animatronic like Balloon Boy (but with pink eyes) is sometimes staring at you from under your desk. JJ doesn't appear elsewhere in the game and cannot kill you.

MAPPING PATHS OF THE WITHERED ANIMATRONICS

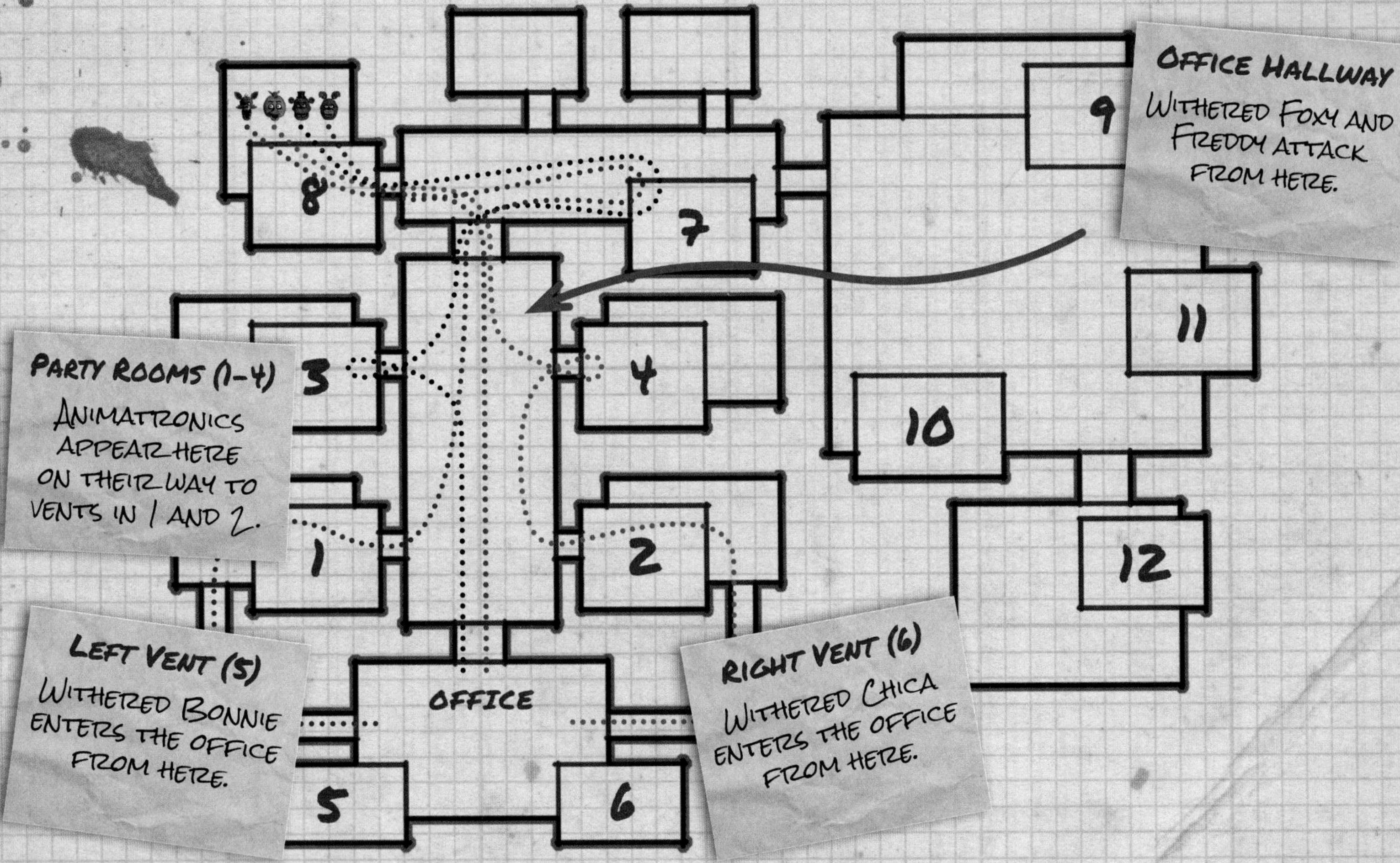

OFFICE HALLWAY
Withered Foxy and Freddy attack from here.

RIGHT VENT (6)
Withered Chica enters the office from here.

PARTY ROOMS (1-4)
Animatronics appear here on their way to vents 1 and 2.

LEFT VENT (5)
Withered Bonnie enters the office from here.

OFFICE

11

12

10

9

7

4

2

8

3

1

6

5

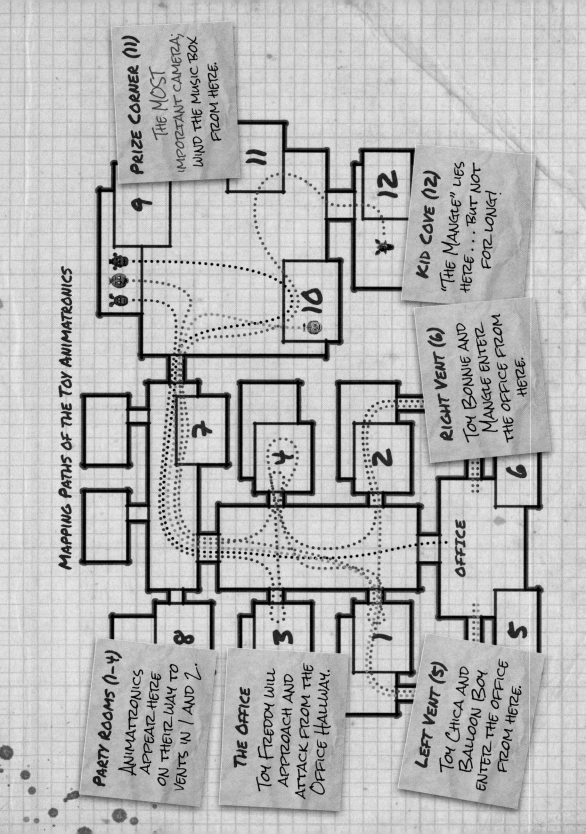

MAPPING PATHS OF THE TOY ANIMATRONICS

PRIZE CORNER (11)
THE MOST
IMPORTANT CAMERA;
WIND THE MUSIC BOX
FROM HERE.

KID COVE (12)
"THE MANGLE" LIES
HERE ... BUT NOT
FOR LONG!

RIGHT VENT (6)
TOY BONNIE AND
MANGLE ENTER
THE OFFICE FROM
HERE.

PARTY ROOMS (1-4)
ANIMATRONICS
APPEAR HERE
ON THEIR WAY TO
VENTS IN 1 AND 2.

THE OFFICE
TOY FREDDY WILL
APPROACH AND
ATTACK FROM THE
OFFICE HALLWAY.

LEFT VENT (5)
TOY CHICA AND
BALLOON BOY
ENTER THE OFFICE
FROM HERE.

OFFICE

Codes, Glitches, and Secrets

RCADE

FNAF·2 RETRO ARCADE

Death Mini game: SAVETHEM

Dying in *FNAF2* might trigger one of several mini games rendered in 8-bit graphics. These are perhaps the most talked-about element of the game because they're so different from anything we've seen before. The first mini game is known as SAVETHEM (the phrase spelled by the letters you will hear being called out). Using the keyboard for movement (W=up, A=left, S=down, D=right), you, as Freddy, follow the Puppet through a map of the restaurant until reaching the Prize Corner. You'll pass slumped-over children and pools of blood along the way.

On rare occasions, "Purple Guy" will end the mini game early. If Purple Guy appears, a scrap of code will appear in the lower left corner following the game crash: "you can't."

ALMOST EVERYTHING ABOUT THIS GAME IS DIFFERENT, BUT ONE THING STAYED THE SAME: CLICK ON THE POSTER IN THE OFFICE TO HONK FREDDY'S NOSE.

FNAF·2 RETRO ARCADE

Death Mini game: Take Cake to the Children

This post-death mini game has Freddy taking cake to six children (with another child visible outside the room). Walking into the room changes the kids' color to green—if you turn them all green at once, you lose control of Freddy. Neglecting the kids changes their color to red. Midway through the game, a car pulls up outside. The aforementioned Purple Guy exits and kills the crying child, who turns gray. The letters being called out are "S-A-V-E-H-I-M"... but you can't. In fact, you move slower and slower until all of the children turn red. The mini game ends with a jump scare courtesy of the Puppet.

It's important to note that Freddy looks slightly different in this mini game than he does in SAVETHEM. The mini game map here is also the smallest. These discrepancies have an important bearing on some fan theories.

Death Mini game: Foxy Go! Go! Go!

Here you'll play as Foxy. Leaving the previous room, you enter a room full of children as party poppers go off. When the last one goes off, you're returned to the starting position and must make your way to the kids once again. And then again. But the last time you do, Purple Guy is visible in the lower left corner of the room. He's smiling. In the next room, the children are dead. This post-death mini game ends with a Foxy jump scare.

RARE SCREEN:
THE LEFT PAPER-PLATE MAN IN PARTY ROOM 4 WILL DISAPPEAR AND REAPPEAR ON THE WALL IN THE OFFICE.

E LIFE

pet. Per the apparently om, you're

Death Mini game: Give Gifts, Give Life

In this post-death mini game, you play as the Puppet. Per the on-screen instructions, you need to give gifts to four apparently dead children. Returning to the center of the room, you're told to "Give Life." As you approach each child, the head of an animatronic appears over the child's head. Once again, letters are being called out: "H-E-L-P-T-H-E-M." You're also earning a score for giving the gifts, but the numbers change to a random sequence when the mini game ends with Golden Freddy's jump scare.

Slowing down the playback of the mini game just before the jump scare reveals a fifth child in the center of the room. Golden Freddy's jump scare originates from the child; perhaps implying that the Puppet placed a fifth animatronic head (Golden Freddy's) on this child.

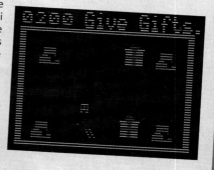

23

Lore and Theories

FAN THEORIES: FREDDY FRANCHISES

Phone Guy tells us on Night I that a previous location was left to rot after something terrible happened there, and then later, on Night 5, we learn there was an original restaurant called "Fredbear's Family Diner," which was apparently franchised out to create the other locations. This was reiterated in *The Silver Eyes* novel, in which Charlie tracked down the old diner, and it was revealed that a single child had gone missing there. *Pizzeria Simulator* picks up that thread with the "HRY223" secret audio file, and the closing sequence of the game.

FAN THEORIES: THE MINI GAMES REVEAL MULTIPLE KILLINGS

A prominent strain of theory maintains that each of the four mini games in *FNAF2* reveals a different set of murders.

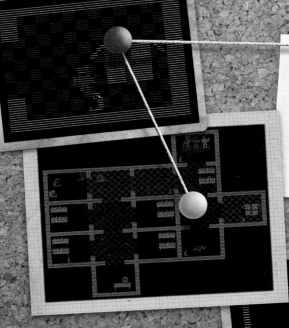

SAVETHEM is believed to be the *FNAF2* restaurant—the mini game map is similar to the camera map. There are five dead children here as well. Purple Guy also looks different; he's now wearing something gold on his chest and holding something in his hand.

FOXY GO! GO! GO! has a completely different map, which now has two rooms (Pirate's Cove and a Party Room). The game reveals that five children are murdered.

Take Cake to the Children

is believed to take place at Fredbear's Family Diner, since the map consists of only one room and a street (denoting a smaller location) and the playable Freddy looks different from the Freddy in SAVETHEM (meaning an older version of Freddy). Theorists assert the game shows Purple Guy's first murder. This seems to be confirmed after *Pizzeria Simulator* showed this child to be the daughter of Cassette Man (Cassette Man is believed to be Henry Emily, the inventor of the animatronics). This child later possessed the Puppet.

Give Gifts, Give Life shows

five dead children as well as the Puppet, but at a seemingly different location (it's one room, but the room's dimensions are different from Take Cake).

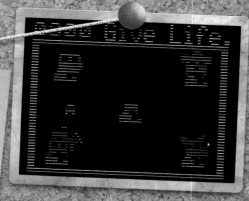

On a final, disturbing note, the models for the dead children are different from game to game, supporting theorists' claims that there could be four unique sets of victims.

Fan Theories: What We Know About the Killer

- He's associated with the color purple. Duh. The real question is, what does the purple coloring mean? This could be part of his uniform, or something else.

- He might be a security guard. In SAVETHEM, Purple Guy has a golden object pinned to his chest. This has led many to believe that he's a security guard and the object is a badge.

- He may know how to work the animatronics. In Night 4, you're instructed not to make eye contact with the animatronics, as "someone may have tampered with their facial recognition systems." All signs point to Purple Guy as the culprit. After all, if he's in the criminal database, he would need to disable their facial recognition to sneak into Freddy's.

- He was likely an employee of Freddy's. Phone Guy on Night 5 warns: "The building is on lockdown, uh, no one is allowed in or out, you know, especially concerning any . . . previous employees." Though it's never explicitly stated, why would Phone Guy give this warning if the wrongdoing wasn't committed by an employee?

♦ He uses a "yellow suit" to kill. On Night 6, Phone Guy tells you that "Someone used one of the suits. We had a spare in the back, a yellow one, someone used it . . . now none of them are acting right." This matches what we know from the newspaper clippings in *FNAF*: "A man dressed as a cartoon mascot [lured the children] into a back room."

♦ So who is he? There are a few theories circulating. Aside from the theory that Purple Guy is just a random security guard at Freddy's operating the day shift, Phone Guy is a suspect for many. People say that the rare Purple Guy kill in SAVETHEM shows Purple Guy holding a phone—a clear link between the two. Others believe Purple Guy could be you—in those end-of-night hallucinations, you're clearly *inside* a mascot costume, just like the killer. Plus maybe those hallucinations of "it's me" are the confessions of a guilty mind: "It's me, I did it. I killed those kids." Yeesh. Talk about a tell-tale heart.

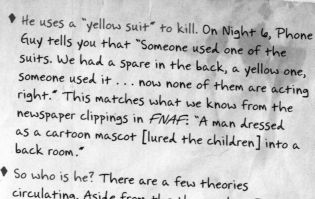

Chapter 3

FIVE NIGHTS AT FREDDY'S 3

If you thought it was impossible for *FNAF* to take a darker turn, allow us to introduce you to *Five Nights at Freddy's 3* (*FNAF3*). Set thirty years after the horrific events that took place at Freddy Fazbear's Pizza (though which *specific* events we're not sure), this game operates on two disturbing levels.

In the present, you're working at a horror attraction built around the mythos of the infamous murders. Only one animatronic is real, but the "phantoms" (read: hallucinations) of other animatronics also appear every now and again to mess with you. A perpetually failing network of ventilation, audio, and cameras adds to the torment, and needs constant attention.

In a series of seven mini games, you're working to gain closure for the souls of the five children who were murdered at the hands of Purple Guy many years ago. The mini games are difficult to access, must be completed in the correct order, and, even after you do successfully complete them, your current night gets reset. It can be a frustrating process, but one that's ultimately satisfying.

The Freddy Scoop

It's the dawn of a new era for *FNAF*, and—since Old Phone Guy is most likely dead—that means a new Phone Guy. New Phone Guy explains that it's been thirty years since the last Freddy Fazbear's Pizza shut down, and a company is trying to capitalize on the restaurant's gruesome past by launching "Fazbear's Fright: The Horror Attraction." The attraction opens next week, so they have to make sure everything works and NOTHING CATCHES ON FIRE. (Always important.) After talking to the original designer of the building, the company finds a boarded-up room inside the restaurant that they're planning to investigate. On Night 2, New Phone Guy reveals they've obtained a real animatronic—Springtrap—which they're using for the attraction. It's loose inside the building, but don't worry . . . it'll find you.

Hey-Hey! Glad you came back for
night! I promise it'll be a lot
interesting this time. We foun
some great new relics over the
And we're out tracking down a
right now. So—uh lemme just
then you can get to wo
tion opens in like
sure everythi

COMING SOON!

Fazbear's
The Horror A

make-
be a part o
really auth
tell you ab
set of draw
head! Whic
then again
cosplay, a
school —

Uh, the
watch f
place
if you
then y
man. K
an eye
somet

nel. Y'k
systems th
trying to
may have o
of this equ
Yeah, I was
tha-that's

THINGS WE LEARN FROM OLD PHONE GUY'S TRAINING CASSETTES

In addition to the Springtrap animatronic, New Phone Guy also found some old training tapes, recorded by—you guessed it—Old Phone Guy!

SPRING LOCK SUITS

♦ At one point, Freddy's had two "spring lock" suits that doubled as animatronics and mascot costumes.

♦ To wear the suits as a costume, you use a handcrank to "recoil and compress the animatronic parts around the sides of the suit." Spring locks must be fastened tight in order to keep the animatronic parts compressed, leaving room for a human occupant. The slightest pressure or moisture can cause the spring locks to trip, releasing the machinery and crushing the person inside the suit.

♦ When the spring lock suits are in animatronic mode, they're pre-set to walk toward any sound they hear.

♦ On Night 4, Old Phone Guy informs you of an incident at the restaurant's "Sister Location" involving multiple spring lock failures, at which point the company deemed the suits unsafe and retired them.

SAFE ROOMS

Also gleaned from Old Phone Guy's audio is the existence of "safe rooms" within each restaurant.

- There is a designated "safe room" in every Freddy's location. This room is not included in the digital map programmed into the animatronics, or in the building's security blueprints. This room is "hidden to customers, invisible to animatronics, and is always off camera," meaning there are no security cameras in these rooms.

- On Night 4, Phone Guy reminds employees, "Under no circumstance should a customer ever be taken into this room and away from the show area."

- On Night 6, it's announced that the room is being sealed, and that employees should never talk to anyone else of its existence. No one is allowed to enter the room to collect their belongings either.

NIGHT END MINI GAMES

At the end of each night, a mini game begins with you in control of an animatronic (Freddy, Bonnie, Chica, Foxy). The goal is to follow Shadow Freddy through the restaurant toward the safe room. After you try to enter the safe room, expect to be dismembered by Purple Guy . . . ending the mini game and the night.

Although you will always need to "die" to continue to the next night, you are still able to wander a short distance. Heading to the left is the Parts/Service Room; among the parts, there appears to be a human skull. If you continue down past the "Pirate Cove" area into a hallway, you'll find hints for unlocking the mini games required to access the "good" ending.

SEE PAGES 36–39 FOR MINI GAME HINTS.

follow me.

follow me.

follow me.

follow me.

NIGHT 5 END MINI GAME

On Night 5, you control a crying child during the post-night mini game. Go toward the safe room as before, and you'll see dismembered animatronics along the way. You're now able to enter the safe room where the animatronics could not go before. Once inside, you'll notice four crying children blocking Purple Guy from leaving the room. Eventually, he dons what appears to be the empty spring lock suit; sure enough, it soon malfunctions and crushes him.

NIGHTMARE MODE!

As with the two prior games, a more difficult night is unlocked after the fifth, called simply (and most appropriately) "Nightmare." On this night, the ventilation system fails a lot more quickly than it normally does, so get ready for a challenge!

If you beat the game's Nightmare mode, regardless of how you played the mini games, you'll see a newspaper informing you that the attraction has burned to the ground due to faulty wiring. But . . . is that Springtrap watching from the background in the article's picture? Maybe this isn't the end of the Freddy's saga after all.

If you play the game straight through, after the Night 5 end mini game, you'll see an image of broken animatronic heads, each with a lit eye. Faded text in the background reads "Bad ending."

THE BLURRED TEXT AROUND THE ARTICLE CONTAINS DEVELOPMENT STORIES FROM GAME CREATOR SCOTT CAWTHON.

IT BURNS!

Fazbear's Fright burns to the ground!

A new local attraction based on an ancient pizzeria chain burned down overnight.

Authorities have not ruled out foul play, but at the moment it seems to have been caused by faulty wiring.

Very little was found at the scene. The few items that were salvaged will be sold at public auction.

REVENGE OF THE MATH

Not counting failure due to a phantom animatronic, you have a certain number of audio uses before the system goes down. Your number of uses changes each night.

	Night 1	Night 2	Night 3	Night 4	Night 5
Audio Uses	unlimited	10	4	3	2

The camera system will go down more rarely than the other systems. This mainly results from overuse. The ventilation system most frequently fails due to phantom animatronics. Similar to the audio, the other two systems fail more frequently as the week progresses.

Note that it takes about five seconds each to restart the cameras, audio, or ventilation. It takes about nine seconds to reboot them all at once. If two or more systems go down, we recommend rebooting everything.

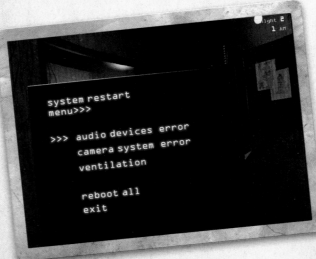

MAPPING THE
ANIMATRONICS AND
SPECIAL EVENTS
IN FNAF3

REMEMBER, SPRINGTRAP CAN
APPEAR ANYWHERE ON THE MAP
AND HAS NO SET PATH.

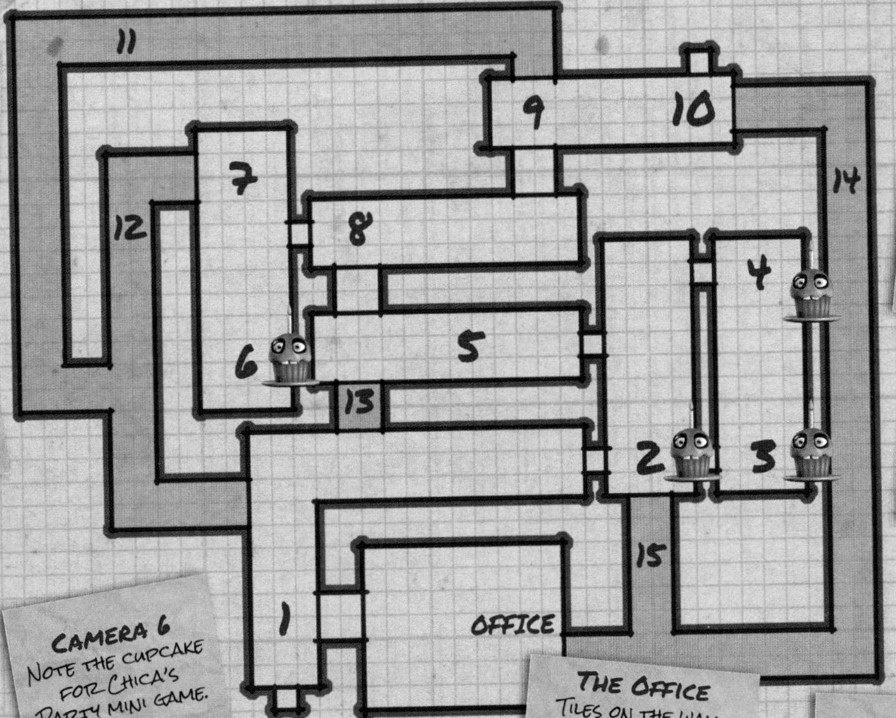

CAMERA 4
PHANTOM MANGLE
APPEARS HERE.

CAMERA 3
CLICK THE PUPPET
POSTER FOR HAPPIEST DAY
MINI GAME.

CAMERA 2
NOTE THE CUPCAKE
FOR CHICA'S
PARTY MINI GAME.

THE OFFICE
TILES ON THE WALL
OPEN (STAGE 01) MINI
GAME, BONNIE'S TOY
ON THE DESK OPENS
THE SHADOW BONNIE
MINI GAME.

VENT
CAMERAS
11-15

CAMERA 8
DOUBLE-CLICK THE
BALLOON BOY
POSTER FOR BB's
AIR ADVENTURE
MINI GAME.

PHANTOM
PUPPET APPEARS
HERE.

CAMERA 7
USE ARCADE
MACHINE TO ACCESS
MANGLE'S QUEST
MINI GAME.

PHANTOM CHICA
APPEARS HERE.

CAMERA 6
NOTE THE CUPCAKE
FOR CHICA'S
PARTY MINI GAME.

14
10
4
2 3
9
5
15
8
13
11
7
6
12
OFFICE
1

SPRINGTRAP

Springtrap is the only real animatronic in this game, and the only one who can kill you. He has no set starting position and can move through every room and the vents.

You can use the audio device to lure Springtrap to adjacent rooms, but it won't work if he's more than one room away. Springtrap only moves to rooms adjacent to his last position or connected to it by an air vent. If Springtrap enters a room with an adjoining vent, it's best to seal it off by double-clicking on that camera.

When Springtrap approaches the office, he'll slink past the window.

PHANTOM ANIMATRONICS

In addition to Springtrap, there are animatronic hallucinations to deal with. All of them will cause systems to malfunction unless you take quick action, and, suspiciously, all the animatronics appear burned.

TRAPPING SPRINGTRAP

It's best to bounce Springtrap between cameras 9 and 10. If he gets closer, use the audio to get Springtrap into the camera 5 room, then close off the vent. You can trap him in there for a while using the audio and keeping the vents closed.

DISABLE VENTILATION

PHANTOM FREDDY

crosses the hallway window before appearing inside the office. Avoid a jump scare by watching the cameras or maintenance panel until he passes.

PHANTOM BALLOON BOY

can appear in any camera except vents.

PHANTOM CHICA

appears on Camera 7 in the arcade machine monitor.

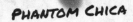

DISABLE CAMERA & VENTILATION

PHANTOM FOXY

randomly appears in the office. Pull up the cameras or maintenance panel to avoid his jump scare.

DISABLE AUDIO

PHANTOM MANGLE

appears on Camera 4, hanging from the ceiling and screeching. She will then appear in the office behind the window unless you lower the monitor or switch cameras as soon as he appears.

DISABLE AUDIO & VENTILATION

PHANTOM PUPPET

appears on Camera 8. Switch to another camera fast or it will appear in the office and block you from using the maintenance panel and monitor.

PATH TO THE GOOD ENDING

To view the game's "good" ending, players must complete mini games in a specific order. Hints appeared throughout the night-end mini games in the walls of a room one left and three down from the Show Stage room.

FNAF·3 RETRO ARCADE

Mini game: BB's Air Adventure

The hint for *BB's Air Adventure* was "BBdblclick"—double-click on the Balloon Boy poster visible on Camera 8. Control Balloon Boy with the keyboard (A=left, D=right, W=jump) and collect all the balloons. Instead of exiting the game, jump onto the platform above the exit and then jump toward the left wall.

Passing through this barrier will send you to a pixelated gray screen with terrifying dead Balloon Boys. Move to the right and you'll find a new playfield containing a rainbow-colored balloon. Jump through the left wall to reenter the mini game and collect the final balloon. This will restart your night in the main game.

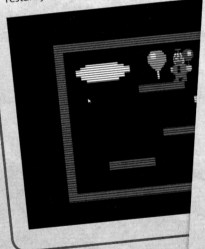

FNAF·3 RETRO ARCADE

Mini game: Mangle's Quest

This game must be accessed on Night 2; its hint was a series of squares that correspond to button presses. On Camera 7, click the arcade machine's buttons in this order: top left, bottom left, top right, bottom right.

Collect all of Mangle's parts without running into a child. Instead of exiting the game, jump through the secret opening above the exit. You'll enter a pixelated red screen with a large, crying version of what looks like the Puppet. Move to the left to enter a new section of the game. Jump onto each balloon platform and a cake will appear at the end of the path. Collect it to reset your night.

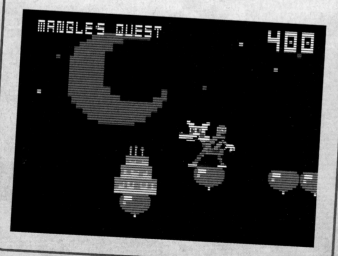

FNAF·3 RETRO ARCADE

Mini game: BB's Air Adventure

Reenter the mini game, the same as the last time you played it. Just like the first time, jump through the secret opening above the exit after collecting the balloons. This time, however, you'll land on a series of balloon platforms that lead to a blue platform with a crying gray child. Since you collected the cake in Mangle's Quest, you can now give it to the child and end the mini game. Your night will reset.

FNAF·3 RETRO ARCADE

Mini game: Chica's Party

This mini game must be accessed on Night 3. The night-end mini game hint for Chica's Party was four cupcakes. To unlock it, click on four cupcakes located throughout the attraction (see page 33).

As Chica, grab all the cupcakes you can find and deliver them to the children in the next room. A hole in the floor leads to two more children and two more cupcakes to deliver.

To get the good ending, jump through the hole in the floor and enter the next screen. Standing on the platform at the top left, jump to the left two more times to enter into a secret screen. On this screen you'll see two more balloon platforms that lead to another child. Walk up to the child to serve them a huge cake. Doing so will end the mini game and reset the night.

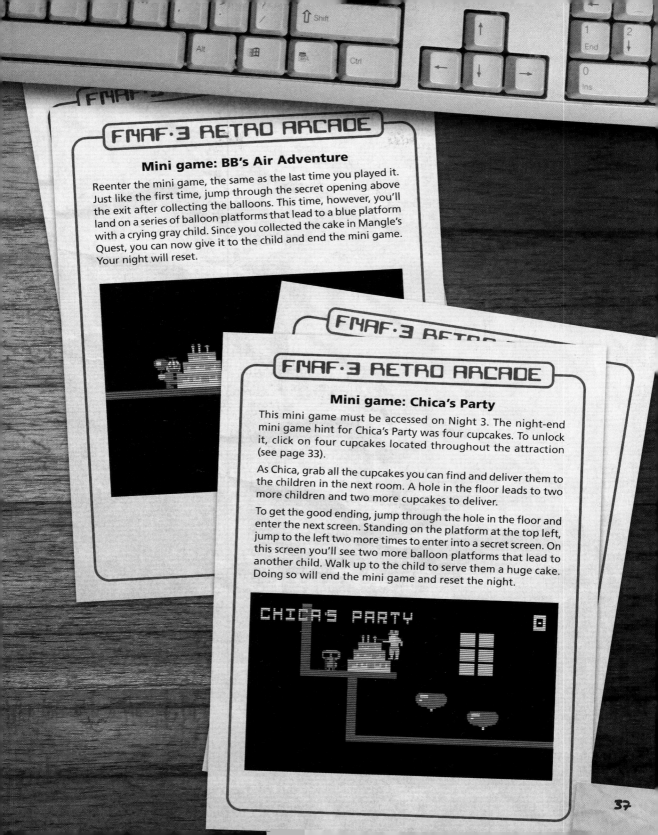

FNAF·3 RETRO ARCADE

Mini game: "Stage 01"

This mini game must be accessed on Night 4. The hint for Stage 01 was a numerical code: 395248. The code corresponds to wall tiles in the office, left of the desk, arranged in a 3 x 3 grid. Click on each tile as you would dial numbers on a phone.

In this mini game, players control Golden Freddy while entertaining children with Springtrap. Jump toward the children to "glitch" through the wall on the left side of the room. As you fall, you'll see that same stage room, twice, until you hit the ground. There are actually nine playing fields arranged in a 3 x 3 grid. All of them are the same except for the top right (3) and middle right (6)—room six only has two children. Follow the path in the map below to get to Room 3 and deliver cake to a lone crying child.

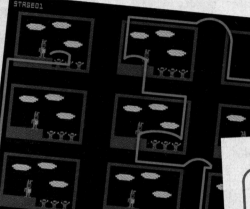

FNAF·3 RETRO ARCADE

Mini game: Shadow Bonnie

The hint for this mini game appeared as a shadow version of Bonnie. To access it, double-click on the shadowed Bonnie figurine on the right side of the office desk on Night 5.

This mini game is a mash-up of all the others. Pressing "S" phases the character from one game setting into a new purple room, and pressing "S" again phases the character into the previously played mini games.

There's a child at the bottom-left corner of the purple room, but outside the walls. To reach it, press "S" until you land in BB's Air Adventure. Jump to the upper left platform and into the wall, passing through it and falling to the ground. Walk to the center of the screen and press "S" to phase back to the purple room. You are now outside the walls and can approach the child to give it cake.

FNAF·3 RETRO ARCADE

Mini game: Happiest Day

This mini game can be accessed any night. On Camera 3, find the two posters on the right side of the room. Double-click the left poster, closest to the center of the room.

As the Puppet, walk past all the partygoers with their cakes. In the last room, a gray crying child sits, watched over by other gray children wearing masks of the animatronics. When you give the child a cake, it stops crying and is given a mask of its own (Golden Freddy). All the masks fall to the ground as the children disappear.

THE GOOD ENDING

If you beat the game after going through the mini games properly, you'll see the same ending image as before, except now there are no lights in the animatronics' eyes. Curiously, the fifth animatronic head (which most believe belongs to Golden Freddy) is missing from the line-up. Faded text in the background reads "the end."

YOU CAN HONK FREDDY'S NOSE IN FNAF3 BY CLICKING ON THE POSTER IN THE OFFICE.

Codes, Glitches, and Secrets

EXTRAS OPTION

There is no "custom night" in *FNAF3*. However, beating Night 5 opens up an Extras option in the main menu. From here, players can view the animatronics' jump scares, play the mini games (as long as the "good" ending was unlocked), and enable some fun cheats. You can speed up time, equip a Springtrap "radar" (to help you find him more easily), and even increase Springtrap's aggression level. (We'll pass on that last one.)

```
EXTRA

    ANIMATRONICS
    MINIGAMES          FAST NIGHTS
    JUMPSCARES         RADAR
    CHEATS             AGGRESSIVE
                       NO ERRORS
    EXIT
```

RARE SPRINGTRAP IMAGES

There are three rare Springtrap images that can appear randomly before the menu screen. All three show that there is someone *inside* the Springtrap suit. Someone long dead.

CAMERA 2
Retro Freddy poster changes to Spring Bonnie.

CAMERA 4
The Bonnie poster will change to a pink cupcake or a golden cupcake.

THE OFFICE
Crumpled Freddy suit sometimes appears in the corner of the office.

THE OFFICE
Two paper plate characters appear on the walls of the office.

CAMERA 10
Retro Freddy poster changes to Spring Bonnie.

41

Lore and Theories

WHO ARE THE SHADOW ANIMATRONICS?

Though introduced in *FNAF2*, Shadow Bonnie and Shadow Freddy don't really take center stage until *FNAF3*. Shadow Freddy plays a crucial role in the night-end mini games, while Shadow Bonnie has his own role to play in the good-ending mini games. Just who are these characters, and what are their intentions?

FORMER EMPLOYEES?: One theory maintains that Shadow Freddy and Shadow Bonnie are the ghosts of the Freddy's employees who were killed by the spring lock suits. On Night 4, Phone Guy mentions "multiple, simultaneous spring lock failures" at Freddy's sister location. Theorists believe this explains why the shadow animatronics help the dead children—as the ghosts of employees, they feel guilty about not being able to stop the murders.

LINK TO THE KILLER?: Interestingly enough, the shadow animatronics take on a purple coloring, which is heavily associated with William Afton. Shadow Bonnie also appears in *Special Delivery*, when a player collects too much negative remnant. Remnant has featured heavily in Afton's plans. But does Shadow Bonnie appear there as an antagonist . . . or as a warning?

WHAT WE KNOW FOR SURE:

♦ Shadow animatronics existed prior to the events of *FNAF2*, based on their appearance in that game.

♦ They don't seem to have a physical form. Unlike the physical animatronics, Shadow Freddy can enter the safe room in *FNAF3* and goes unnoticed by Purple Guy. In the mini games, Shadow Bonnie's figure seems to dissipate and re-form often. He is also able to travel to different mini games, something none of the other mini game animatronics can do.

♦ They help the children. In the night-end mini games, Shadow Freddy tries to lead you to the killer, who's hiding out in the safe room. In his mini game, Shadow Bonnie gives cake to one of the children.

FAN THEORIES: GOLDEN FREDDY WAS A SPRING LOCK SUIT

There's been a lot of speculation about Golden Freddy—where he came from, why he seemingly can't move, and why he appears and disappears randomly. One theory says that *FNAF3* provides us with the answer: Golden Freddy is a spring lock suit.

Theorists point to the crumpled sitting position of Golden Freddy, and how it matches the sitting position of the empty Springtrap suit in the night-end mini game on Night 5. Fans also believe this could answer why Golden Freddy appears and disappears like a hallucination—the spring lock suits were retired (and presumably destroyed) long ago. All that would remain is a ghost of the animatronic.

This point seems more solid considering the unique Fredbear encounter in *Ultimate Custom Night*. The animatronic can only be seen by setting Golden Freddy to one and all other animatronics to zero, then giving Golden Freddy a Death Coin when he appears. Could this allude to Golden Freddy's origins as a Fredbear spring lock suit?

Still, others reject this idea on the basis that Golden Freddy has four-fingered hands, which would be awkward for a human occupant. Springtrap has five fingers.

Chapter 4

FIVE NIGHTS AT FREDDY'S 4

Five Nights at Freddy's 4 (*FNAF4*) marks a huge next step for the series. Gone are the security office, the stationary playable character, and the . . . well, the paycheck wasn't worth much to begin with. But for all this change, *FNAF4* kept the elements players like best: 8-bit mini games at the end of each night, perhaps the most nightmare-inducing animatronics of any game to date, and mysterious Easter eggs that have become the hallmark of the series.

That said, this game is punishing. It forces you to crank up the volume in order to hear a variety of subtly distinct sounds. Failing to respond correctly to those sounds results in an eardrum-shattering jump scare that will likely send you (and possibly your keyboard) flying.

Beyond the gameplay, there's a lot to be gleaned here in terms of lore, and *FNAF4* kicked off one of the most intense fan-theory debates in the series' history—The Bite of '87 vs. The Bite of '83—as well as the million simultaneous cries of "What's in the box?"

Let's dig into some of these questions and more.

The Freddy Scoop

FNAF4 begins with a screen that announces "5 days until the party" followed by an 8-bit image of a little yellow Freddy wearing a purple hat. His name is Fredbear, and he reveals that you've been locked in your room.

The screen dissolves, and you'll see yourself as a crying (but alive) child in a bedroom with plush toys. The aforementioned Fredbear is a stuffed animal on your bed whose creepy eyes follow your every movement . . .

Using the keyboard (W=up, A=left, S=down, D=right), make your way toward the (locked) bedroom door. You won't be able to open it, but that's okay. The screen dissolves—tomorrow is another day.

After the mini game, you'll find yourself launched into the primary gameplay. You're playing as a child, trying to ward off nightmare versions of the animatronics who are attacking you in your bedroom.

Like the other games, you need to survive from midnight until 6:00 a.m. by checking your closet, the hallways outside your room, and your bed, where the nightmare animatronics lurk. Before each night begins, you'll also have the chance to skip two hours by playing a mini game with a plush version of Springtrap.

YOUR ALARM CLOCK WILL FLASH A RANDOM SERIES OF NUMBERS AT THE END OF EACH NIGHT BEFORE HITTING 6:00 A.M.

FNAF·4 RETRO ARCADE

Night 1 End Mini game

Four days until the party. Your bedroom door is now unlocked. Fredbear tells you that someone is hiding, and he won't stop until you find him. Exit your room to explore the house. Heading back and to the left, you'll end up in a living room with a TV. Walk to the TV to be jump-scared by your older brother and end the mini game.

NOTE THE DISMEMBERED MANGLE TOY ON THE FLOOR.

FNAF·4 RETRO ARCADE

Night 2 End Mini game

Three days until the party. Tonight you're at a Freddy's restaurant, but someone has left without you. The game urges you to run toward the exit. If you go left, the game prompts you with "No! Don't you remember what you saw?" A man in a Fredbear suit blocks the exit to your right. The game urges, "Find someone who will help! You know what will happen if he catches you!" On the next screen, you're told to run past a silhouetted Freddy and Spring Bonnie, but walking forward ends the mini game.

FNAF·4 RETRO ARCADE

Night 3 End Mini game

Two days until the party. You're back at the pizzeria, but this time you can escape. On the way home, talk to the kids you see—one reveals that the upcoming party is for you. At home, head to your bedroom to be jump-scared and end the mini game.

FNAF·4 RETRO ARCADE

Night 4 End Mini game

One day until the party. You're locked in the spare parts/maintenance room of the pizzeria. Unable to escape, you once again end up crying on the floor, begging to be let out, until the mini game ends.

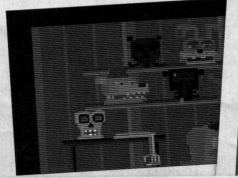

FNAF·4 RETRO ARCADE

Night 5 End Mini game

Zero days until the party. Tonight you're back at the pizzeria with no control—you just have to watch. Your brother and his friends (all wearing animatronic masks) tease you with the Fredbear animatronic. Your head ends up in Fredbear's mouth, followed by a sickening crunch as the animatronic bites down.

FNAF·4 RETRO ARCADE

Night 6 End Mini game

Sitting with the plush Fredbear, someone tells you they're sorry. Then someone tells you that you're broken, but that the speaker will put you back together. You can hear the sound of a heart monitor flatlining.

You're broken.

NIGHT 7 END MINI GAME

Beating Night 7 brings up an image of a locked box. You can click the locks to rattle them, but they won't open. The text reads, "Perhaps some things are best left forgotten, for now."

47

Gameplay and Strategy

SOUNDS

Like we said, this game is punishing on sound—you need to learn how to tune your ear to hear *everything*. Here's a list of what to listen for.

SOUNDS YOU SHOULD DISREGARD:

♦ Dog barking

♦ Clock chimes
(Good luck. Those chimes are *loud*.)

♦ Distorted radio

SOUNDS TO LISTEN FOR:

♦ Breathing: Before you turn on your flashlight at the doorway, be sure to listen for breathing as it means an animatronic is outside your room. If you hear it, shut the door and don't open it until you hear . . .

♦ Footsteps on gravel: This means an animatronic is walking away from or toward your room.

♦ Deep, slow-motion laugh: Nightmare Fredbear/Nightmare has entered your room.

♦ Metallic-sounding giggles: Freddles are accumulating on the bed behind you.

♦ Dishes clanking: Chica is in the kitchen . . . for now.

♦ Pitter-patter running, followed by a creak: Nightmare Foxy has entered your closet.

Sound is oriented to where you are in the room, so if you hear a sound from your left, you should check the left door. This includes when you're at the door and can hear breathing, laughing, or other sounds.

AND OF COURSE, LISTEN CAREFULLY FOR THE SWEETEST SOUND OF ALL:

The alarm clock hitting 6:00 a.m.

HOURS ARE EXACTLY SIXTY SECONDS LONG, MAKING EACH NIGHT LAST EXACTLY SIX MINUTES.

RIGHT HALLWAY
Nightmare Chica only enters from this side.

YOU ARE HERE!

CLOSET
Nightmare Foxy hides here if he enters your room.

LEFT HALLWAY
Nightmare Bonnie only enters from this side.

BED
Nightmare Freddy only approaches from the bed.

Be sure to clear the Freddles!

NIGHTMARE FREDBEAR AND NIGHTMARE CAN APPEAR ANYWHERE!!!

ANIMATRONICS

♦ **FREDDLES** appear on the bed, but flee when you shine the flashlight on them. The more Freddles there are, the longer it takes to clear them. **NIGHTMARE FREDDY** will attack if you do not check under the bed often enough.

If your flashlight flickers, it means your Freddle count is increasing

♦ **NIGHTMARE BONNIE** attacks from the left hallway or the center of the bedroom. Nightmare Bonnie is very active on the first few nights; check the left hallway often to avoid a jump scare.

♦ **NIGHTMARE CHICA** is very active on the first few nights, and attacks players from the right hallway. While she does not enter the bedroom, her **CUPCAKE** does, and its jump scare is just as bad.

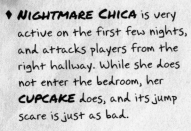

Something interesting to note—the full-size animatronics in *FNAF4* have five fingers, whereas most of the previous games' animatronics (except Springtrap) have four.

Nightmare Bonnie and Nightmare Chica stick to the same sides of the map as their *FNAF* counterparts.

♦ **NIGHTMARE FOXY** doesn't appear until Night 2. Listen for fast footsteps followed by a creak, or watch for the closet door to open or close slightly. Nightmare Foxy goes through a sequence before attacking: starting as a plush, next in his normal form standing upright, then in a crouching position, and finally, with his head poking out of the closet (watch out for a mini jump scare). To placate Nightmare Foxy, hold the closet doors closed until he resets.

♦ **NIGHTMARE FREDBEAR** shows up on Night 5 and Night 6 (after 4:00 a.m.) and can attack from anywhere. When he's around, however, none of the others will be. Audio clues are your friend: If you hear laughter, check the bed or closet. If you hear laughter followed by footsteps, check the hallway.

♦ As with Nightmare Fredbear, **NIGHTMARE** appears from both hallways (but closer), in the closet, and on the bed. Nightmare only appears on Night 7 and Night 8 after 4:ØØ a.m. and has the same audio clues as Nightmare Fredbear.

NIGHTMARE IS MUCH HARDER TO SEE AT A GLANCE, SINCE HE BLENDS IN WITH THE SHADOWS.

MINI GAME: FUN WITH PLUSHTRAP

Between nights, you can play a mini game called *Fun with Plushtrap* to remove two hours from the clock (game starts at 2:ØØ a.m.). Your goal is to get Plushtrap to land on an X on the floor of the darkened hallway. When you flick the flashlight on, Plushtrap will either go limp or hide in an adjacent room. If you don't check on him enough, Plushtrap will jump-scare you; check on him too often and he won't make it to the X within the time limit. To win, try turning on your flashlight each time you hear a few seconds of running to judge his location.

Codes, Glitches, and Secrets

EXTRAS MENU

Beating Night 5 unlocks the Extras menu, allowing players to view animatronics, a "Making of . . ." gallery progression, jump scares, mini games, Nightmare mode, and cheats. Some of these options remain locked until players complete Night 6.

Cheats include a map of the house with a "radar" of the animatronics, faster nights (thirty seconds instead of sixty seconds each), and a danger indicator near the hallway doors.

NIGHT 8

Though there is no "Custom Mode" in *FNAF4*, there is still a way to play 20/20/20/20. Enter the new Extras menu and type "20202020" to access this final challenge. All the animatronics are set to their maximum difficulty level, and Nightmare does appear after 4:00 a.m.

RARE SCREENS

Don't miss these rare screens in *FNAF4*, which point to a darker plot twist. Turning around to clear Freddles from the bed, you may get one of these three rare screens, which show a pill bottle, an IV, and a vase of flowers on your bedside table.

NIGHT-END MINI GAME EASTER EGGS

Night 2: When you're urged to run past a silhouetted Freddy and Spring Bonnie, turn back to the right first to get a glimpse of Purple Guy helping someone into the Spring Bonnie suit. This is our only glimpse of Purple Guy in *FNAF4*.

Night 3: The girl with pigtails along your walk home reveals that the animatronics "come to life at night" and that "if you die, they hide your body and never tell anyone." On the previous screen, a kid holds a Spring Bonnie plush.

Night 3: Click on the TV in the living room to watch the *Fredbear & Friends* TV show. Notice the copyright date: 1983.

HALLOWEEN EDITION

The *FNAF4* Halloween update replaces Nightmare with Nightmarionne, Nightmare Bonnie, and Nightmare Chica—each with their own jack-o'-lantern version, and Nightmare Foxy with Nightmare Mangle. The Fun with Plushtrap mini game becomes Fun with Balloon Boy.

The update also alters the night-end mini games to fit the Halloween theme (check out the Halloween decor in the house and at Freddy's).

Explore the Extras menu for terrifying new challenges including Blind Mode, Mad Freddy, Insta-Foxy, and All Nightmare.

> TRY CLICKING THE NOSE OF THE PLUSH FREDDY ON THE BED.

Lore and Theories

THE BITE OF '83

It's now widely accepted among fans that *FNAF4* doesn't show the infamous Bite of '87, but instead a different "Bite of '83." The evidence?

♦ **Fredbear & Friends:** In the Night 3 mini game, the TV plays a show with a 1983 copyright date.

♦ **Responsibility:** The Bite of '87 forced management to introduce new rules for the animatronics. If Fredbear was stationary at the time of the bite, why restrict the animatronics' movement?

♦ **Frontal Lobe:** The Bite of '87 victim lost their frontal lobe. When you remove the frontal lobe from the brain, it no longer feels fear. This seems inconsistent with our apparent gameplay as the bitten child.

♦ **Secret Cameras:** In the Private Room of *Sister Location*, a remote control is held by the Fredbear plush that we see in the *FNAF4* night-end mini games. A secret keypad on the wall has the passcode "1983"; the keypad brings up a security camera feed . . . of the *FNAF4* house.

♦ **Cameo:** The *Curse of Dreadbear* seemingly takes place during "Fall Fest '83." The *FNAF4* house appears on a hill in the distance.

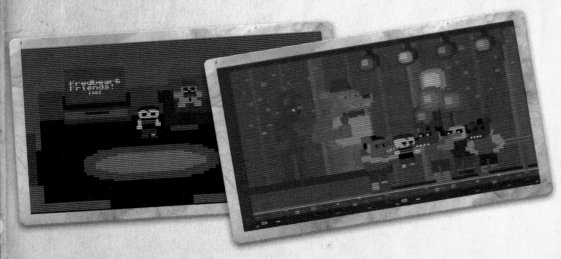

Fan Theories:
What's up with Fredbear?

It seems clear someone is spying on the bite victim, between the creepy way the Fredbear plush follows him around in the *FNAF4* night-end mini games and the *FNAF4* camera feed in *Sister Location*'s Private Room. Why though? Could it be because of what the child saw at the pizzeria? Or because the keeper of the cameras knows how dangerous the animatronics are?

At the end of the game, the Fredbear plush does give you a clue as to the bite victim's fate:

"You're broken . . . I'm still here.
I will put you back together."

Some interesting theories:

♦ Based on a similar wording in *Sister Location*, could this mean whoever is spying wants to put the bite victim's soul into an animatronic?

♦ Is this line coming from one of the creators of the animatronics, either Henry or William Afton?

♦ Could the bite victim ultimately possess Golden Freddy, whom many fans believe to be an old Fredbear spring lock suit?

I will put you back together.

Chapter 5

FIVE NIGHTS AT FREDDY'S: SISTER LOCATION

If you thought *FNAF4* was a departure, allow us to introduce you to *Five Nights at Freddy's: Sister Location*, the game that took the series in a completely different direction. For the first time in *FNAF*, you're out of the one-room setup and allowed (mostly) free rein of the building. Added to your night-guard duties are various maintenance tasks, including repairing the animatronics, which you somehow have to do *without* getting murdered by them.

The series continues to get darker with the introduction of Ennard (try explaining this character to your grandma) as well as a number of mysterious Easter eggs that have launched a whole new string of theories. This game also features a full cast of voice characters in the animatronics who are—not surprisingly—pretty talkative. With the added dialogue comes some quirky humor, a refreshing light in this deep and winding saga.

But perhaps the biggest change for the series is the absence of, well, Freddy's. *Sister Location* is set at Circus Baby's Pizza World—an apparent warehouse of animatronics. The animatronics live here, but they're rented out for parties.

There's a lot to unpack, so let's get started.

The Freddy Scoop

As you boot up the game, you'll overhear a conversation. An unnamed man questions a "Mr. Afton" on some of his animatronic design choices, but you never hear the end of the conversation.

Similar flashback audio plays before each night, but this time you'll hear a little girl— Mr. Afton's daughter—talking. She begs her father to play with Circus Baby, at one point asking, "Didn't you make her just for me?" At the end of Night 5, you'll hear an ominous line implying the girl may have been killed by the animatronic. "Don't tell Daddy that I'm here . . . I don't know why he won't let me come see you . . . Where did the other children go?"

WELCOME TO CIRCUS BABY'S PIZZA WORLD!

The game begins in an elevator, where you meet the Handyman's Robotics and Unit Repair System Model 5 (aka HandUnit). Your first task is to enter your name in the system, but it autocorrects to "Eggs Benedict." When you get to the bottom, head toward the caution tape to crawl through the vent.

As you crawl, HandUnit explains that Freddy Fazbear's Pizza was a huge success until it was closed down, at which point there was room for a "new contender in children's entertainment." The animatronics here are rented out for parties; your job is to keep them working.

NIGHT 1

Follow HandUnit's directions to administer a "controlled shock" to Ballora and Funtime Foxy, summoning them to their stages. Once they appear, crawl through the vent to the Circus Gallery Control Module (aka Circus Control) to summon Circus Baby. She won't appear.

NIGHT 1

NIGHT 2

On your elevator ride, select a new voice for HandUnit. Whatever button you press, it autocorrects to "angsty teen."

In the Primary Control Module, follow HandUnit's instructions. Trying to summon Funtime Foxy and Ballora to the stage will cause a glitch, restoring HandUnit's default voice. Head through the vents to summon Circus Baby. This time, however, as you try to "motivate" Circus Baby, there's a power malfunction. HandUnit reboots the system, which also takes down the security doors, vent locks, and oxygen!

Circus Baby tells you to hide in a space under the desk that a previous guard created. After hiding there, pull on the metal sheet to close off the space, and keep it closed when BidyBabs start tugging on it.

After the BidyBabs retreat, Circus Baby tells you not to listen to HandUnit's instructions about Ballora. Seconds later, HandUnit returns—you'll need to restart the system manually in the Breaker Room. As you cross Ballora Gallery, ignore HandUnit's urging to speed up. Ballora is triggered by sound, so advance across the gallery slowly and stop if Ballora's music gets louder.

In the Breaker Room, click and hold the buttons on the left side of the map to restore power to each area. Listen for Funtime Freddy's approach and play audio to distract him. Once the breakers are back on, your shift is over. Exit through Ballora Gallery.

NIGHT 3

Your elevator trip includes a musical selection: "Casual Bongos." Tonight you're performing maintenance work on Funtime Freddy. You may not be qualified to do this, but that's okay!

At the control center, check on Ballora and Funtime Foxy. Ballora is on the stage in pieces. Funtime Foxy isn't there, but HandUnit doesn't notice. HandUnit tells you not to visit Circus Baby. Proceed into the right vent.

To maintenance Freddy, you'll have to make it past Funtime Auditorium . . . and Funtime Foxy. Her auditorium is dark, but you can use the flash beacon as needed. Funtime Foxy is motion-activated, so be patient and move in short bursts, flashing your light periodically. If you see him, stop and wait until she moves away.

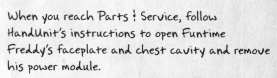

When you reach Parts & Service, follow HandUnit's instructions to open Funtime Freddy's faceplate and chest cavity and remove his power module.

Now you must collect the secondary power module on the Bon-Bon puppet. Bon-Bon hides from your flashlight, so wait for him to appear at the edge of the light. When Bon-Bon's chest is visible, click on the button below his bow tie to complete the repair.

Exit through Funtime Auditorium, but don't worry about moving slowly— it's impossible to avoid triggering Funtime Foxy's jump scare, which ends the night.

NIGHT 4

When you awake, you're inside a spring lock suit, compliments of Circus Baby. You watch as two technicians bring Ballora into the Scooping Room, where the "Scooper" machine rips Ballora's endoskeleton out of her body. After the techs leave, Circus Baby opens the spring lock suit's faceplates so the company can find you on the security cameras. You'll have to survive in the meantime.

There are ten spring locks—five on each side—and they turn red when they're about to trip. Click and hold the spring locks to keep them wound, and beware the Minireenas closing in. Shaking them off causes the spring locks to unwind faster, but you'll need to do so to avoid a jump scare.

NIGHT 5

To celebrate the end of your first week, the company is sending a gift basket of . . . Exotic Butters. HandUnit reveals that there are still two technicians on site. When you check on Funtime Foxy and Ballora, you'll find the techs—hanging from the show stage.

Pass through the empty Funtime Auditorium to enter Parts ¦ Service and perform maintenance on Circus Baby. There Circus Baby tells you she's broken and they want to scoop her, but that won't solve the problem. She asks you to save the good parts of her so the bad will be destroyed.

Following her instructions, pull up Baby's hidden keypad and enter the code quickly and correctly. Failing to input the code results in an endoskeleton jump scare. Open the hatch on her arm, take the glowing green card, and press the button on the conveyor belt.

As you send Circus Baby to be scooped, you can see the endoskeleton retreating into the darkness.

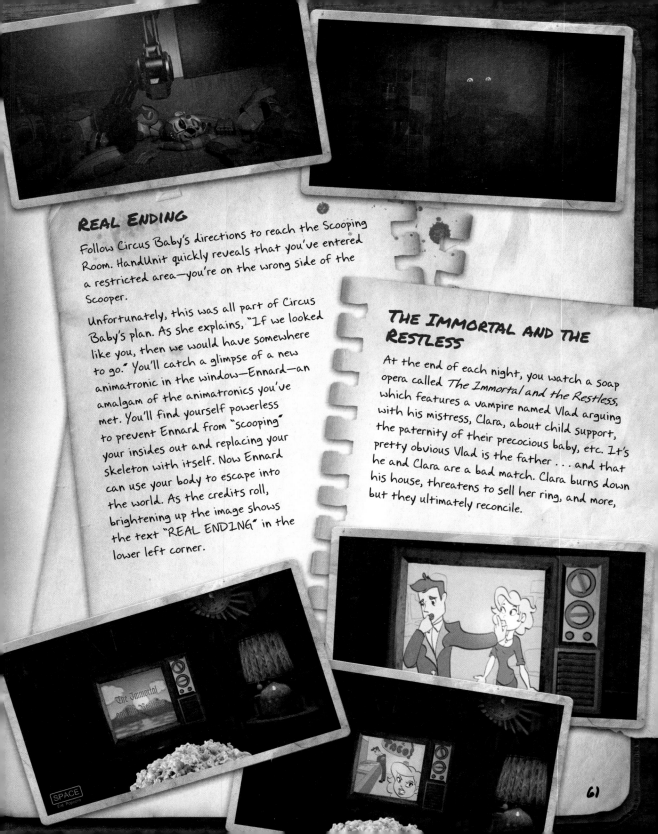

REAL ENDING

Follow Circus Baby's directions to reach the Scooping Room. HandUnit quickly reveals that you've entered a restricted area—you're on the wrong side of the Scooper.

Unfortunately, this was all part of Circus Baby's plan. As she explains, "If we looked like you, then we would have somewhere to go." You'll catch a glimpse of a new animatronic in the window—Ennard—an amalgam of the animatronics you've met. You'll find yourself powerless to prevent Ennard from "scooping" your insides out and replacing your skeleton with itself. Now Ennard can use your body to escape into the world. As the credits roll, brightening up the image shows the text "REAL ENDING" in the lower left corner.

THE IMMORTAL AND THE RESTLESS

At the end of each night, you watch a soap opera called *The Immortal and the Restless*, which features a vampire named Vlad arguing with his mistress, Clara, about child support, the paternity of their precocious baby, etc. It's pretty obvious Vlad is the father . . . and that he and Clara are a bad match. Clara burns down his house, threatens to sell her ring, and more, but they ultimately reconcile.

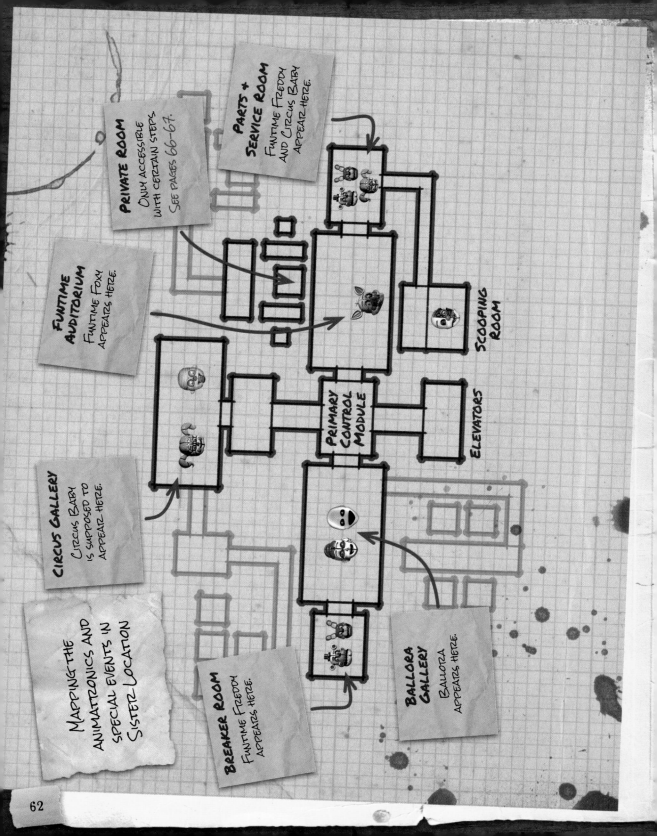

PARTS +
SERVICE ROOM
FUNTIME FREDDY
AND CIRCUS BABY
APPEAR HERE.

PRIVATE ROOM
ONLY ACCESSIBLE
WITH CERTAIN STEPS.
SEE PAGES 66-67.

FUNTIME
AUDITORIUM
FUNTIME FOXY
APPEARS HERE.

CIRCUS GALLERY
CIRCUS BABY
IS SUPPOSED TO
APPEAR HERE.

MAPPING THE
ANIMATRONICS AND
SPECIAL EVENTS IN
SISTER LOCATION

BREAKER ROOM
FUNTIME FREDDY
APPEARS HERE.

BALLORA GALLERY
BALLORA
APPEARS HERE.

SCOOPING
ROOM

PRIMARY
CONTROL
MODULE

ELEVATORS

Codes, Glitches, and Secrets

BLUEPRINTS

Blueprints for Circus Baby, Funtime Freddy, Ballora, and Funtime Foxy can rarely be found on the game load screen. Their design choices seem meant to lure children in to be kidnapped, and are no doubt what the technicians were referencing in the prologue.

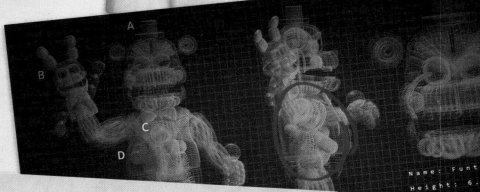

Name: Funtime Fred
Height: 6.0 ft
Weight: 350 lbs

A: Proximity Sensor/
   Grouping Coordinati
B: Parental Tracking/
   360 Pivot
C: Voice Mimic/ Luring
D: Storage Tank

ROAD TO THE SECRET ENDING!

On Night 3, before heading to Funtime Auditorium, go to the Circus Gallery Control Room and enter the crawl space under the desk. Circus Baby will tell you about the first and only night she was on stage. Part of her programming requires her to count children. As soon as there was only one child left in the room with her, she lost control of herself. Her stomach opened and made an ice-cream cone. Then she pulled the unfortunate little girl inside herself. Baby is still haunted by her screams.

IS THAT A KID IN FREDDY'S STORAGE TANK??

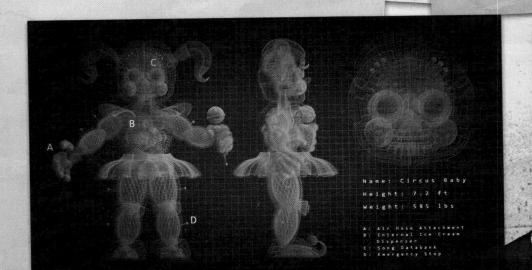

Name: Circus Baby
Height: 7.2 ft
Weight: 585 lbs

A: Air Hose Attachment
B: Internal Ice Cream
   Dispenser
C: Song Databank
D: Emergency Stop

FNAF·SL RETRO ARCADE

Circus Baby Mini game

The Circus Baby mini game may appear after a jump scare. In order to unlock the secret ending, you need to fully complete this mini game. Playing as Circus Baby, you must collect food and give it to children within a limited amount of time. Each kid needs to be fed two cupcakes, unless you hit them with a green cupcake. Their color will change from green to red when they've had their fill.

Collectible Food:
- **Pink Cupcake:** Single throw cupcakes
- **Blue Cupcake:** Triple throw; can feed kids lined up vertically
- **Green Cupcake:** Single throw; can fully feed multiple kids lined up horizontally
- **Ice-Cream Cone:** Unlocks secret child

Jump to grab the pink cupcakes, and throw two at the first child and then another two at the next child. Continue right into the next area, but do *NOT* target the kids on the lower level! Instead, jump up and throw another two cupcakes each at the kids on the platforms.

From the upper-right platform, jump right into the next screen to leap over a blue cupcake and land on a middle island. Proceed right to the next area, and throw your last two pink cupcakes right as you jump to the first platform.

FNAF·SL RETRO ARCADE

Return left to grab the blue cupcake, then head right again. Jump to the middle platform and throw twice to hit all three kids lined up vertically at the same time. Continue to the right, but do not grab the green cupcake. Hop onto the left edge of the platform to jump over it. In the next area, jump and throw twice to hit the three kids arranged vertically.

Now return left to collect the green cupcake. Continue left until you reach the area where you ignored the two unfed kids. Throw a green cupcake at them. Quickly return to the right, jumping all of the gaps. In the area where you hit the last set of three kids arranged vertically, there is a gap at the far end. Jump it, and immediately throw a cupcake to hit the kids in the next room! Continue to the right, jumping gaps and throwing cupcakes as necessary.

At the end of the screen, take the ice-cream cone but *don't* exit to the GOAL. Instead, run all the way back to the left. You'll reach the end with only seconds to spare, but as long as the timer doesn't expire, a girl will come out for the ice cream. Circus Baby grabs her with a terrible scream.

To access the game quickly, go to the Extras menu and move your mouse to the lower left corner. Click on the icon of Circus Baby when it appears.

PRIVATE ROOM

After completing the Circus Baby mini game, you can disobey Baby's directions on Night 5. Move right in Funtime Auditorium to find the Private Room. HandUnit will inform you that you're not allowed to leave until 6:00 a.m. Sound familiar?

Your task is to survive the night against Ennard in a manner similar to *FNAF*. Listen carefully for sound clues to determine Ennard's whereabouts and use the monitor and doors sparingly. Survive the night and you'll be treated to a final installment of *The Immortal and the Restless*—complete with your "Exotic Butters" gift basket—but you're not alone. Ennard has followed you.

ENTER 1-9-8-3 ON THE KEYPAD TO BRING UP *FNAF4* CAMERA FEEDS ON THE DESK MONITORS!

NOTICE THE FAMILIAR FREDBEAR PLUSH ON THE DESK.

CUSTOM NIGHT

Defeating Ennard unlocks a series of custom nights with preset AI difficulties. You must defeat each on V. Hard to access bonus cut scenes.

	Ballora	Funtime Freddy	Yenndo	Funtime Foxy	Bonnet	BidyBab	Electrobab	Lolbit	Minireena	Minireena 2
Angry Ballet	X								X	X
Freddy & Co.		X	X	X	X					
Funtime Frenzy		X	X	X				X		
Dolls, Attack!						X	X		X	X
Girls' Night	X				X	X	X		X	X
Weirdos			X			X		X	X	X
Top Shelf	X	X	X	X	X				X	
Bottom Shelf						X	X	X	X	X
Cupcake Challenge	X	X		X	X			X	X	X
Golden Freddy		X	X	X	X	X	X	X	X	X

A
B
C

Name: Funtime Foxy
Height: 5.9 ft
Weight: 290 lbs

ation Sensor
ice Sync
cent Release
or Anchor
us Baby dir07

copyright © xxxx A

CHECK OUT THE CREEPY PUPPETS IN THE CIRCUS GALLERY CONTROL ROOM.

Try clicking around the Primary Control Module. You can honk the masks' noses, make beeping sounds with the buttons, and more.

♦ Ballora: approaches from East or West Hall; close the door when her music gets louder.

♦ Funtime Freddy/Bon-Bon: hides in the closets outside either door; when he commands Bon-Bon to attack, close the corresponding door; if he shouts "surprise," close the opposite door.

♦ Yenndo: appears at random in the office; open the monitor to make him disappear.

♦ Funtime Foxy: sits in "Funtime Cove"; follows same rules as FNAF Foxy.

♦ Bonnet: rushes through your office; click on her nose to stop her.

♦ BidyBab: enters from the vent above your desk; close the vent when it gets too close.

♦ Electrobab: drains your power; administer a controlled shock to stop it.

♦ Lolbit: distracts you with audio and visuals; type L-O-L to stop it.

♦ Minireenas: drain your oxygen until you black out; administer a controlled shock to stop them.

♦ Minireenas 2: randomly appear over your line of sight; cannot be stopped.

NOTE THAT NONE OF THE Custom Night GAMEPLAY IS CONSIDERED CANON. (SORRY TO THE LOLBIT FANS.)

ON NIGHT 5, THE ENNARD MASK IN THE PRIMARY CONTROL MODULE IS MISSING, THOUGH IT WILL SOMETIMES CHANGE TO A LOLBIT MASK.

FINAL CUT SCENES

After defeating each of the first nine custom nights, you'll watch one of seven 8-bit cut scenes. Ennard (who now occupies your body) is going through the world like normal, only, your body is decaying. Ennard's endoskeleton eventually leaves in search of a fresher body, but strangely, your body comes back to life.

Defeating the Golden Freddy custom night unlocks something even more earth-shattering: this message from Michael.

"Father, it's me, Michael. I did it. I found it—it was right where you said it would be. They were all there. They didn't recognize me at first, but then they thought I was you. And I found her. I put her back together, just like you asked me to. She's free now. But something is wrong with me. I should be dead, but I'm not. I've been living in shadows. There is only one thing left for me to do now. I'm going to come find you. I'm going to come find you."

Lore and Theories

MICHAEL . . . AFTON?

The second secret ending of *Sister Location* was quite a doozy, confirming that William Afton's son, Michael, is out there, possibly helping his father. Since then, many theories have popped up about Michael's role in the *FNAF* universe.

One strain of theories posits that Michael is the player character across *FNAF*, *FNAF2*, *FNAF3*, and *Sister Location*.

♦ Aliases: Fans use the fact Michael goes by "Mike" in *Sister Location* to link him to the guard "Mike Schmidt" from *FNAF*. The names on the paychecks in *FNAF2* (Jeremy, Fritz) interestingly match the first names of some of the murder victims we see on the gravestones screen from *Pizzeria Simulator*.

♦ Pink Slips: The player character is repeatedly fired for tampering with the animatronics—which, aside from alluding to the Custom Night and knowledge of animatronics, could point to turning off their facial recognition or collecting Remnant. Another reason cited in *FNAF2* is "odor"—which could link to Michael's decomposing body.

Fan Theories: A Family Affair

Many theorists insist that *Sister Location* proves that *FNAF* is truly a "family affair." Some theorists purport that *FNAF4* introduces us to the family of William Afton, and *Sister Location* shows us where they end up.

The Younger Son: The Bite Victim

William Afton seems to have been watching the bite victim in *FNAF4*, between the camera feeds in the Private Room and parts of the Breaker Room map matching up with the layout of the *FNAF4* house. Plush Fredbear's line at the close of *FNAF4* says, "I will put you back together." Sound familiar?

It's the same thing Michael Afton says during the last custom night cut scene in *Sister Location*: "I put her back together, just like you asked me to." Could this mean that the younger son was also put back together in a similar manner, and is possessing an animatronic?

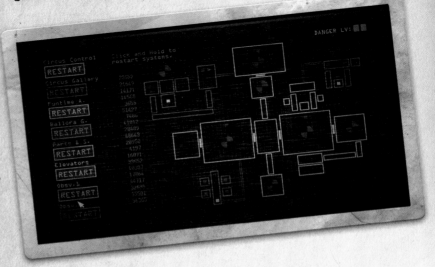

The Older Son: Michael Afton, aka, You

This theory seems confirmed by the game. In the final cut scene, you call William Afton "father," and state your name—"Michael." (Remember how we saw "Mike" taped to the keypad in the elevator?) Strangely, in the 8-bit Ennard cut scene, when you come back to life, it's Circus Baby's voice—your sister's voice— that seems to bring you back.

THE DAUGHTER: ELIZABETH AFTON, AKA CIRCUS BABY

At the end of each night in *Sister Location*, we overhear a girl pleading with her father to let her play with Circus Baby. On the final night, she is left alone with Circus Baby, and we know from Circus Baby's dialogue on Night 3 how that ended. Further proof comes from Circus Baby's eye color, which changes in her mini game to match that of the little girl. From the novel series and *Pizzeria Simulator*, we get seeming confirmation that Circus Baby is indeed Afton's daughter, Elizabeth.

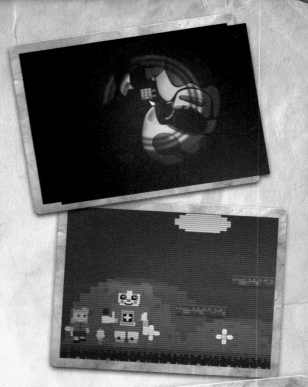

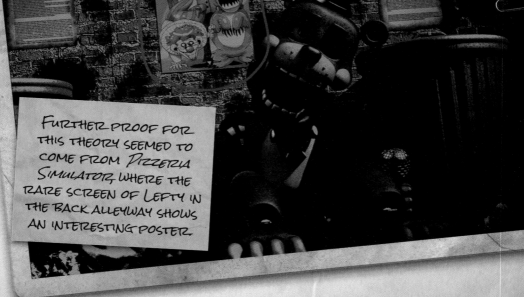

FURTHER PROOF FOR THIS THEORY SEEMED TO COME FROM *PIZZERIA SIMULATOR*, WHERE THE RARE SCREEN OF LEFTY IN THE BACK ALLEYWAY SHOWS AN INTERESTING POSTER.

Chapter 6
FREDDY FAZBEAR'S PIZZERIA SIMULATOR

CONGRATULATIONS! You, yes, you, have been chosen as the newest franchise owner of a Fazbear Entertainment restaurant! The sixth game in the Five Nights at Freddy's series, *Freddy Fazbear's Pizzeria Simulator*, puts you in the driver's seat of your very own restaurant. Choose the decor, the games, the entertainment; the possibilities are endless!

But it's not all fun and games. Split into three parts, the gameplay consists first of restaurant management, where you buy and place animatronics, games, and decor. The next stage is office maintenance, where hard-core *FNAF* fans are sure to shine. Your goal seems innocent enough: complete the tasks assigned to you in your dark office. But depending on your choices, you could find yourself fighting for your life against a horde of vicious animatronics, including some, er, not-so-friendly faces. The final part of your day is salvaging, where you must sort through and test old animatronics that were found outside your door.

Pizzeria Simulator shocked and delighted fans with its new concept, allowing for near-infinite possibilities and a variety of different endings. Though first appearing as a fun and funny new take on the mythos of *FNAF*, the game quickly takes a dark turn. With creepy mini games that both answer old questions and open up new ones, and a "good" ending that seemingly wraps up some of the many mysteries of the franchise, *Pizzeria Simulator* is sure to keep you on your toes . . . and keep you up at night.

The Freddy Scoop

The game starts with an 8-bit mini game where, after you choose toppings for your own pizza, Freddy has to deliver pizzas to hungry customers. As the levels increase, a shadow Freddy will appear and try to block you from delivering the pizzas. As you continue to get past him, the game suddenly glitches, causing multiple shadow Freddys to appear until the screen cuts to black.

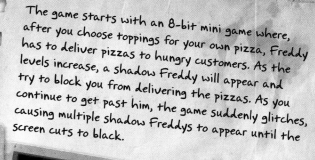

When the screen flickers back to life, you'll see Scrap Baby, a broken-down version of Circus Baby. Look down to find a piece of paper and a tape recorder. The tape recorder plays and the Cassette Man asks you to document the responses of the animatronic based on various aural stimuli. Two noises play and seemingly nothing happens, so you can check "No," "Yes," or "Maybe" in each box. On the third test, the pitch of a creepy song rises and rises until the screen cuts to a training video.

The training video informs you that you are now a franchisee of Fazbear Entertainment. Congratulations! You'll be in charge of your very own pizzeria, which means you'll be required to buy equipment for entertainment purposes while also cutting costs to make a profit. Make sure not to cut too many costs, though, as you don't want to be liable for any "accidents."

DAY 1: MONDAY

On the Restaurant Management screen, you can buy equipment for your restaurant. After buying the franchise license, you have $100 left, which means only items from "Dumpster Diver Weekly" are affordable. As you buy more expensive items, better categories become available. Each item has a value for Atmosphere, Health & Sanitation, Entertainment, Bonus Revenue, and Liability.

When you're done buying, move to **Blueprint Mode** to place equipment in your restaurant. There's a blinking "Sponsorship Offer" in the top-right corner, which gives you extra money. Testing the games also nets bonus revenue.

When you're done, click "Finished!" in the bottom-right corner to move to the next phase: **the office.** Here you must do all the tasks on the computer terminal. Click on a task to start it. Your tasks don't cost money to complete, but you can spend money to upgrade your equipment to make it quieter or more efficient.

Tutorial Unit warns that your terminal and ventilation system are loud, so disable them if the noise draws unwanted attention. Be careful about keeping the ventilation system off, though, as the room will heat up.

You can keep track of what's going on in the vents to your left and right by checking a motion detector, deploying an audio decoy, or using a secondary ventilation system. If all else fails, shine your flashlight into the vent to scare off any visitors.

HONK THE NOSE ON THE HELPY DOLL ON TOP OF YOUR TERMINAL.

After finishing your tasks, log off. The Tutorial Unit congratulates you on a job well done, but reminds you that you must get through the full week in order to prove yourself. There's a big party this Saturday, and if you are successful, you'll be rewarded.

The final phase of the day is **salvaging**. You're brought back to the dimly lit desk, a piece of paper and a recorder in front of you. Only this time you're facing Molten Freddy, a broken-down Funtime Freddy.

Cassette Man tells you to inspect the animatronics found by the back door. No one knows why they're there, but they can be used for spare parts. You can either salvage them for extra money or throw them away. If the animatronic attacks, you can shock it. If you shock it more than three times, you will irreparably damage the hardware and its value will decrease.

Fail this phase and you will receive a jump scare and a notification: you lost the salvage, and now something is loose in your pizzeria.

Make it through all five stimuli, shocking each time the animatronic moves, and you will receive money. As the screen cuts to black, a distorted voice is heard saying, "Thanks for letting me join the party. I'll try not to disappoint." The animatronic is still loose in your pizzeria.

The day ends with a summary screen totaling the amount of money you made from your restaurant for that day. Great job!

Summary		
New Visitors		20
Returning Visitors		0
Turned Away		0
Total Visitors		20
Food Revenue	$	183
Bonus Revenue	$	0
Salvage Revenue	$	0
Total Revenue	$	183
New Lawsuits		

GREAT JOB!

DAY 2: TUESDAY

Welcome back! On the Restaurant Management screen, you can buy better equipment with yesterday's profits. Watch the liability ratings on the items, particularly if it says something undesirable might be hiding inside.

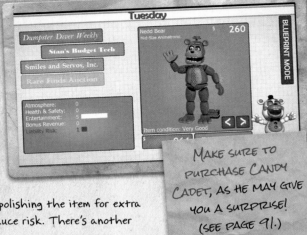

On the Blueprint screen, you can now modify what you've bought by adding coin slots for bonus revenue, cleaning and polishing the item for extra atmosphere, or adding safety straps to reduce risk. There's another sponsorship offer as well.

Make sure to purchase Candy Cadet, as he may give you a surprise! (See page 91.)

Once finished, you're brought back to your office. If you salvaged an animatronic or purchased a high-liability animatronic, it will come for you through the vents. Complete your tasks quickly while monitoring the vents.

You can pause a task or shut down your terminal completely if you need to check the vents. The animatronics are attracted to sound, so use an audio decoy to distract them. Beware of sponsorships, as your tasks can be interrupted by a loud advertisement on your terminal if you took one. Be sure to monitor the temperature, too, though the fans and vents can be pretty loud.

After completing your tasks, you're brought to the Salvage screen again, where you can choose to salvage Scraptrap or throw him away. If you salvage successfully, Scraptrap can be heard saying, "What a deceptive calling. I knew it was a lie the moment I heard it, obviously. But it is intriguing nonetheless . . ."

The Tutorial Unit reminds you, "Don't forget: Saturday, you want them to all be in one place!"

DAY 3: WEDNESDAY

Halfway there! You're once more brought to the Restaurant Management and Blueprint screens. Note that you can upgrade the size of your restaurant to accommodate more items, or take another sponsorship to earn more cash.

Buy and test the arcade games Midnight Motorist and Fruity Maze for a special surprise!
(See pages 82, 84, 86, 88, and 92-93.)

Now back to the office! If you attempted to salvage both animatronics, you'll notice things have gotten a little harder. Complete your tasks without dying and you're brought to the Salvage screen, where you can choose to salvage Scrap Baby, whom you saw at the beginning of the game. If you salvage successfully, you can hear her say, "You don't really know your employer, do you?" as the screen cuts to black.

Depending on what you bought and the liability issues associated with the equipment, you might find yourself presented with several lawsuits on the Summary screen that you can choose to either fight or settle.

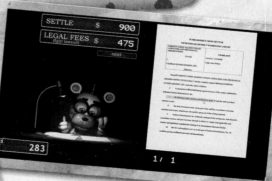

DAY 4: THURSDAY

Another day, another dollar! You're brought back to the Management screen, where you can continue to buy equipment and change the blueprint of your restaurant, upgrading as you see fit. The office will get even more difficult if you salvaged Scrap Baby.

If you're able to make enough money through salvaging, sponsorships, and bonus revenue from testing your products, purchase the Security Puppet for a surprise! (See page 82, 87, 88, 90, and 282.)

Security Puppet
$ 12500
Item condition: Very Good

< >

On tonight's Salvage screen, you're presented with Lefty. If you purchased him from the store, you'll be presented with a sign of a winking smiley face that says, "No one is here. I'm already inside." You know the drill; if you choose to salvage him, tase Lefty every time he moves, but not more than three times or you'll reduce his value.

DAY 5: FRIDAY

Keep on keeping on. Buy all the new things! Blueprint those things! Be careful in your office. Lucky you—no salvages today!

DAY 6: SATURDAY

Go about your business filling your restaurant with all the goodies your money can buy. Move along to the office and stay alive through your tasks.

REAL ENDING

After you complete your tasks for the night, the screen goes dark and you'll hear Scrap Baby's voice: "You played right into our hands . . . You gathered them all together in one place, just like he asked you to. All of those little souls in one place. Just for us. A gift. Now we can do what we were created to do and be complete . . ."

Cassette Man interrupts Scrap Baby, calling her Elizabeth. He explains that all the animatronics carrying trapped souls have been brought here and sealed inside as the restaurant is set on fire. Scrap Baby, Scraptrap, Lefty, and Molten Freddy are shown burning as they try to escape, along with images of the various 8-bit mini games from past *FNAF* games.

Cassette Man further states that the restaurant was made to lure the animatronics inside and destroy them so the souls can be freed. All except for one. "The darkest pit of Hell has opened to swallow you whole, so don't keep the Devil waiting, old friend," he says as Scraptrap burns.

Addressing the player, he goes on to say that he had designated an escape route for you, but has a feeling you don't want to leave. Lastly, Cassette Man talks to his daughter and apologizes for not being able to save her.

As the feed cuts out, you're presented with a new voice-over, congratulating you with a certificate of completion.

Gameplay and Strategy

Money Money Money

♦ Use all ten daily tokens to test out games in the pizzeria. You make bonus revenue if you perform well!

The Office

♦ Monitor the motion sensor and watch out for blips on the screen, indicating an animatronic's location.

♦ Use the audio decoy to move animatronics away from you. Use the decoy within an animatronic's circular audio range; otherwise, it won't hear the decoy!

♦ Listen closely to distinguish between the sounds of animatronics entering the hall, entering the vent, and shuffling out of the vent!

Don't Tase Me!

♦ During salvage, the animatronics only move when you check off their responses. If the animatronic is suddenly sitting upright, shock it!

Animatronics

♦ **Molten Freddy** is worth $500 and can be salvaged on the first night, unless you buy the Discount Ball Pit on Monday—he'll enter the restaurant by hiding in the ball pit. He doesn't speak or make any sound as he climbs through the vents.

♦ **Scraptrap** appears on the second night and is worth $1,000. If you purchase the Nedd Bear animatronic on Tuesday, Scraptrap won't appear, implying that he hides inside Nedd Bear during the day. As he approaches you from the vents, he makes a loud clamoring sound and says, "You may not recognize me at first, but I assure you, it's still me."

♦ **SCRAP BABY** can be salvaged on the third night and is worth $2,000. As she approaches in the vents, she can be heard saying, "I heard your call!" and "It feels like . . . my birthday. Did you have a gift for me?"

♦ **LEFTY** can either be bought for $5 with a liability rating of 9, the highest of any piece of equipment, or salvaged on the fourth night for $5,000. Similar to Molten Freddy, he doesn't speak when he is in the vents.

MAPPING
ANIMATRONICS AND
TIPS IN FREDDY
FAZBEAR'S PIZZERIA
SIMULATOR

THIS IS THE SAFEST PLACE TO PLAY AN AUDIO CUE, AS IT'S THE FARTHEST FROM YOU.

THIS BIG SQUARE IS THE RESTAURANT.

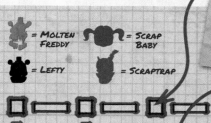

= MOLTEN FREDDY   = SCRAP BABY

= LEFTY   = SCRAPTRAP

ANIMATRONICS CAN TAKE ANY PATH TO YOU!

YOU ARE HERE.

YOU'LL HEAR AUDIO CUES FROM SCRAP BABY AND SCRAPTRAP WHEN THE ANIMATRONICS ARE IN THESE VENTS.

Codes, Glitches, and Secrets

♦ If you refrain from buying or salvaging anything, you are awarded the **Certificate of Mediocrity** and the "lazy" ending, where you're fired from the restaurant.

♦ If you run out of money, either by purchasing expensive equipment or incurring lawsuits, you are awarded the **Certificate of Bankruptcy** and fired from the restaurant.

♦ If you end the game with a risk rating of fifty or higher and win (i.e., don't go bankrupt), you're awarded the **Blacklisted Certificate** and can never work for a Fazbear Entertainment establishment ever again.

♦ If you unlock the secrets of Midnight Motorist, Fruity Maze, and Security Puppet, and get the "real ending," you're awarded the **Lorekeeper Certificate** and a secret ending screen after the credits roll.

♦ Obtain the **Certificate of Insanity** by buying and placing Egg Baby (aka Data Archive) in your restaurant. When you get to the office, turn off the monitor by pressing "Z," then click and hold the power button on the monitor, and press "Z" again. An audio file called "HRY223" plays, and secret blueprints of several animatronics and devices come onto the screen. After listening to the file, you're awarded the certificate and told that no one will believe you.

82

ACHIEVEMENT BADGES

To unlock the **Trash and the Gang** achievement badge, place Bucket Bob on the Star Curtain Stage and the rest of the "trash" animatronics on the Deluxe Concert Stage.

Trash and the Gang

To unlock the **Mediocre Melodies** achievement badge, place Orville Elephant on the Star Curtain Stage and the rest of the cheaper animatronics on the Deluxe Concert Stage.

Mediocre Melodies

Rockstars Assemble

To unlock the **Rockstars Assemble** achievement badge, place Lefty on the Star Curtain Stage and the rest of the Rockstar animatronics on the Deluxe Concert Stage.

To unlock the **Posh Pizzeria** achievement badge, place the three most expensive animatronics (El Chip, Funtime Chica, Music Man) on the Deluxe Concert Stage.

Posh Pizzeria

PURCHASE AND PLAY PRIZE KING TO WIN FUNTIME CHICA AT NO ADDITIONAL COST.

FFPS RETRO ARCADE

Midnight Motorist

During the fourth lap of *Midnight Motorist*, hit other cars to slow down, then drive across to the bottom lane. Eventually you'll see there is an opening at the bottom of the screen you can enter.

You'll be led to another screen, where it's raining and you're just one purple car driving along a winding road. As you drive to the U-shaped bend in the road, crash your car into the dark clearing in the trees. You can get out (you'll find that your character is yellow, not purple!) and walk to an open spot in the trees. In the upper left corner, there's an unmarked pile of dirt.

Get back in your car and you'll reach a fork in the road where you can either go left or continue straight. If you turn left, you're brought to a parking lot where there's a restaurant called JR's. There's a green man standing outside the restaurant. Park and get out of the car.

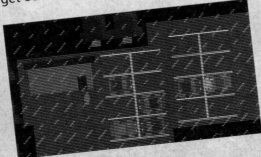

As you approach the green man, he says, "Come on, you know you can't be here. Don't make this more difficult than it has to be." Nothing else happens.

FFPS RETRO ARCADE

Get back in your car and turn right. Keep driving until you reach a blue house. You can get out of your car and walk around the house. The sound of music fades away and is replaced with the sound of rain. The closer you get to the house, the more it zooms in on your character. Go to the front door and enter the house. The game falls silent. There's a person dressed in gray sitting in a chair in front of a TV. The gray person says, "Leave him alone tonight. He had a rough day."

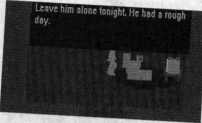

Go down the hall and knock on the door. You'll shout, "I told you not to close your door." Then, "This is my house. He can't ignore me like that." Then "OPEN THE DOOR," and finally, "I'll find a way in from outside."

Leave the house and walk around to the back. The window is broken and there are two sets of footprints, one human and one animatronic. Your character says: "Ran off to that place again. He'll be sorry when he gets back."

85

FFPS RETRO ARCADE

Fruity Maze

On the first level, hit a magnet to attract nearby fruits and a big purple slug to walk through walls. Collect all the fruits before the time runs out to advance to the next level. You'll see a reflection in the screen of a happy blonde girl.

As you start the second level, the music sounds slowed down. This time you're collecting bloodied dogs along with fruits. Now when the screen flashes, the little girl is frowning.

As you start the third and final round, you're collecting dead dogs, flowers, and white boxes. You leave behind bloody footprints as you walk. The music is slowed down even more and you'll find you can't use any magnets or slug power-ups. As the screen flashes, you'll see the girl crying with Springtrap lurking behind her.

Suddenly, a car horn starts honking. Time ended! The game disappears and the text on the screen reads, "He's not really dead . . . ," "He is over here," and "Follow me . . ." as the screen starts flickering.

FFPS RETRO ARCADE

Security Puppet

You're brought to a screen with directions to not let your assigned child reach the exit. Your child's code is green. Near the exit there's a large purple-and-white wrapped present. Every now and then the lid lifts up and the Puppet's green eyes peek out. After a couple of rounds pass with no sight of a child with a green armband, the screen cuts to black.

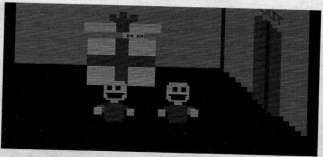

Next, the game opens and a child wearing the green armband is outside in the rain, looking in the window. There's another box on top of the purple one. Suddenly, the Puppet leaps out of the purple box and floats toward the child at the window.

The Puppet exits the building in the rain. The Puppet keeps walking, but then slumps over. Eventually its green eyes die out and it becomes grayer and grayer as it short-circuits. The Puppet drags itself forward. There's a gray child on the ground. The Puppet slumps over and dies holding the child.

GRAVESTONES

If you play the *Midnight Motorist*, *Fruity Maze*, and *Security Puppet* games and receive the Lorekeeper Certificate, you're rewarded with this rare screen after the credits. The names on the graves are Gabriel, Fritz, Susie, and Jeremy—whom fans believe to be the victims of the original killings. One of the graves is hidden from view. The last grave is on the hill in the background.

Some fans believe that the distant grave is Charlie, or Charlotte, implying that Henry's daughter is still watching over the children. The hidden grave is also believed to be Golden Freddy's. To uncover the secret of the hidden grave, check out the *Survival Logbook*.

PICKLES ARE THE ONLY ITEM WITH A HAPPINESS RATING, BUT THEY'RE SOLD OUT FOR THE ENTIRE GAME. TO UNLOCK THEM, BUY ALL THE ITEMS IN THE CATALOG AND UNLOCK THE *POSH PIZZERIA* ACHIEVEMENT BADGE. AFTER THAT, THE PICKLES ARE PURCHASABLE FOR $15!

RARE SCREENS

Besides the Gravestones screen, the Springtrap/Little Blonde Girl Fruity Maze screen, and the "I'm already inside" salvaging screen, there are four rare screens showing the animatronics waiting to be salvaged in the alleyway.

Molten Freddy is seen here resembling Ennard from *Sister Location*. You can spot a yellow-orange eye from Funtime Foxy, a magenta eye from Bon-Bon, a blue eye from Funtime Freddy, and a purple eye from Ballora. Molten Freddy's blueprint, which accompanies the HRY223 audio, also confirms that the animatronics fused together to create this new one.

Scrap Baby is seen with four posters on the wall behind her. One is of a clown laughing, two appear to be contracts, and another looks like Twisted Wolf from *The Twisted Ones* novel.

Scraptrap's rare screen shows four posters behind him, including two posters of contract pages. The other two posters depict a Halloween "Spook-Fest" and a building with gargoyle lions flanking a set of stairs. Some fans have connected the Spook-Fest to either *FNAF3*'s Fazbear Fright attraction or the "Fall Fest '83" seen in *The Curse of Dreadbear*. The poster of the building bears some interesting, if possibly coincidental, resemblance to Heracles Hospital from the short story "The Man in Room 1280."

On Lefty's rare screen, you can spot a thin-striped appendage—reminiscent of the Puppet—poking out of his arm. A poster to the right depicts a puppet as well. Some fans suggest the poster behind Lefty represents William Afton and his children. William would be the elderly ventriloquist; Michael, the talking dummy who resembles the old man; Elizabeth, believed to possess Circus Baby, is the clown; and the bear with the razor-sharp teeth is the third Afton child, considered by many to be the bite victim from *FNAF4*.

Lore and Theories

So . . . What Does It All Mean?

Pizzeria Simulator revealed a lot of lore, and seemingly closed the book on one chapter of the franchise. There's a lot of evidence to support that . . .

♦ Henry is Cassette Man: Henry is known from the novel series as Afton's old business partner, and the inventor of the animatronics. He calls Afton "old friend" and the animatronics "small souls trapped in prisons of my own making." The secret audio file is also labeled "HRY223," which fans have speculated means "Henry 2023."

♦ Connections to Past Games: "2023" could imply that *Pizzeria Simulator* follows *FNAF3*, which takes place thirty years after *FNAF*. The HRY223 audio file also seems to confirm that William Afton was collecting remnant from the possessed animatronics:

  ♦ "He lured them all back, back to a familiar place, back with familiar traits. He brought them all together . . . He set some kind of trap, I don't know what it was, but he led them there, again. He overpowered them, again. And he robbed them of the only thing that they had, again."

♦ Henry's Daughter, the First Victim, the Puppet: Cassette Man insists he must "heal this wound, a wound first inflicted on me, but then one that I let bleed out to cause all this." The events of the Security Puppet mini game, coupled with the *Take Cake to the Children* mini game from *FNAF2*, seem to confirm this. While Charlotte waited outside in the rain, she was murdered by Afton, and her body was thrown in the alleyway. The Security Puppet tried to save her, but short-circuited while holding her, allowing her spirit to merge with the Puppet.

♦ The Puppet Is Inside Lefty: The final HRY223 blueprint also reveals that Lefty is an acronym: "Lure Encapsulate Fuse Transport : Extract." This animatronic seems designed to trap and placate the Puppet, so it can't interfere with Cassette Man's plan.

♦ Remnant: From the HRY223 blueprints, you learn that the Scooper from *Sister Location* infuses things with soul energy, or "Remnant." Remnant can be destroyed by overheating, thus the fire. Remnant is featured heavily in *The Fourth Closet* novel, the *Special Delivery* game, and the stingers of the Fazbear Frights short story series.

CANDY CADET

If you spend a token on Candy Cadet, there's a chance he may reveal a secret story to you. These stories seem connected to Remnant and possibly the HRY223 audio—the idea of luring five things together and combining them.

♦ The first story is about a young woman who is sealed in a small room and given five keys. Each key opens the door to a child, but she can save only one. She melts the keys into one, hoping to save all five. Unfortunately, the key now opens none of the doors and all the children die.

♦ The second story is about a boy who owns a hungry snake. One day he finds five kittens and keeps them in a shoebox. Each night for five nights, the snake sneaks out of its cage and eats a kitten. Filled with regret, the boy cuts open the snake and sews together the remains of the five kittens, putting them back in the shoebox.

♦ The last story is about a kind man who adopted five orphans to protect them from the world. While the man is away, a criminal breaks into his home and kills the children. The man can afford only one coffin, so he stitches the children together to form one body. That night, there was a knock at the door . . .

FAN THEORIES: THE ARCADE MINI GAMES

These arcade machines can be purchased in the Restaurant Management Catalog.

FRUITY MAZE

In *Fruity Maze*, you're shown flashes of a blonde girl smiling as she collects fruits. In the next levels, she gradually gets sadder as she collects dead and dying dogs. Some fans theorize that this girl is one of the original kidnapping victims—"Susie"—whose name appears on one of the gravestones at the end of the game. *The Fourth Closet* novel supports this theory—one of the original missing kids, Susie, talks about how Spring Bonnie helped her find her dog. Susie's story is further explored in the "Coming Home" Fazbear Frights short story.

Another popular theory posits that Mangle from *FNAF2* is the girl's dog. Fans believe the girl's dog died and she was lured away by William Afton to watch him reanimate it as an animatronic. Fans point to the fact that the dog in the game is missing an eye, like Mangle, and that Mangle is unlike other animatronics in that he doesn't speak, only makes garbled radio noises.

MIDNIGHT MOTORIST

Midnight Motorist surprised fans by revealing that the driver of the purple car was yellow instead of the much-anticipated Purple Guy. Since then, a flurry of conversation has arisen around his identity.

♦ Some have theorized that the yellow guy is still William Afton (Springtrap is yellow, after all) and that the gray person watching TV in the house is his son Michael. The runaway son is believed to be the bite victim, who was stolen by the animatronic, as there were two sets of footprints—one human and one animatronic—leading away from the broken window.

♦ Another interesting theory posits that the yellow man isn't Afton at all, but the father of one of the kidnapping victims. The animatronic footprints were made by Afton, wearing the Springtrap suit, who broke into the house and stole the child from his bed.

♦ Other theories have also popped up around the secret grave in the clearing, with many fans linking it to the twisted animatronics from *The Twisted Ones* novel, who would bury themselves to hide during the day.

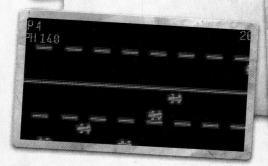

Chapter 7

ULTIMATE CUSTOM NIGHT

You asked for it, you got it! *Ultimate Custom Night* is the seventh and arguably most difficult of the *FNAF* games to date.

You're once again stuck in an office with murderous animatronics, but this time, there are more than fifty of them roaming the building . . . and they each have their own way of attacking, distracting, and annoying you! Lucky for you, you can set their difficulty from zero to twenty and decide whom you want to fight, or have a go at one of sixteen themed challenges. As you rack up points, you unlock cut scenes and lore, possibly relating to who you are and what you're doing.

From your office you need to keep an eye on doors, vents, and air hoses that allow those pesky animatronics to get in. You also need to monitor the heater, air-conditioning, music box, and power generator, as well as the camera, ventilation, and air duct systems. (You know, for those animatronics that are heat or sound sensitive.)

But don't worry, you'll learn on your feet. At least you get a Freddy mask and a flashlight! Don't forget to set those laser traps in the vents, purchase items from the Prize Counter, and watch those Pirate Cove curtains closely, all while collecting Faz-Coins.

Like we said: you asked for it.

The Freddy Scoop

Gameplay begins with the character screen, where you have the option to set fifty animatronics to difficulty levels ranging from zero to twenty. On the sidebar you have the option to set them all to zero, five, ten, or twenty, or to add one individually. You can also see how many points you would receive for a perfect score based on the difficulty of the animatronics. The game will record your highest score along with your best time for that particular difficulty setting. When you've made your selections, press "Go!"

You're greeted by the Controls screen, which will help you react quickly to the various animatronics. Press "Go!" when you're ready to be brought to your office. There are doors on your left and right, along with a vent in front of you and to your right. There are also two duct hoses coming down from the ceiling. Your job is to fight off the animatronics, which differ in number and difficulty based on your character settings. This means the gameplay will change for every setting but the controls remain the same.

HONK THE NOSE
OF THE LITTLE
FREDDY FAZBEAR
ON YOUR DESK

1- Power Generator
2- Silent Ventilation
3- Heater
4- Power AC
5- Global Music Box
6- All OFF
X- All OFF
Z- Flashlight

W- Close Forward Vent
A- Close Left Door
S- Monitor
D- Close Right Door
F- Close Side Vent
C- Catch Fish (Old Man Con.)
Enter- Close Ad (El Chip)
Spacebar- Desk Fan ON/OFF
Hold Esc.- Return to Menu

GO!

Gameplay and Strategy

YOUR BASIC SCREEN shows you the number of Faz-Coins you have in the top left corner, your power usage and percentage along with noise level in the bottom left corner, the time in the top right corner, and the temperature in the bottom right corner.

YOUR POWER INDICATOR appears in the bottom left corner of your screen, showing how much power you have left, and how much power you're using. The ventilation and monitor consume the most power. You can turn the ventilation off until the temperature reaches eighty, but you will attract heat-sensitive animatronics. Also, don't forget that the ventilation system needs to be reset every thirty seconds!

The longer the doors and vents are shut, the more power you lose. While you can't get power back, you can potentially receive a booster the more often you play (even if you lose), or by clicking on Rockstar Foxy's parrot, which will summon him and offer you one of four power-ups, including 1 percent more power. The only way to slow down power consumption is to use the additional power generator, which can be activated by pulling up your monitor and clicking on the "Power Generator" button in the top right of your screen. But be careful—the generator causes a lot of noise.

Number of power bars	Average time it takes to drain 1%	Power drained per hour
Idle	10 seconds	4.5%
1	3 seconds	15%
2	1.25 seconds	36%
3	0.75 seconds	64.29%
4	0.5 seconds	90%
5	0.33 seconds	136%
6	0.25 seconds	180%

YOUR MONITORING SYSTEM is activated by swiping down on the right white arrow at the bottom of your screen. There you can monitor the camera, ventilation, and duct systems. You can also reset or silence the ventilation, enable the power generator, enable the heater or air-conditioning, and turn on the Global Music Box.

THE CAMERA SYSTEM shows eight cameras used to monitor the animatronics.

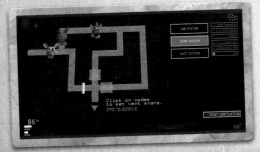

THE VENTILATION SYSTEM shows a small icon of any animatronics that are in the vents. You can deploy vent snares to trap certain animatronics. If there's not enough oxygen, you will need to reset the ventilation.

THE DUCT SYSTEM shows a series of colored caution symbols that correspond to the animatronics in the ducts. You can close only one duct at a time, or you can set an audio lure or turn on the heat to push the animatronics back.

NOISE LEVEL AND TEMPERATURE go hand in hand. Everything that cools or heats the office causes noise, and everything that stops noise makes the temperature rise. The noise can be monitored in the bottom left corner, the temperature in the bottom right. Almost every action makes noise temporarily, including closing the doors.

Collect **FAZ-COINS** by clicking on them as they appear on the cameras or by asking Rockstar Foxy. Coins are also awarded as a power-up at the beginning of the game, depending on how often you play and what bonuses you achieve. Keep track of your coins in the top left corner of your screen.

THE DEATH COIN can be purchased for ten Faz-Coins on Camera 7, but can be used only once per night. It allows you to eliminate certain animatronics without removing points.

THE GLOBAL MUSIC BOX soothes certain animatronics. It doesn't change your noise level, but increases power consumption.

THE FREDDY MASK is enabled by swiping down on the left reddish arrow; this also prevents jump scares from certain animatronics.

BONUSES appear to you after every game played, regardless of performance.

 "Frigid" allows you to start playing at a temperature of fifty degrees.

 "3 Coins" allows you to start the game with three Faz-Coins.

 "Battery" gives you bonus power, totaling 102 percent.

 "Dee Dee Repel" prevents Dee Dee and her friends from appearing during the game.

ANIMATRONICS

♦ **FREDDY** approaches from the left hall, advancing in stages. Watch him on the monitor and shut the door when he reaches in the doorway. He moves faster as the building gets warmer; keep him at a cool sixty degrees Fahrenheit.

♦ **BONNIE AND FOXY** are in Pirate's Cove.

  ♦ Watch for a figurine on your desk. If the figure is Bonnie, avoid looking at Camera 5 (Pirate's Cove). If you do, he'll disable all cameras for some time.

  ♦ If the figure is Foxy, check Camera 5. If you don't, he breaks apart and slips pieces into your office. Once he reassembles himself, he'll jump-scare you.

♦ **CHICA** stays in the kitchen; you can listen to her on Camera 4. Keep the music box wound for both her and the Puppet. If you stop hearing the noise from the kitchen, change the music by pressing the button below the Puppet's windup button. If you don't change it, Chica will jump-scare you.

♦ **GOLDEN FREDDY** appears at random in your office. Stare at him for too long and he'll jump-scare you. Instead, put your monitor or tablet up, or put on the Freddy mask.

TOY FREDDY plays *Five Nights with Mr. Hugs* on Camera 8. In the game, there are three ways into the office and only one door can be closed. Click the cams on Toy Freddy's monitor and close the correct door to block Mr. Hugs. If you check on Toy Freddy and see "Game Over" on his screen, that means he lost . . . and he's coming for you.

TOY BONNIE and **WITHERED BONNIE** sneak in through a trapdoor to your right, and both can be cleared by donning the Freddy mask. Toy Bonnie's coming is signaled by a low buzzing sound and flickering lights. Withered Bonnie will similarly cause audio distortions and disrupt your screen.

TOY CHICA is very active, sneaking in through a trapdoor on your left. Put on the Freddy mask and look directly at her.

WITHERED CHICA enters through the vents, but can be blocked using the Vent Snare. If she reaches the office, she'll become stuck, preventing you from closing it. While this also temporarily prevents other animatronics (except Mangle) from entering through the vents, Withered Chica will eventually wiggle free and jump-scare you.

♦ **MANGLE** climbs through the vents and can be stopped using the vent snare. Once the vent door in your office opens, she'll hang from the ceiling, cause audio distortions, and jump-scare you.

♦ **THE PUPPET** stays in its music box as usual. Make sure the music box is wound.

♦ **BB** and **JJ** will try to sneak in through the side vent. Keep it closed until you hear a thud, indicating he or she is gone. If BB slips in, he'll disable your flashlight. If JJ sneaks in, she'll disable the door controls.

♦ **SPRINGTRAP** climbs silently through the front vent. Close the door when you see him.

♦ **PHANTOM MANGLE** appears at random on your monitor. If you close your monitor or switch viewing modes, he'll disappear. Leave her too long, and he'll come into your office and make noise.

♦ **PHANTOM FREDDY** materializes at random in your office. Shine your flashlight at him quickly or he'll jump-scare you, causing you to black out for a short period.

♦ **PHANTOM BB** appears at random on your monitor. Close the monitor or switch viewing modes to avoid a jump scare and blackout.

♦ **FREDDLES** will populate your office at random. Shine your flashlight to make them disappear. If too many Freddles accumulate, **Nightmare Freddy** will jump-scare you.

♦ **NIGHTMARE FREDBEAR** and **NIGHTMARE** appear as a duo. Fredbear appears in the left doorway, Nightmare in the right. Shut the doors as soon as you see their glowing eyes or hear a deep laugh sound cue.

♦ **NIGHTMARE BONNIE** and **NIGHTMARE MANGLE** each attack once per night from the right hall. To fend them off, purchase their plush toys on Camera 7 with Faz-Coins (the amount varies based on the difficulty).

♦ As the heat rises in the office, **JACK-O-CHICA** will appear in the right and left doors at the same time. Close the doors before the temperature reaches one hundred degrees Fahrenheit.

♦ **NIGHTMARIONNE** appears at random in different areas of the office. Avoid leaving your cursor over it.

♦ **NIGHTMARE BALLOON BOY** sits slumped over in your office. Do not shine your light on him if he's sitting. If he stands, shine your light on him to return him to the sitting position.

♦ **CIRCUS BABY** attacks only once per night, from the Right Hall. Fend her off by purchasing her plush toy on Camera Ø7.

♦ **BALLORA** approaches from the left or right hall, disabling your camera feeds. Listen to her music to determine which side she's approaching from, and close the correct door.

♦ **FUNTIME FOXY** hides behind the curtain in Funtime Cove. The sign outside lists a "showtime" when Funtime Foxy will find you. Watch her as the time approaches and until the time passes. This will buy you a few hours until a new time is listed.

♦ **ENNARD** approaches from the vents and can be tracked only when in motion. Close the vents when you hear a squeaking noise.

♦ **HAPPY FROG, MR. HIPPO**, and **PIGPATCH** use the duct system and hoses to drop into your office. An audio lure will keep Happy Frog away, while the heater or audio lure can be used to deter Mr. Hippo and Pigpatch.

♦ **NEDD BEAR** also uses the duct system and hoses, but he's only fooled by the audio decoy half of the time. Use heat to deter him.

♦ **ORVILLE ELEPHANT** is the same as the other Mediocre animatronics, but he's only fooled by audio 1Ø percent of the time and is much faster. Use the heater to repel him!

♦ **ROCKSTAR FREDDY** remains in the office. When he activates, he'll demand a payment of five Faz-Coins. Turn up the heat to make him malfunction.

♦ **ROCKSTAR BONNIE** appears in your office without his guitar. Find and double-click it on the camera system to make him go away.

♦ **ROCKSTAR CHICA** waits outside the left or right doorway. Double-click the wet floor sign to put it in front of the door and make her leave.

♦ **ROCKSTAR FOXY'S** parrot will fly across the screen in your office; if you click on it, Rockstar Foxy will appear and either jump-scare you or offer you one of four upgrades: adding 1 percent to your power, resetting the office temperature to sixty degrees Fahrenheit, soundproofing the office, or granting you ten Faz-Coins.

♦ **EL CHIP** periodically interrupts you with advertisements for his restaurant, El Chip's Fiesta Buffet. Click "Skip" or press "Enter" to get rid of them. The higher his difficulty, the more often his ads will appear.

♦ Make a lot of noise and **MUSIC MAN** becomes active, eventually jump-scaring you. Reducing noise will make him calm down.

♦ **FUNTIME CHICA** will occasionally appear and pose, accompanied by camera flashes, which will disorient you.

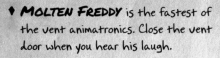

MOLTEN FREDDY is the fastest of the vent animatronics. Close the vent door when you hear his laugh.

SCRAP BABY appears by the side of your desk, slumped over, once per night. Only shock her if you see her move, as it will drain 1 percent of your power.

SCRAPTRAP/WILLIAM AFTON attacks only once per night, from the right vent. Close the vent if you hear a loud clamoring sound and see flickering lights.

LEFTY stays in the closet on Camera 3. If the office becomes too noisy or too hot, he'll jump-scare you. Soothe him by switching on the Global Music Box, but watch your power supply.

PHONE GUY's calls make noise. You have a few seconds to mute his call or you have to listen to his entire message.

TRASH AND THE GANG appear in the office at random and create loud noise while blocking your screen. Mr. Can-Do appears on the camera.

There's a chance that **OLD MAN CONSEQUENCES'S** subscreen will appear in the top-left corner of your screen. Your goal is to press "C" when the fish is on the red dot. If you catch the fish, the screen disappears; otherwise, your camera will be inaccessible for some time.

HELPY appears in the top-right corner of your office, on the back desk. Click on him to avoid being jump-scared with an air horn.

DEE DEE appears at random and adds new animatronics to your game at difficulty levels one through ten. She can either add a character from the Start screen or a special character from her own roster . . .

♦ **RWQFSFASXC** makes your office go dark for ten seconds, once per night.

♦ **PLUSHTRAP** appears on Camera 6, sitting in his chair. Scare him away by clicking on him.

♦ **BONNET** walks across the screen at random. Click her nose or you'll be jump-scared.

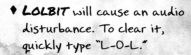

♦ **NIGHTMARE CHICA'S** jaws will close slowly around your field of vision until she jump-scares you. Stop her by using the heater or Power A/C.

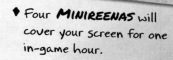

♦ Four **MINIREENAS** will cover your screen for one in-game hour.

♦ **LOLBIT** will cause an audio disturbance. To clear it, quickly type "L-O-L."

FREDBEAR can be summoned by setting all animatronics to zero and Golden Freddy to one. If Dee Dee summons another animatronic, you'll need to restart the night. Purchase a Death Coin with ten Faz-Coins, then wait for Golden Freddy to show up. When he does, use the Death Coin on him and you'll be jump-scared by Fredbear.

POINTS AND TROPHIES

Point totals must be accumulated to unlock "Intermissions," office skins, and trophies.

An intermission appears for every 700 points earned. These include *Toy Chica: The High School Years, Bear of Vengeance*, and a twitching Golden Freddy.

Office skins can also be unlocked. The *Sister Location* skin costs 2,000 points, the *FNAF3* skin costs 5,000, and the *FNAF4* skin costs 8,000.

You can also receive three trophies in bronze, silver, and gold if you win against a certain number of animatronics cranked up to 20 difficulty. Bronze is awarded for winning 40/20 mode, silver for 45/20 mode, and gold for 50/20 mode.

Codes, Glitches, and Secrets

XOR/Shadow Dee Dee

Sounds to Listen For:

When playing in 50/20 mode, a new animatronic called XOR, or Shadow Dee Dee, will appear, even if Dee Dee Repel is active. She is colorless and eyeless, and arrives accompanied by garbled audio. She eventually calls her entire roster of animatronics, with around seven seconds between the spawn of each. The order goes: RWQFSFASXC, Plushtrap, Nightmare Chica, Bonnet, Minireenas, and Lolbit. She can also very rarely appear in normal play.

Death Lines

Most of the animatronics have "death lines" dialogue they speak after killing you.

♦ Mangle: "He's here and always watching. The one you shouldn't have killed."

♦ Nightmare: "I am your wickedness made flesh."

♦ The Puppet: "The others are like animals, but I am very aware."

♦ Withered Chica: "I was the first. I saw everything."

♦ Ballora: "Admit it, you wanted to let me in."

If you're treated to one of Mr. Hippo's extended death lin Elephant. Don't bother trying to skip through it; just sit back, relax, and let Mr. Hippo have his moment.

Old Man Consequences

If all other characters are set to zero and Old Man Consequences is set to one, catching a fish will result in being sent to Old Man Consequences's pond. Old Man Consequences will ask you to "come and sit with me a while," prompting you to press "Enter." When this is done, Old Man Consequences concludes, "Leave the demon to his demons. Rest your own soul. There is nothing else."

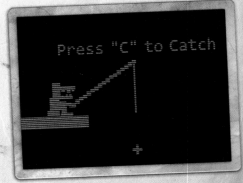

Some players have said that by pressing "A" and "D" above the pond, the game will crash. Music can apparently be heard in the background that sounds like robotic screaming.

MAPPING THE ANIMATRONICS IN UCN

SCRAPTRAP, WITHERED CHICA, MANGLE, AND MOLTEN FREDDY ALL USE THE VENTS.

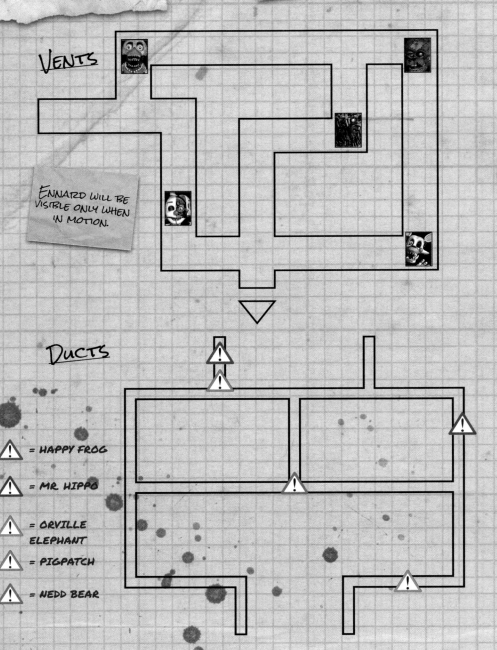

VENTS

ENNARD WILL BE VISIBLE ONLY WHEN IN MOTION.

DUCTS

⚠ = HAPPY FROG

⚠ = MR. HIPPO

⚠ = ORVILLE ELEPHANT

⚠ = PIGPATCH

⚠ = NEDD BEAR

ALL ANIMATRONICS CAN COME FROM EITHER DUCT.

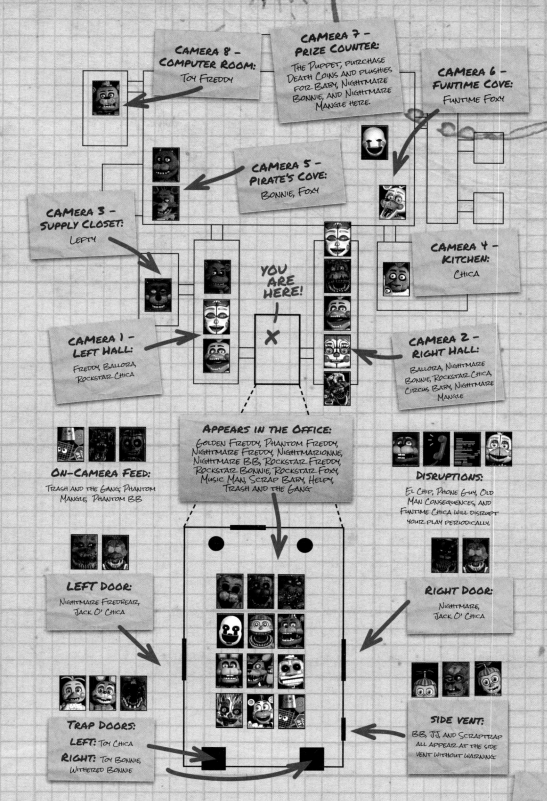

CAMERA 8 – COMPUTER ROOM: Toy Freddy

CAMERA 7 – PRIZE COUNTER: The Puppet, purchase Death Coins and plushies for Baby, Nightmare Bonnie, and Nightmare Mangle here.

CAMERA 6 – FUNTIME COVE: Funtime Foxy

CAMERA 5 – PIRATE'S COVE: Bonnie, Foxy

CAMERA 3 – SUPPLY CLOSET: Lefty

CAMERA 4 – KITCHEN: Chica

YOU ARE HERE!

CAMERA 1 – LEFT HALL: Freddy, Ballora, Rockstar Chica

CAMERA 2 – RIGHT HALL: Ballora, Nightmare Bonnie, Rockstar Chica, Circus Baby, Nightmare Mangle

APPEARS IN THE OFFICE: Golden Freddy, Phantom Freddy, Nightmare Freddy, Nightmarionne, Nightmare BB, Rockstar Freddy, Rockstar Bonnie, Rockstar Foxy, Music Man, Scrap Baby, Helpy, Trash and the Gang

ON-CAMERA FEED: Trash and the Gang, Phantom Mangle, Phantom BB

DISRUPTIONS: El Chip, Phone Guy, Old Man Consequences, and Funtime Chica will disrupt your play periodically.

LEFT DOOR: Nightmare Fredbear, Jack O' Chica

RIGHT DOOR: Nightmare, Jack O' Chica

TRAP DOORS:
LEFT: Toy Chica
RIGHT: Toy Bonnie, Withered Bonnie

SIDE VENT: BB, JJ, and Scraptrap all appear at the side vent without warning

109

Lore and Theories

INTERMISSIONS:
TOY CHICA: THE HIGH SCHOOL YEARS

The first unlockable intermission portrays Toy Chica as a high school student who obsesses over various other "boys" at her school, including Freddy, Toy Bonnie, the Puppet, Funtime Foxy, Pigpatch, and the Twisted Wolf from *The Twisted Ones*. She details in her diary entries how she plans to lure the boys inside and then they'll be hers "forever." Each entry explains, "There is only one thing that could possibly go wrong," before everything resets and Toy Chica has a new target.

In the last cut scene, Toy Chica explains that she's once again brokenhearted, but that tomorrow is another day and that she knows she'll find another guy for her. As she writes in her diary against a tree, her school bag can be seen behind her filled with body parts of the various "guys" (animatronics) she loved.

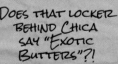

DOES THAT LOCKER BEHIND CHICA SAY "EXOTIC BUTTERS"?!

110

INTERMISSIONS: BEAR OF VENGEANCE

This intermission shows various cut scenes portraying Freddy and Foxy as enemies in feudal Japan. Every time Freddy confronts Foxy, he ends up having to perform some sort of household chore for the villain after being defeated in battle. Freddy always vows to seek vengeance the next time.

The title screens are in Japanese, and Freddy's and Foxy's lines are spoken in Japanese; however there are English subtitles. Some fans have noted that the English subtitles don't quite match the spoken Japanese.

FINAL INTERMISSION: GOLDEN FREDDY

After unlocking all the cut scenes from both intermissions, you will be shown Golden Freddy sitting in darkness. He twitches violently as he approaches the screen before fading away into the darkness.

FAN THEORIES

◆ WHO ARE YOU AND WHERE ARE YOU?

Many fans posit that the animatronics' death lines indicate you are playing as William Afton, trapped in Hell. Support for their theory comes from Cassette Man, whom fans believe to be Henry, Afton's old partner, condemning his "old friend" to "burn" at the end of *Pizzeria Simulator*. Some of the animatronics' death lines include the words burn and flame and fire.

Others have pointed to "The Man in Room 1280" short story, which many presume shows that Afton somehow survived the fire in *Pizzeria Simulator*. These theorists believe that Afton is experiencing this while in some kind of coma, as the nurses state that the man has been in the hospital for years.

◆ GOLDEN FREDDY

Some fans believe that Golden Freddy's final cut scene, where he twitches and retreats into darkness, means that his spirit has not been put to rest and that he is, or will be, seeking revenge.

◆ THE ONE YOU SHOULD NOT HAVE KILLED

A few different animatronics' death lines use the phrase "the one you should not have killed." Mangle and Withered Chica's death lines suggest this person is a boy, but who exactly is the one you should not have killed? Some fans believe it's Golden Freddy. One of Orville Elephant's death lines says, "He tried to release you, he tried to release us. But I'm not gonna let that happen. I will hold you here, I will keep you here, no matter how many times they burn us." Is the person whom you should not have killed residing in "Hell," haunting and torturing Afton, as some fans suggest?

◆ THE FACE

Some players have noted that a child's face appears in the game at random intervals. Could this be "the one you should not have killed"?

♦ TOY CHICA'S HIGH SCHOOL YEARS
Some fans suggest that the different methods laid out by Toy Chica to lure the boys "inside" may be ways that William Afton lured children to him in order to kill them.

♦ BEAR OF VENGEANCE
Fans theorize that the Foxy vs. Freddy drama is actually portraying Freddy as Henry and Foxy as William Afton.

♦ MEDIOCRES DEATH LINES
During the deaths of Happy Frog and her friends, some fans have suggested that a young girl's voice can be heard echoing what the animatronics are saying. Some have even said that the voice resembles that of Scrap Baby from *Pizzeria Simulator*.

♦ NIGHTMARE FREDBEAR'S DEATH LINE
One of Nightmare Fredbear's death lines says, "Let me put you back together, then take you apart all over again." Some fans believe that this ties into the iconic Fredbear plushie quote from *FNAF4*: "I will put you back together."

Chapter 8

HELP WANTED

Seems like a no-brainer, right? Transporting one of the most popular horror games of all time to virtual reality, where fans can fall in love with the terror all over again. But what started out as a fun new way to play *FNAF* quickly morphed into a chilling new chapter for the series.

The setup for *FNAF* games usually involve filling an open position at Fazbear Entertainment—whether you're a night guard, a technician, or even a franchise owner. Here, you're playing a lot of roles: security guard, vent tech, animatronic maintenance . . . but there's another job you hear about: game tester. That's right. *Help Wanted* had a bit of a bumpy road to development, and there might still be some glitches left behind by the game team. But as with every *FNAF* entry, things aren't quite as they appear.

Lurking beneath familiar faces, fun new game modes, and more *FNAF*-themed snacks than you can eat in a lifetime . . . something is festering at the heart of the game. Can you find what it is before it spreads too far? Or is it already too late?

The Freddy Scoop

Fazbear Entertainment is excited to join the digital age, and what better way to do that...

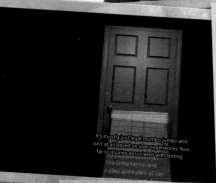

It's mostly just legal mumbo jumbo and isn't at all based on user experiences thus far or injuries associated with testing.

THE FREDDY FAZBEAR VIRTUAL EXPERIENCE

Welcome to *The Freddy Fazbear Virtual Experience!* Fazbear Entertainment has had a rough few decades, thanks in part to some lunatic spreading lies about them through indie video games. But thankfully, the company isn't above laughing at itself, which is the reason for this VR game. At the end of the introduction, the company signs your virtual waiver for you (something-something digital consciousness transference, something-something real-world manifestations of digital characters), and you're good to go.

MAIN HUB

You land in a new home base of sorts, situated out in what's usually the dining area at Freddy Fazbear's Pizza. Behind you are tables and chairs and the Prize Counter. To your left is Pirate Cove. To your right, in the doorway, a rabbit figure is watching. In front of you is the main show stage as well as a desk, set with several buttons, switches, and monitors.

♦ Party Machine: Throw the switch on your left to enter Nightmare Mode, a more difficult challenge mode of the existing mini games.

♦ Go to Gallery: This button appears after beating the *Pizza Party* mini game. It takes you to a gallery to view the models of the animatronics.

♦ Prize Counter: This button moves you to the Prize Counter.

♦ Virtual Menu: Use this console to select a mini game. As you complete mini games, more are unlocked (up to thirty). There is a secret button on the left side of the console that we'll get to later.

♦ Showtime: This button activates the animatronics show, but it's out of order.

♦ Replay Title: This button replays the Title screen.

♦ Token Counter: To your right, this monitor tracks how many Faz-Tokens you've collected (see page 134).

LOOKING FOR FOXY ON THE MENU SCREEN? TURN AROUND.

PRIZE COUNTER

Prizes are unlocked by opening a present (similar in style to the Puppet's present) with a hand crank at the end of each mini game. Certain prizes can be eaten, some can be eaten, and some you can choke on if you try to eat it three times.

At the Prize Counter, you can collect the prizes you've unlocked. Special prizes become available by collecting the Faz-Tokens hidden throughout the mini games. Use the console on your right to review the prizes and select them. The only prize available at game start is the basketball.

Occasionally, you can earn a jump scare prize, where Plushtrap or Bon-Bon will simply jump-scare you upon opening the prize.

Fazbear Entertainment
Where Fantasy and Fun Come to Life
Prize Catalog COLLECT THEM ALL!

FOOD/DRINK

☐ BONNIE BITES

☐ BUTTER FOR ONE

☐ CHICA CHUG

☐ DISAPPOINTMENT CHIPS

☐ EL CHIP'S TORTILLA CHIPS

☐ EL CHIP'S TORTILLA CHIPS BOLD AND SPICY

☐ EXOTIC BEVERAGE

☐ FAZBAR

☐ FOXY COVE COOLER

☐ FREDDY FUDGEBAR

☐ LEMON CHICA BAR

☐ MEAT BITES

☐ MEAT BITES XL

☐ MIXED NUTS

☐ PIRATE PLUNDERBAR

☐ SLICE OF CAKE

☐ STICK OF BUTTER

☐ SODARONI

PLUSHIES

☐ BONNIE

☐ CHICA

☐ FOXY

☐ FREDDY FAZBEAR

☐ THE PUPPET

☐ TOY BONNIE

☐ TOY CHICA

❏ TOY FREDDY

❏ NIGHTMARIONNE

❏ CIRCUS BABY

❏ FUNTIME FOXY

❏ FUNTIME FREDDY

❏ SCRAP BABY

ACTION FIGURES (for ages 3 and up)

❏ FREDDY FAZBEAR

❏ ENNARD

❏ MANGLE

❏ TOY FREDDY

❏ TOY BONNIE

❏ TOY CHICA

❏ BALLOON BOY

❏ PUPPET

❏ BONNIE

❏ CHICA

❏ FOXY

❏ NIGHTMARIONNE

❏ CIRCUS BABY

❏ FUNTIME FOXY

❏ FUNTIME FREDDY

❏ NIGHTMARE FREDBEAR

❏ PLUSHTRAP

❏ BON-BON

TOYS (for ages 3 and up)

❏ BALLOON

❏ CUPCAKE

❏ CATERPILLAR

❏ PHONE

❏ ROBOT

UNLOCKABLE WITH FAZ-COINS

❏ BASKETBALL (FREE)

❏ DEAD COCKROACH (5, EDIBLE)

❏ PLASTIC CUP (8)

❏ DESK FAN (10)

❏ ROLLED PAPER (15)

❏ FREDDY MASK (20)

❏ 8-BALL (22)

❏ HELPY (25)

BOBBLEHEADS

❏ BONNIE

❏ CHICA

❏ FREDDY FAZBEAR

Gameplay and Strategy

FNAF 1-3

The *FNAF* game modes follow similar rules to their original counterparts, where you need to stay alive until 6 a.m. while defending against the animatronics from each game. Check out the Gameplay & Strategy sections on pages 6, 18, 32, 48, 80, and 96 for tips and tricks to these modes. Note that there are a few key differences in *Help Wanted*:

♦ Only the first four nights are playable in normal mode.

♦ In *FNAF1* and *FNAF2*, the animatronics are active on night 1 (no freebies here).

♦ *FNAF3* gives you a bit of a break. Instead of a pop-up window, you reboot your systems on a terminal to your left. This means you're able to keep watch in the office and view the camera while rebooting systems.

♦ In *Help Wanted*, fans can watch the animatronics walking toward them and are able to peek out into the hallways, look behind them, and interact with more items on the desk.

♦ The game's original rare screens and secrets do not appear, including Golden Freddy and the *FNAF2* and *FNAF3* mini games.

FNAF1 FOXY'S SPEED IS PUNISHING IN VR. KEEP AN EYE ON PIRATE COVE.

NIGHTMARE MODE

Nightmare Modes for *FNAF1*, *FNAF2*, and *FNAF3* each take place on Night 5 (and Night 6 for *FNAF2*), making Nightmare Mode inherently more difficult. The game also throws a few more curveballs at you.

♦ *FNAF1*: The screen is now black and white, similar to your security monitor feeds. Your doors and lights are broken, activating randomly.

- o Keep an eye on Freddy, as it will slow him down, and listen for his laugh. He's at the right door by his fifth laugh, and doesn't leave, so keep the door closed.

- o Chica is pretty quiet, but she and Bonnie have similar sound cues: footsteps. Focus on listening for them and closing the doors when you hear them.

- o Keeping an eye on Freddy and Foxy is tough. Ignore Foxy's camera entirely, and focus on listening for his footsteps in the hall instead.

IN *FNAF1*, THE CUPCAKE ON YOUR DESK APPEARS AS NIGHTMARE CUPCAKE.

♦ *FNAF2*

- o Night 5: The room is dark, like it's under a black light, making it difficult to spot the various animatronics coming at you from the hall, vents, etc. Night 5 does not include the withered animatronics, so no need to worry about them.

- o Withered: The room is now almost completely dark, but what you can see is cast in an eerie purple glow. Withered is much more difficult, as it features all animatronics.

♦ *FNAF3*:

- ♦ This mode seems to be taking place during the fire that we know occurs at Fazbear's Fright at the end of *FNAF3*. The room is now red and you can see flames through the vents. Springtrap moves much faster, so try to trap him early between Cameras 9 and 10, and keep rebooting your systems.

119

PLUSHTRAP

LAND ON THE X

Similar to the night-start mini games from *FNAF4*, the animatronic starts at the end of the hallway. Shining your flashlight causes them to stop in their tracks. Listen for the audio cues and get them to land on the X in front of you before time runs out.

NIGHTMARE BB

NIGHTMARE MODE: NIGHTMARE BB

In Nightmare Mode, you are lower on the ground, and the hallway is filled with balloons.

NIGHTMARE MODE: PLUSHTRAP

In Nightmare Mode, you are lower on the ground, and there are toys obscuring the two nearest rooms.

SURVIVE 'TIL 6 A.M.

Similar to clearing Freddles in *FNAF4*, you must shine your flashlight to clear the toys approaching you. The flashlight has limited battery life that recharges over time, so use the flashlight sparingly.

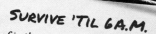

PLUSHBABY

NIGHTMARE MODE: PLUSHBABY

In Nightmare Mode, the room is filled with Circus Baby plushes, and the approaching toys are Scrap Baby plushes.

CROSS THE ROOM

Similar to the Funtime Auditorium level in *Sister Location*, the animatronic in the room with you is motion activated, so the room is dark. Use your Flash Beacon to navigate the darkness. If you see an animatronic in your path, freeze and wait for it to leave. Slow and steady wins.

FUNTIME FOXY

NIGHTMARE MODE: FUNTIME FOXY

In Nightmare Mode, the room is filled with Circus Baby, Funtime Freddy, and Funtime Foxy animatronics, but Lolbit is the only motion-activated animatronic.

Fazbear Entertainment

Animatronic Technician Manual

Parts & Service

Hearkening back to your technician tasks in *Sister Location*, your job is to make sure the animatronics are clean, safe, and functioning properly. Follow the instructions exactly if you want to survive.

Bonnie

Bonnie's guitar is out of tune and needs to be recalibrated. To do this, you'll need to access his harmonization module, located in his secondary throat pipe. Start by removing Bonnie's eyes and placing them in the cleaning receptacles. Then press the two buttons on Bonnie's jaw to open his faceplate. Once open, press the blinking button to enter calibration mode. Watch the colors that correspond to the notes to find which note is out of tune, then turn the correctly colored knob on his guitar. Replace Bonnie's eyes, click the buttons on his jaw, and he's good to go.

- **Nightmare Mode:** Bonnie appears under a black light, with a shower of confetti and background music playing. Good luck with that color-coded harmony calibration.

Chica

There have been customer complaints about Chica's acrid smell. Remove all food particles from Chica and put them in the trash bin. Press the two buttons on the side of her head to open her beak. To remove Chica's cockroach infestation, apply the Fazbear Entertainment Restaurant-Grade Chemispray to Chica's exterior by pressing the button under the hanging canister. Avoid inhaling the chemispray, as exposure may result in respiratory problems or skin or eye irritation. Carefully reattach Chica's arm and then her cupcake plate. Reapply the chemispray to

Fazbear Entertainment

clear another round of cockroaches. When the cupcake jumps away, return it to Chica's plate.

- **Nightmare Mode:** The room is completely dark, and Chica's cupcake is now its nightmare counterpart. The chemispray is no longer effective, so you must remove the cockroach infestation by hand.

Freddy

It looks like a guest has left a personal item on the star attraction. Grab and remove the child's hat from Freddy's mouth and place it in the lost-and-found bin. Grab Freddy's bow tie and pull outward to open Freddy's chest cavity. Inside, remove the child's watch from the left side of his chest and place it in the lost and found. Remove Freddy's music box, press the red button to reset the safety latch, then remove the child's shoe. Carefully replace Freddy's music box and then touch Freddy's nose. Your pay will be docked for mishandling of parts.

- **Nightmare Mode:** Freddy is in a dark room, surrounded by high-contrast static screens. Light is coming from his eyes and mouth, and many animatronic parts and toys are strewn about the floor.

Foxy

Foxy has been out of commission for quite some time. It's your job to return him to full working condition so that Pirate Cove can be reopened. Begin by placing Foxy's head on his endoskeleton. Doing so prompts a malfunction of his proprietary servo motors. You'll need to place new control fuses in the exposed receptacles, beginning with his legs. Inside the chest, a former employee placed the wrong fuse there. Remove the incorrect fuse and place it in the upper arm. Now insert new fuses for the chest. Finally, place an eye in his right eye socket.

- **Nightmare Mode:** Foxy is completely burned and the workroom is on fire.

Fazbear Entertainment

Vent Technician Certification Program

Vent Repair

Many *FNAF* games feature animatronics that are sensitive to heat, or require activating ventilation systems to keep yourself cool. This mode extends that mission into a series of puzzles in dark, cramped spaces, all in an effort to get the facility to a perfect seventy-two degrees Fahrenheit.

Mangle

Start by pushing the flashing button to hear from Tutorial Unit. You'll then descend to the first set of puzzles. When the service elevator stops, push the second flashing button to open a compartment with a lever. Flip the lever to activate your headlight and scare off Mangle. Listen carefully for Mangle's cues, and shoo him away by turning your headlight on her.

On this level, you must throw four levers to advance. Reach into the second vent that opens and flip the switch on the ceiling. Flip the second lever when it appears on the left side of the vent. Inside the central elevator, find and turn two yellow valves (one above and one below) and a third level will appear. Throw this lever and press the yellow flashing button above you. The final vent will now open. Above the final vent, open the hatch to reveal a blinking light inside the vent that changes colors. You must match the given order on the keypad to your right. Doing so will reveal the final lever. Throw it to complete your task.

- **Nightmare Mode:** A darker level with black-light coloring, and all three vents are open at the same time. Both Mangle and Shadow Mangle are active to attack you.

Fazbear Entertainment

Ennard

Hit the flashing yellow button to begin. On the first level, as each light turns red, follow the tangled cord from each breaker box to the corresponding button. Hit the buttons in the correct order to open another vent. Solve the same but more complicated puzzle to open a third vent. The third vent has an even more complicated puzzle, and the room is dark, lit only by stray voltage, and Ennard is approaching you. Once solved, Ennard will try to open the doors as you descend to the next level.

In the second level, you must use a small, medium, and finally a large gear to get the machinery up and running. Ennard is present and can attack. Start in the left panel. Grab the small gear and place it in the machinery to access the medium gear. In the middle panel, place the medium gear straight ahead to open a gate on the right side. Now that it's accessible, place the small gear in the top-right side of the machinery, and the medium gear in the top left. This will cause the large gear to drop. Still in the middle panel, replace the medium gear straight ahead to reach the large and small gears. In the right panel, place the large gear on the far left, the small gear one peg below the large gear, and the medium gear on the remaining upper peg. Now the machinery is in working order.

In the boiler room, align the pipes properly to run the gas. There are multiple solutions to these puzzles, but one path is as follows. In the left panel, press buttons 3, 1, 2 in order to open the middle panel. Here, you can press rotate, rotate, rotate, 2. In the right panel, press the button to set fire to Ennard.

- **Nightmare Mode:** This mode is similarly dark and cluttered with animatronic parts. The mode is also played upside down; though the puzzles have the same solutions, you may have to take additional steps or think differently to complete them. On the first level, when the second vent opens, Springtrap approaches, limiting your time. After successfully completing the game, Ennard jumps at you, implying that he survived the fire. The elevator crashes.

NIGHT TERRORS

This game mode hearkens back to *FNAF4* with some familiar and not-so-familiar faces. As with that game, keep an open ear for audio cues.

FUNTIME FREDDY

Funtime Freddy, Bon-Bon, and Bonnet haunt this game. Funtime Freddy will approach with Bon-Bon from either hall, so be sure to listen at the door before shining your light. Bonnet hides in the dresser drawers and the closet. Shine your flashlight on her or she'll jump-scare you. Note that Bonnet's and Bon-Bon's jump scares can't harm you.

NIGHTMARIONNE

Players will hear "My Grandfather's Clock" (the Puppet's song) playing. Nightmarionne can appear from anywhere—the halls, bed, closet, and a disturbing hole in the ceiling. When it appears at the door, its eyes will be visible in the dark. Shine your flashlight on Nightmarionne's tentacles to repel attacks from the bed, closet, and ceiling. The tentacles are punishing; you may need to hold the door shut against a Nightmarionne attack while removing tentacles from the room.

CIRCUS BABY

In this game, you play from inside the closet, with Circus Baby looking for you. If she sees you, close the door as she runs your way. But be wary: Closing the door for too long will attract attention from the PlushBabies surrounding you. Best to wait until Circus Baby is close to the closet, as the PlushBabies can jump-scare you, even if you're holding the door shut against Circus Baby's attack.

NIGHTMARE FREDBEAR

As in *FNAF4*, Nightmare Fredbear can attack from all directions. When he's on the bed, shine your flashlight to ward him off. But when he's in the hallways, it's best to look for his red glowing eyes, or use a quick burst of light to scan the area. The flashlight makes Fredbear move faster in the hall. If he's at the hall or closet doors, hold them closed to keep him from getting to you.

Animatronic	Funtime Freddy	Nightmarionne	Circus Baby	Nightmare Fredbear
Length of Nights	3 minutes	3.5 minutes	2 minutes	3 minutes

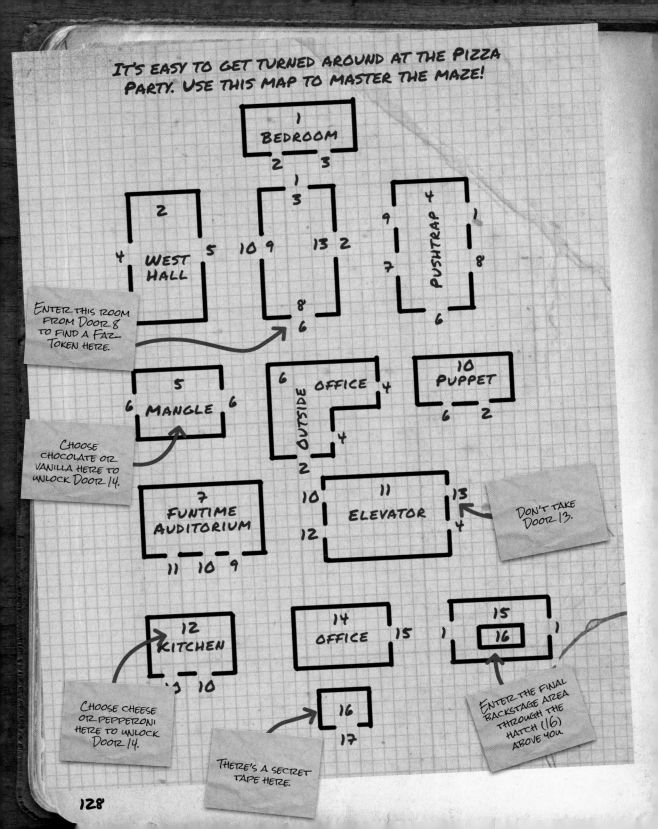

It's easy to get turned around at the Pizza Party. Use this map to master the maze!

1
BEDROOM
2   3

1
3

2
WEST HALL
4   5   10 9   13 2

4
PUSHTRAP
9   1

7   8

8

6

6

Enter this room from Door 8 to find a Faz-Token here.

5
MANGLE
6   6

6   OUTSIDE OFFICE   4
     2

10
PUPPET
6   2

4

Choose chocolate or vanilla here to unlock Door 14.

7
FUNTIME AUDITORIUM
11   10   9

10
11
ELEVATOR
13

12   4

Don't take Door 13.

12
KITCHEN

9   10

Choose cheese or pepperoni here to unlock Door 14.

14
OFFICE   15   1

15
16   1

Enter the final backstage area through the hatch (16) above you.

16
17

There's a secret tape here.

128

NIGHT TERRORS

NIGHTMARE MODE: PIZZA PARTY

This terrifying free-roam game brings you to the first ending of *Help Wanted*. Navigate the surreal black-light maze, which takes you through various locations you've seen throughout the *FNAF* series. Your goal is to reach the kitchen and Mangle rooms via Doors 12 and 5, so you can choose the flavors for your cake and pizza. Once you've made your choices, return to the outside office room and take the newly available Door 14. This will lead you through the *FNAF 3* office into a new room. Look up and crawl through the hatch to reach Backstage, and your pizza party.

THE FIRST ENDING

The backstage area is filled with cake and presents. Eat as much as you like. Glitchtrap appears, and gestures for you to follow him. Once you do, the screen goes black. You reawaken onstage, presumably stuffed into a Freddy Fazbear suit, performing for an empty pizzeria as Glitchtrap dances in the background. After the credits roll, HandUnit congratulates you.

Congratulations on completing the Freddy Fazbear virtual experience. You did an amazing job. You might be wondering if you missed anything, or if there's anything left to see. So just take my word for it: You didn't miss anything, and there's nothing left to see. We're looking forward to a fresh start with you, now that we've had a good laugh at these tall tales, and now that you realize that Fazbear Entertainment is a safe, family-friendly brand with no skeletons in our closet. So good-bye for now, and we'll see you on the toy aisle. Bye-bye. Bye-bye. Bye-Bye. Buh-bye. Take care now.

Codes, Glitches, and Secrets

THE GALLERY

Once you complete the Pizza Party level, a new button appears on your desk: Go to Gallery. Here, you can take your time looking at the models for the game's animatronics.

THE SECRET TAPES

There are two other endings for *Help Wanted*. To get them, you'll need to obtain the secret tapes hidden throughout the game.

THE TAPE PLAYER

To listen to the tapes, head to the Prize Counter. Throw a basketball at the tape player (to the right of the Chica plush) to obtain it. When you return to the main hub, activate the Party Machine and a glitching purple tape player will be sitting on top of your Faz-Token counter. Click it to enter the secret room and listen to the tapes.

INVENTORY LOG

Fazbear Entertainment

Item No.	Description	Location
1	The tapes were created to warn about a malicious code in the game files that the game team is unable to understand or contain.	Intro Sequence, left rail just before waiver appears
2	The malicious code manifests as a character, and it was watching what Tape Girl was doing.	Prize Counter, under the Disappointment Chips
3	Tape Girl overheard a conversation between her manager and someone else. There's a lawsuit and the project is on the line. It seems to involve Jeremy, who warned that something was wrong.	Prize Counter, inside the left gumball machine
4	Describes the guillotine paper slicer in the supply room, and how Jeremy used to do design work, which is how he knew it was there.	*FNAF1*, right side of the desk
5	The client came to the office and emptied things out, including some old game hardware that the team had scanned into the game files. That was when the anomaly began.	*FNAF3*, desktop behind the maintenance panel
6	Talks about that morning, and how Tape Girl saw Jeremy in the testing room, with the supply room lit brightly.	Dark Rooms, PlushBaby, right of the alarm clock
7	Jeremy had nightmares. The company told Tape Girl to leave him alone, like they knew he'd need to be replaced soon.	Dark Rooms, Funtime Foxy, left wall
8	The company started making a case to fire Jeremy, but Tape Girl believes this was more because of something he'd seen, like they needed to discredit him.	Parts & Service, Chica, refuse bin
9	A seeming continuation of Tape 6, Tape Girl finding Jeremy and thinking that ink had spilled everywhere.	Parts & Service, Freddy, under Freddy's right leg
10	Tape Girl takes over Jeremy's work. Another studio is buying Fazbear Entertainment out and will finish the game. She's trying to isolate the anomaly so the next person who tests it can destroy it.	Parts & Service, Foxy, floor left of Foxy
11	The anomaly seems to have attached itself to these logs; Tape Girl resolves to destroy them.	Vent Repair, Mangle, under the right pipes
12	Tape Girl is unable to delete them, but she has another idea.	Vent Repair, Ennard Nightmare Mode, Nightmare Fredbear's mouth, middle panel, descending between the intro and first puzzle level
13	Tape Girl discovers some old files showing that Fazbear Entertainment was working with the "rogue indie developer" to make light of the past and rebrand the company.	Night Terrors, Circus Baby, on the shelf behind you
14	Tape Girl ran a fragmentation program on the logs, hoping to render the anomaly harmless. It also destroyed her warnings.	Night Terrors, Nightmare Fredbear, behind toy telephone
15	Tape Girl seems to change her tune here—she tells you not to reassemble the logs, as doing so will reassemble the anomaly.	Night Terrors, Nightmare Mode Pizza Party, Backstage beside the pizza box
16	Tape Girl now tells you to let the anomaly try to leave the game through you, then use the emergency disconnect switch by the main stage to cause a hard restart and kill it.	Gallery, inside the cabinet under the monitor

MERGE ENDING

To obtain the merge ending, don't follow the instructions on Tape 16. At some point when you load into the main hub area, Glitchtrap will approach you. When he does, your view will slowly darken to purple and your screen will glitch, implying that the merge was successful and Glitchtrap can escape into the real world. You're then led to a Game Over screen.

TRAPPED ENDING

To view the trapped ending, follow the instructions on Tape 16. When Glitchtrap reaches out toward you, flip the Party Machine lever to off, press the Showtime button, reach around the left side of your monitor and hit the secret button there, and then hit the Prize Counter button. Your screen will fade to black, and then you'll be taken to a metal door covered in handprints and scratch marks. Interact with the lock, and a panel slides back. On the other side of the door, Glitchtrap shushes you and walks away.

Replaying Pizza Party after beating the level gains you access to a door in the backstage area. It says EMPLOYEES ONLY and opening it takes you outside. Snow is blowing and there's a billboard that says COMING SOON! with a massive building under construction in the background.

132

PRINCESS QUEST

In the mobile port of *Help Wanted*, the secret tapes are replaced with a mini game called *Princess Quest*. To gain access to the game, you must zoom in on a glitching object at the Prize Counter (this occurs occasionally). The screen will fade to black and reopen on the main hub, where *Princess Quest* is now shown on the right monitor.

The game plays like a classic dungeon crawler, and you need to light torches scattered throughout the ten rooms while avoiding the various Glitchtrap enemies. The game ends with the princess unlocking a door covered in purple overgrowth. At the end of the room is a distorted purple bunny monster, and dialogue appears on the screen, but it doesn't look to be written in a language we can understand. Some sleuthing from fans revealed that the text in the dialogue box is "I ALWAYS COME BACK." The distorted voicelines heard here say, "I always come back. Let me out."

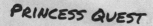

This door appears to be locked.

MANY FANS BELIEVE THE SIX TORCHES IN THE GRAVEYARD ARE SYMBOLIC OF THE MISSING CHILDREN.

Room	1	2	3	4	5	6	7	8 (Graveyard)	9	10
Torches to light	0	2	5	0	7	0	0	5 (1 does not produce flame)	1	1 (cannot be lit)
Enemies	0	0	7	5	5	0	7	0	0	1
Hearts	1	0	0	0	0	0	1	1	0	0
Keys	0	0	0	1	0	0	0	0	1	0

133

FAZ-TOKENS

Gold Faz-Tokens appear throughout the game, and collecting them can net you some interesting secrets as well as unlocking hidden prizes at the Prize Counter. Nab all thirty and a basket of exotic butters will appear on the Prize Counter. Empty out the basket and press the red button at the bottom to activate the TV—the TV has shown different things throughout various patches, including the final room of the Pizza Party level and a tease for *The Curse of Dreadbear*.

Fazbear  Entertainment

Item No.	Game Mode/Area	Location
1	Prize Counter	On the counter in front of the monitor
2	FNAF1	In the bottom-left desk drawer
3	FNAF1	Under the cupcake on the right monitor
4	FNAF1	At 3 a.m., reach inside the right monitor
5	FNAF2	Between the camera monitor and buttons
6	FNAF2	Put on the Freddy mask. Coin will appear on the desk.
7	FNAF2	Allow the music box to unwind. As the Puppet approaches, a coin appears in front of the telephone.
8	FNAF3	Left of the camera monitor
9	FNAF3	Tiles above the vent monitor form a number pad; dial 395248
10	FNAF3	During a ventilation error, check the vent on the right
11	Dark Rooms, Nightmare BB	Point the flashlight at the ceiling fan, a coin will drop
12	Parts & Service, Bonnie	Beside the right eye cleaner
13	Parts & Service, Bonnie	Under the Bonnie plush on the left
14	Parts & Service, Bonnie	Strum Bonnie's guitar three times, then a coin appears on the left workbench
15	Parts & Service, Chica	In the trash can on the right

Item No.	Game Mode/Area	Location
16	Parts & Service, Chica	Behind the soda can on the left
17	Parts & Service, Chica	After completing the game, feed Chica pizza. A coin appears on the left.
18	Parts & Service, Freddy	Behind Freddy's head
19	Parts & Service, Freddy	Under a music box on the lower left workbench
20	Parts & Service, Foxy	Under the gears atop the right workbench
21	Parts & Service, Foxy	Wear Foxy's head, and it appears on the left workbench
22	Vent Repair, Mangle	Behind the second panel, between the gears and wall
23	Vent Repair, Ennard	Second set of puzzles, in the gear respawn box
24	Vent Repair, Nightmare Mode, Ennard	As the elevator travels between the intro and first set of puzzles, watch the right wall. There's a coin in Bonnet's eye.
25	Night Terrors, Circus Baby	Right side of the closet, on a wooden box
26	Night Terrors, Circus Baby	Left side of the closet, behind the centermost PlushBaby
27	Night Terrors, Circus Baby	Left side of the closet, on the left side of the box that the centermost PlushBaby is on
28	Night Terrors, Nightmare Mode, Pizza Party	Hallway outside the *FNAF3* office, on the floor of the vent to your left
29	Night Terrors, Nightmare Mode, Pizza Party	From Plushtrap's hallway, take the top-left door (8 on the map); a token will appear atop the present to your right
30	Gallery	In the top drawer of left table

EASTER EGGS

HELPY

MAIN HUB:
Helpy appears to the left of the virtual menu, acting as a hint for the trapped ending, pointing to both the secret button on the side of the monitor and the Party Machine switch.

FNAF2:
Nightmare Mode, Withered: Helpy will rarely appear behind you, to your left.

COFFEE

FNAF3:
Rarely, Coffee from Scott's previous game *The Desolate Hope* will appear on the desk.

PRIZE COUNTER:
Rarely, Coffee will appear on the floor behind the Prize Counter.

THEY'RE WATCHING

FNAF1:
If you look away from the cupcake, its eyes will be focused on you when you next see it.

PARTS & SERVICE:
The animatronics' eyes follow you.

DEATH SCREEN:
Nightmare Cupcake sometimes appears atop the monitor instead of the normal cupcake.

SISTER LOCATION

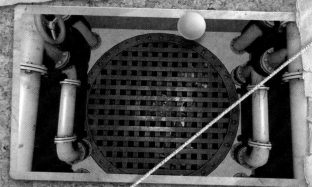

NIGHT TERRORS: CIRCUS BABY:

A Bidybab will sometimes appear beside the flashlight on the floor.

DARK ROOMS: PLUSHTRAP:

There's a rare chance that a Minireena will be peeking in from the far left room.

FNAF2:

Endo Ø2 will rarely make an appearance, looming over the right side of your desk.

ENDO

VENT REPAIR: ENNARD:

Endo Ø2 can rarely be seen peering up at you from the grating below.

VENT REPAIR: MANGLE

A new animatronic, Nightmare Endo, can be found in this mode.

YOU CAN HONK FREDDY'S NOSE ON THE MENU SCREEN.

137

SHOWTIME

Avid fans found a few interesting tidbits in digging through *Help Wanted*'s game files. The Showtime button remains one of the most talked-about unused features of the game. If you move forward far enough, you can see Freddy, Bonnie, and Chica through the main stage curtain. Animations for the animatronics in the songs are present in the game files, as well as a placeholder recording of the Freddy Fazbear's Pizza theme song.

...ls, Fazbear Entertainment
...r the one, the only,

...a good time? I know I am!

...umber

...the singer
...bear, but

...a cotton
...listen to

...Freddy

...reat!

BIRD WHO LIKES TO

...for a hand! He hangs

...you've met all the members of the band!

All: WOO-HOO!! Freddy Fazbear's Pizza, the fun just can't be beat! Freddy Fazbear's Pizza! It's time for us to eat!

Advertiser 1: For the next hour, add meat to any kids' pizza for just a dollar!

Advertiser 2: And if your parents really love you, they'll buy you a thirty-two ounce Freddy Fountain drink!

Advertiser 3: And don't forget: All the popular kids sign up for our mailing list.

All: And get free stuff on their birthday!

Advertiser 1: Freddy Fazbear's Pizza!

All: Where fantasy meets fun! Freddy Fazbear! Freddy Fazbear! Freddy Fazbear Pizza! Freddy Fazbear! Freddy Fazbear! Freddy Fazbear Pizza! Freddy Fazbear! Freddy Fazbear! Freddy Fazbear Pizza!

ACHIEVEMENTS

 I SCREAM. YOU SCREAM . . . : Get jump-scared.

 NOW I WILL TELL YOU A STORY: Eat a piece of candy.

 POP GOES THE WEASEL . . . : Get a jump-scare prize! (Get jump-scared while opening a prize.)

 YOUR SPECIAL DAY!: Activate the Party Machine.

 SHOWTIME!: Re-create the main stage show. (You can do this by placing action figures of Freddy, Bonnie, and Chica on the Prize Counter.)

 LET'S EAT!: Consume all possible edibles in the game. (Eat all food prizes plus the edible cockroach.)

 PLAY!: Complete the Prize Counter.

 NUMISMATIST: Find all tokens.

 CELEBRATE!: Unlock all achievements.

 LET'S PARTY!: Find a hidden token.

 EXOTIC BUTTERS: Finish the game. (Complete the Pizza Party mini game.)

 STAY PUT!: That is why you don't leave the office. (In *FNAF1*, step outside the office to prompt a jump scare.)

 ROCK!: Strum Bonnie's guitar. (In Parts ¦ Service: Bonnie, reach out and strum his guitar.)

 PEST CONTROL: Pull 25 roaches off Chica. (In Parts ¦ Service: Chica, manually pick 25 cockroaches off Chica.)

 CHOKING HAZARD: For ages 3 and up. (Eat an action figure.)

Lore and Theories

TAPE GIRL

Many theories have popped up around the girl who made the secret tapes scattered throughout *Help Wanted*. The tapes seem to confirm that:

♦ Tape Girl was a QA tester for the original game development team. She had a manager, Dale, and a coworker, Jeremy, who tested the game before her.

♦ The client (assumed to be Fazbear Entertainment) gave the development team old circuit boards to scan, some of which had code on them to use for the game. After it was downloaded, an anomaly began to appear.

♦ Jeremy complained of nightmares and had seen something in the game that disturbed him. The company was putting together a case of minor offenses to use as evidence to either fire or discredit him.

♦ Something terrible happened to Jeremy, something that seemingly resulted in a lawsuit, and may be why Fazbear Entertainment handed off development to another company.

♦ Tape Girl discovered that Fazbear Entertainment was actually *working with* the indie game developer that they claimed to want to discredit. It was all an elaborate cover-up and rebrand scheme.

♦ Tape Girl was given three days to finish up Jeremy's work before the game development was taken over by a new studio. She decided to try to isolate and delete the anomaly, which she described as a character who watched her while she worked.

♦ She later discovered that the anomaly had attached itself to her audio logs. She tried to destroy the logs, but was unsuccessful. She ultimately ran a fragmentation program on the files to break them up, rendering the anomaly harmless. She urged whoever was listening to not reassemble the tapes, as doing so will reassemble the anomaly.

FRIEND OR FOE?

Fans have turned a spotlight on Tapes 1 and 15, since Tape Girl seems to introduce herself in both tapes, but gives contradicting directions (find the tapes vs. don't). This, coupled with the secret merge ending and the note on the waiver about "digital consciousness transference," seems to imply that Tape Girl herself may be corrupted by the Glitchtrap anomaly.

142

DATE 11-12-1987

PAY TO THE ORDER OF _Jeremy Fitzgerald_ $ 100.50

One hundred dollars and 50/100   DOLLARS

MEMO _Welcome to the family!_   _Fazbear Entertainment_

AND WHO'S JEREMY?

Theorists were quick to probe Jeremy's relation to the other two Jeremys in the *FNAF* canon: Jeremy Fitzgerald, the night guard from *FNAF2*, and the missing child confirmed on the tombstone in *Pizzeria Simulator*. The community seems to have reached the conclusion that the duplicate name is just a coincidence.

THE INDIE GAMES

At the start of *Help Wanted*, HandUnit explains that an indie game developer created games that were loosely based on real events. Fazbear Entertainment insists that they're currently suing him for the damage he did to their name, but this is later shown to be a lie. In Tape 13, Tape Girl says "They lied to us . . . Fazbear Entertainment hired the game developer. Those indie games were designed to conceal and make light of what happened. This isn't just an attempt to rebrand. It's an elaborate cover-up. A campaign to discredit everything."

Mystery solved, but one question still remains: Which games is she referring to? Theorists have a few ideas . . .

- All *FNAF* Games Up to Now: While this theory was popular upon the release of *Help Wanted*, most fans have since discredited it.

- The 8-bit Mini Games: *FNAF 2-4* and *Sister Location* feature a variety of 8-bit mini games that seemingly tell the truth about the horrific murders at the various *FNAF* locations. These games could certainly fit the bill.

- *FNAF World*: *FNAF World* has been ruled as existing outside of *FNAF*'s canon, but that doesn't necessarily mean the game as a game isn't canonical.

Is Scott Cawthon canon? Scott is confirmed to portray the indie developer referenced in the opening, but Scott himself is not canon.

Five
Nights
at
Freddy's

>> New Game
Continue

Unlocks

© 2014-2019 Scott Cawthon

v 1.0

FNAF WORLD

MANGLE'S QUEST

400

143

Chapter 9

THE CURSE OF DREADBEAR

Five Nights at Freddy's

HELP WANTED

CURSE OF

DREAD BEAR

Five Nights at Freddy's is no stranger to Halloween-themed DLC. All the way back in *FNAF*, Halloween decorations went up in the office like clockwork every October 31. This trend continued through future games, including a particularly robust DLC for *FNAF4*, which featured new animatronics. But *The Curse of Dreadbear* takes the meaning of DLC to a different level.

Far from a re-skin, this expansion throws in three entirely new game modes: Afraid of the Dark, Spooky Mansion, and Danger! Keep Out!, for a total of ten new games. The games, Easter eggs, and new ending have the potential to change the course of future *FNAF* games, with huge implications for lore. And if you're not into the lore, well, Foxy's Pirate Adventure should keep you chasing a twisting road to that high score.

The Freddy Scoop

Welcome to the Halloween Hub, themed around Fallfest '83. The hub here is similar to the main hub in *Help Wanted*, but a little sparser. Gone are the tape player, Faz-Token counter, and most of the buttons. The virtual menu (to select a level), Party Machine (note there are no Nightmare Mode games), go to title button (to return to the Title screen), and candy bucket (to return to *Help Wanted*) remain. Note that there are no Faz-Tokens in the DLC, but there is technically one more secret audio.

PRIZES

It's not Halloween without treats—check out the new Halloween-themed prizes!

Fazbear Entertainment
Where Fantasy and Fun Come to Life
Prize Catalog COLLECT THEM ALL!

TREATS

 ☐ BITE LATE NIGHT

 ☐ CRUDLET

 ☐ GOBBLINZ

☐ KATZ BLACK LICORICE

 ☐ LAVENDER DOLLOP

☐ SLOPPY

 ☐ SQUIRMY

 ☐ THIRD EYE

 ☐ CHEWY TREAT

 ☐ DEVLISH DELIGHT

 ☐ EAT 'N' CRY

 ☐ FAZZIES

 ☐ MOON DROP

 ☐ TEETHY CHEW

☐ BUCCANEER BOUNTY

☐ CHICA OF THE SEA

ACTION FIGURES (for ages 3 and up)

 ☐ DREADBEAR

 ☐ GRIMM FOXY

 ☐ JACK-O-BONNIE

 ☐ JACK-O-CHICA

 ☐ NIGHTMARE BONNIE

 ☐ NIGHTMARE CHICA

 ☐ NIGHTMARE FOXY

 ☐ NIGHTMARE FREDDY

 ☐ WITHERED BONNIE

 ☐ WITHERED CHICA

 ☐ WITHERED FOXY

☐ WITHERED FREDDY

MASKS

 ☐ BALLOON BOY

☐ BONNIE

 ☐ CHICA

 ☐ FOXY

 ☐ FREDDY

☐ MANGLE

MISC.

 ☐ CUPCAKE CANDY PAIL

PUMPKINS

 ☐ BONNIE

 ☐ CHICA

 ☐ FOXY

 ☐ FREDDY

Gameplay and Strategy

AFRAID OF THE DARK: PLUSHKIN PATCH

Plushkins are one of the three *Curse of Dreadbear* animatronics new to *FNAF*. They appear to be PlushBabies who wear the masks of other characters (specifically Balloon Boy, Chica, Foxy, and Freddy).

This game mode is similar to PlushBaby's Dark Rooms game from *Help Wanted*. Only, instead of a long, narrow hall, you're situated in a wide-open pumpkin patch. The different dimensions of the screen mean there's more square footage to scan. You'll need to scan vertically, too, since PlushBabies can hide in the trees as well as behind pumpkins. If you see one, shine your flashlight to clear it, but be careful as your battery life is limited. You need to survive until 6 a.m.

AFRAID OF THE DARK: PIRATE RIDE

Welcome aboard Cap'n Foxy's Pirate Adventure! Ye can help me with this here adventure by shootin' the targets with that there hand cannon. Do yer best, or I'll send ye to Davy Jones's Locker. For yer safety, keep yer hands inside the ride at all times, or you'll end up like me. Hahahaha!

That's right—it's a classic dark ride featuring Cap'n Foxy on a pirate adventure. Your mission is to shoot the color-coded targets around the ride to earn the high score. Hit all the targets in a room and you activate a bonus round to double your score.

During a normal run, the highest-possible score is 3,425 (First Mate). After earning different rankings, four different Helpy cutouts will appear throughout the ride. Shooting him so he points left will take the cart on a different track, to behind-the-scenes areas where high-point values can be found . . . along with Jack-O-Bonnie and Jack-O-Chica.

- ♦ Backroom: Hit Helpy in Ride Start. Exits to Underwater.
- ♦ The Office: Hit Helpy in Kraken Attack! Exits to Outside.
- ♦ Kitchen: Hit Helpy in Underwater. Exits to Set Sail.
- ♦ Boiler Room: Hit Helpy in Outside. Exits to Ride Start.

The highest-possible score is 11,150, but the maximum score that can be tallied is 9,975. Exceeding this will cause the score to reset to zero.

Though you can take a route that hits all four Helpys, the highest-scoring path doesn't require it: Ride Start (0) → Set Sail (850) → The Storm (450) → Kraken Attack! (500, hit Helpy) → The Office (2,400) → Outside (0, you reenter the track after the target has passed) → Underwater (850, hit Helpy) → Kitchen (2,500) → Set Sail (850) → The Storm (450) → Kraken Attack! (500) → Fight the Kraken (700) → Outside (100, hit Helpy) → Boiler Room (1,000) → End

Rooms	Blue (25)	Green (50)	Yellow (75)	Pink (100)	Total/Bonus
Ride Start	1 (no points)	1 (no points)	1 (no points)	1 (no points)	0
Set Sail	4	2	3	0	425/850
The Storm	5	2	0	0	225/450
Kraken Attack!	6	2	0	0	250/500
Fight the Kraken	2	3	2	0	350/700
Outside	0	0	1	0	75
Underwater	4	5	1	0	425/850
Backroom	0	0	0	14	1,400
The Office	0	0	0	24	2,400
Kitchen	0	2	0	24	2,500
Boiler Room	0	0	0	10	1,000

At the end of your ride, your score nets you a new title:

- Bilge Rat: 0+
- Scallywag: 1,000+
- Buccaneer: 2,000+
- First Mate: 3,000+
- Captain: 7,000+
- Admiral: 8,325+

SCORING UNDER 1,000 OR 10,000–10,975 WILL EARN YOU A FOXY JUMP SCARE.

AFRAID OF THE DARK: CORN MAZE

In what is perhaps the most frightening game of the lot, you're dropped in the center of a maze of wooden fences. There are four color-coded gates (red, blue, yellow, green) at the north, east, south, and west sides of the maze. The catch? You'll need the correct key to open the gate. The keys spawn at random in different locations, so you'll need to navigate the maze differently with each playthrough, which is tricky with the animatronic on your tail. There are some general rules for key locations though:

♦ Red Spider Key spawns near the yellow gate

♦ Blue Book Key spawns near the green gate

♦ Yellow Pumpkin Key spawns near the red gate

♦ Green Tombstone Key spawns near the blue gate

As you collect keys, an icon for each is added to your flashlight.

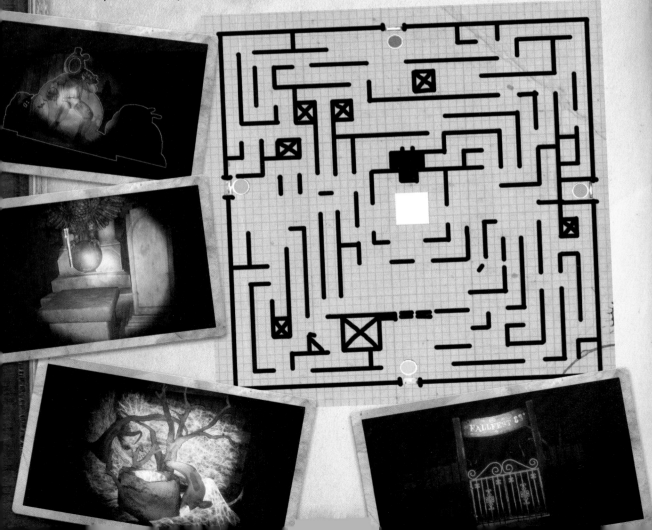

If you get turned around, a good shorthand to reorient yourself is to look for some of the taller objects, like the windmill, which appears by the red gate, or the water tower, which appears by the yellow gate.

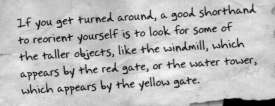

GRIMM FOXY

Meet another terrifying new addition to the *FNAF* canon: Grimm Foxy. Grimm Foxy is on fire, and he has a large scythe in place of the usual hook. He chases you, and can only be avoided by hiding behind one of the many painted cutouts in the maze. Listen closely for his singing when he draws near, and never be far from a cutout. When in doubt, reset Grimm Foxy by letting him see you and then hiding. This will buy you about fifteen seconds of exploration time, and becomes more necessary as the maze goes on and Foxy is more active.

THE FIFTH EXIT

After collecting all four keys, a fifth, the purple key, becomes available. You have the option of leaving via one of the gates that matches the key you collected (to win a prize), or you can collect the purple key and continue on to the secret ending.

To use the purple key, return to the center of the maze and use it to unlock the cellar doors.

Inside the cellar is a secret prize room, but the prize here has already been opened: a white rabbit mask sits inside. Put it on to finish the game and return to the Title screen.

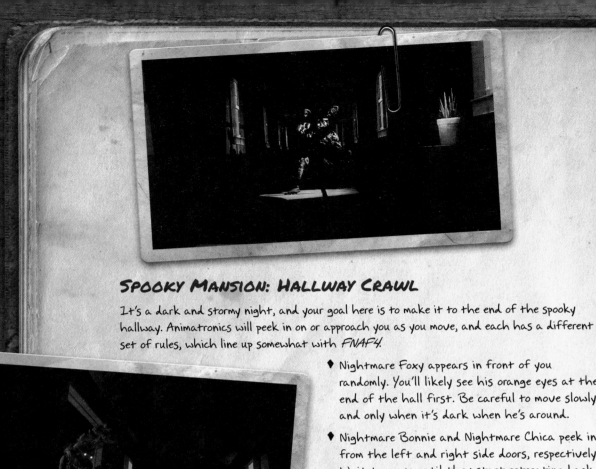

SPOOKY MANSION: HALLWAY CRAWL

It's a dark and stormy night, and your goal here is to make it to the end of the spooky hallway. Animatronics will peek in on or approach you as you move, and each has a different set of rules, which line up somewhat with *FNAF4*.

♦ Nightmare Foxy appears in front of you randomly. You'll likely see his orange eyes at the end of the hall first. Be careful to move slowly, and only when it's dark when he's around.

♦ Nightmare Bonnie and Nightmare Chica peek in from the left and right side doors, respectively. Wait to move until they start retreating back into their rooms.

♦ Halfway down the hallway, Nightmare Freddy announces his presence via his trademark laugh, and a metallic screeching that gets louder as he nears. If you don't keep moving, Nightmare Freddy will catch up to you.

Interestingly enough, the door at the end of the hallway accesses the bedroom from *FNAF4*!

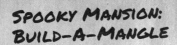

SPOOKY MANSION: BUILD-A-MANGLE

Welcome to the Fazbear Entertainment Fulfillment Center. Today, we are assembling animatronic performers. Each animatronic unit will bring joy to the children at one of our many Freddy Fazbear locations. Just place the necessary components in the assembly chute, conveniently located at the front of your workstation. Each work order is unique, so gather only the components as shown on the quad monitor array. Use the high-voltage shock buttons to gently remove any unwanted critters that stumbled onto the assembly line. Now let's get to work.

You'll need to grab ten pieces off the conveyor belt to assemble Mangle properly, and only seven of those ten pieces need to match what was shown on the quad monitor. The quad monitor can be a challenge to manage, but suffice it to say that the monitor cycles through a list of parts, so if you see it on the monitor, grab it, even if it's not currently displayed. You have one minute to grab the necessary parts, so be mindful of your time. Shock the Freddle animatronics when they appear on the conveyor belt; otherwise, you're in for a jump scare.

MANGLE

If you grab too many incorrect pieces, Mangle will crawl out of the air duct above the monitors and stare at you. Three more incorrect pieces will trigger a Mangle jump scare. Mangle will also jump-scare you if you accumulate fewer than seven pieces, either correct or incorrect.

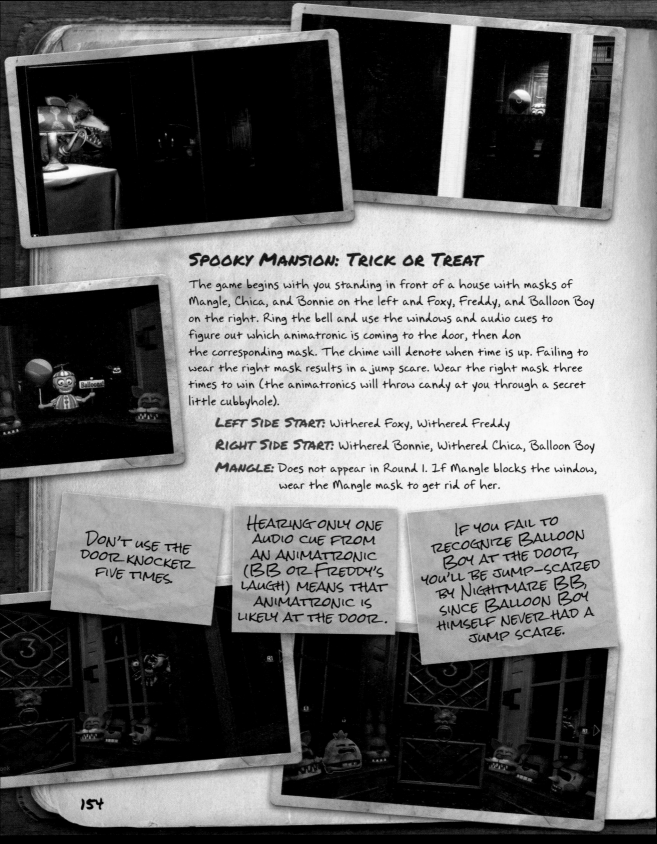

SPOOKY MANSION: TRICK OR TREAT

The game begins with you standing in front of a house with masks of Mangle, Chica, and Bonnie on the left and Foxy, Freddy, and Balloon Boy on the right. Ring the bell and use the windows and audio cues to figure out which animatronic is coming to the door, then don the corresponding mask. The chime will denote when time is up. Failing to wear the right mask results in a jump scare. Wear the right mask three times to win (the animatronics will throw candy at you through a secret little cubbyhole).

LEFT SIDE START: Withered Foxy, Withered Freddy

RIGHT SIDE START: Withered Bonnie, Withered Chica, Balloon Boy

MANGLE: Does not appear in Round 1. If Mangle blocks the window, wear the Mangle mask to get rid of her.

DON'T USE THE DOOR KNOCKER FIVE TIMES.

HEARING ONLY ONE AUDIO CUE FROM AN ANIMATRONIC (BB OR FREDDY'S LAUGH) MEANS THAT ANIMATRONIC IS LIKELY AT THE DOOR.

IF YOU FAIL TO RECOGNIZE BALLOON BOY AT THE DOOR, YOU'LL BE JUMP-SCARED BY NIGHTMARE BB, SINCE BALLOON BOY HIMSELF NEVER HAD A JUMP SCARE.

SPOOKY MANSION: DREADBEAR

Begin by turning the left crank to lower the final new animatronic of the DLC, Dreadbear, into place. Once properly positioned, give him a controlled shock with the switch on your forward right.

Today, you'll be working on Dreadbear's control module (his brain). Start by coloring the ten sections of his brain to match the blueprint on the left monitor. Under the blueprint, you'll see a scale with a yellow charge number and a red goal number. Use the red diode to increase the charge or the blue diode to decrease the charge until the yellow number matches the red number. Now place the white diode in the brain to view the neural feedback loop. Use the button on the top left of the console to show the goal in red, then manipulate the three dials to match the neural wavelengths with the goal. When finished, place the brain in Dreadbear's head.

As time goes on, you'll lose power, so be sure to move quickly and efficiently. You can use the controlled shock switch to reset the power, but note that shocking Dreadbear five times (this includes the initial shock) will result in a jump scare.

155

DANGER! KEEP OUT!

NIGHT 01

You're in the office from *FNAF*, tasked with staying alive until 6 a.m., but instead of doors, the doorways on your left and right sides are boarded up. You can still access the camera system, and the lights on the left and right that can be used to fend off the animatronics. You also have lights on the cameras themselves that can be used to push the animatronics back. In this mode, the lights function more as flashbulbs, similar to the Funtime Foxy level in *Sister Location*.

> Power Supply: The camera system doesn't drain your power, but each flash performed drains your power by 20 percent. After using five flashes, you'll need to reset the power system, which takes about eight seconds.

Night 01 only features Jack-O-Bonnie and Jack-O-Chica, who approach from left and right, respectively. If they make it to the boards, flash them, or they will break the boards down until they reach you. Best advice: Stay on top of your power supply. After flashing both animatronics, reset your power. You don't want to be under attack and unable to use your only defense.

NIGHT 02

Same rules apply as Night 01, only now Grimm Foxy has been added to the mix in Pirate Cove. You can use the light button on the cameras to reset his usual cycle, though it's recommended to wait until he's fully in view before flashing him. The animatronics also seem to move faster on this night.

NIGHT 03

Dreadbear appears starting on this night, moving slowly toward you. He cannot be stopped, only slowed using the flash. If you hear a lightbulb shatter, that's your cue that Dreadbear is in the East Hall, and you don't have much longer before his attack. Keep track of him as well as the other animatronics, which are now more aggressive.

Codes, Glitches, and Secrets

FNAF4 HOUSE

The *FNAF4* house sits on the hill ahead of you. This is especially clear when the sky loads in red (it can also load as green, orange, or purple).

HALLOWEEN HUB

PARTY MACHINE

Turn on the Party Machine, and press the secret button on the left side of the monitor. Look behind you at the car on the hill; its headlights are now purple. If you look in the distance on the hill with the *FNAF4* house, you can see Glitchtrap dancing.

FALLFEST '83

If this DLC takes place in 1983, does it have something to tell us about the Bite of '83?

PRIZE ROOM

If a clown poster appears, you can honk its nose.

Rarely, Dreadbear will rise from the lake and walk behind you, into the barn.

FOXY'S SHIP

Foxy's pirate ship sometimes appears on the lake, but it will eventually be dragged under by a kraken.

PRIZE SCREEN

Rarely, three clown posters will spawn in the Prize Room. Hit each poster with a dart and the room will turn purple, as though under a black light. The banner's text changes to "IT'S ME."

DANGER! KEEP OUT!: NIGHT 03

Rarely, if you pick up the phone and hold it up, a dial tone will play. The textures on all the objects in the room will then go static, with certain objects (ones with lighting effects) turning purple. The monitor will then say, "Scanning for glitches" and "No glitches found" after completing its scan. You'll then be taken to the Title screen.

GAME OVER SCREEN

A green-and-purple glitching grave, which appears to have a similar texture as the secret tapes and Glitchtrap plush from *Help Wanted*, appears under Dreadbear's hand. The monitor on the table will sometimes say, "Report glitches before they spread" or "Purging system . . ."

RELUCTANT FOLLOWER

After locating the original sixteen secret tapes in *Help Wanted* and completing the fifth exit in the Corn Maze level of *Dreadbear*, fans can unlock a secret final tape. To listen, head back to the Prize Counter in *Help Wanted*. The white rabbit mask you obtained in Corn Maze will be sitting there. Take it back with you to the main hub, and wear it while holding the Glitchtrap plush you obtained to hear the audio.

Yes, I hear you. I know . . . No. There's no miscommunication. I understand. Yes, I have it. I made it myself. I think you would like it . . . No, no one suspects anything. Don't worry, I'll be ready, and I won't let you down. It will be fun.

Lore and Theories

THE RELUCTANT FOLLOWER

♦ The Mask: The secrets revealed in the Corn Maze level were certainly unnerving. Fans were quick to point out that Tape Girl talked about a Halloween mask on Tape 9, and that there seemed to be another voice looming in the background of that tape.

♦ The Audio: The secret audio is certainly disturbing, with this character seemingly taking orders from someone and forming some sort of secret plan. When put together, many fans believe that the Reluctant Follower is Tape Girl, under the influence of the Glitchtrap code.

♦ The Grave: Could the glitching grave on the hill belong to the Reluctant Follower? Or could this be a reference to Afton himself? Interestingly enough, the glitching tombstone is surrounded by seven other tombstones, as opposed to the usual six.

FALLFEST '83

References to 1983 aren't usually dropped into *FNAF* games at random. Most fans accept that the events of *FNAF4* take place in 1983, and this game did have quite a few *FNAF4* references:

- Hallway Crawl takes place in the *FNAF4* house.

- The masks in Trick or Treat look to be the real versions of the masks worn by the bullies in the *FNAF4* night-end mini games.

- The *FNAF4* house appears on the hill in front of the monitor, and there's a Glitchtrap Easter egg that shows him dancing beside the house.

Certain fans have drawn a connection between *FNAF4*'s "I will put you back together" and the theming around Dreadbear. The idea of taking something inanimate, something dead, and giving it new life through an animatronic rang more than a few bells for theorists. We've seen some definite mad-scientist moments from William Afton, particularly in *The Fourth Closet*. But whether this is just an interesting idea, or a spooky tale that could be dropping a hint, remains to be seen. Food for thought: In an earlier patch of the game, it wasn't Glitchtrap on the hill with the *FNAF4* house . . . it was Dreadbear.

Chapter 10
SPECIAL DELIVERY

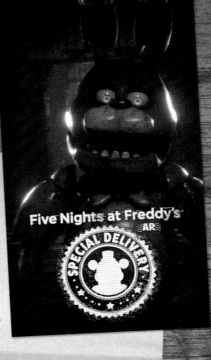

Five Nights at Freddy's
AR
SPECIAL DELIVERY

The VR format of *Help Wanted* and *Curse of Dreadbear* allowed players to insert themselves into the terrifying world of *FNAF*, but with the success of the game, an interesting question arose. What if fans could insert *FNAF* into the real world?

Special Delivery aimed to answer this question with a horrifying new premise and a massive expansion of game lore. You play as a user of Fazbear Funtime Service, in which animatronics are sent to your home at random or by other players. But something is wrong—far from delivering a gift or performing, these animatronics arrive with more sinister aims. Fending off enemies nets you components to build animatronics of your own to send after your friends or to go salvaging for more parts. But as with any *FNAF* game, things aren't as they appear.

Fazbear Entertainment outsourced the Fazbear Funtime Service to an independent company. Through leaked and glitching emails, it's clear the company is having some problems with a virus . . . and with a troubled employee named "Ness."

FAZBEAR FUNTIME SERVICE

The game begins with an advertisement for Fazbear Entertainment's new Fazbear Funtime Service, a subscription that sends animatronics to your home to deliver gifts. Although the service seems harmless at first, a series of rapid-fire messages reveal some kinks in the system.

The first pop-up subscribes you for the eternal package, meaning an endless stream of animatronics. The company then appears to override and reboot the system. The system seems to right itself, but it is then followed by a stream of glitches. The first encourages you to deploy your animatronic to salvage for parts. The second encourages you to collect Remnant, glowing orbs of light that longtime fans of the series will recognize.

"You'll never be alone again! It's guaranteed with our exclusive animatronics, you'll always have someone watching your back! They'll provide you with hours of fun fun fun entertainment and companionship! You can't hide from a future of fun! Our special delivery will make you jump with excitement. Subscribe today! Don't miss this opportunity! And remember, we're always watching over you."

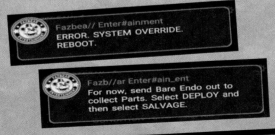

Fazbea// Enter#ainment
ERROR. SYSTEM OVERRIDE. REBOOT.

Fazb//ar Enter#ain_ent
For now, send Bare Endo out to collect Parts. Select DEPLOY and then select SALVAGE.

Faz//...ar Ent##ain_int
While you're waiting for more fun to arrive, why not try out Remnant collection?

Gameplay and Strategy

BARE ENDO
OWNER: FAZBEAR ENTERTAINMENT

PERCEPTION
AGGRESSION
DURABILITY
ATTACK

JAMMER   ENCOUNT

150

23:49:35

DEVICES
(0)

MAP

On the map, icons with question marks will appear. Clicking on them prompts an event—you could receive an item, be invited to collect Remnant, or encounter an animatronic. Each animatronic has a perception and aggression rating to help you judge the difficulty of the encounter. Once an encounter is clicked, you must engage in the encounter or use Faz-Coins to purchase a jammer to escape.

CONTROLS

Fortunately, Fazbear Entertainment hasn't left you totally defenseless. Enter the Diagnostic and Repair Multitool 2.0.

♦ **Battery Power:** At left, it shows how much power you have for your shocker and flashlight. Battery is very important, and it needs time to recharge. To the right you'll see your spare batteries, which can be used if you run out of power.

♦ **Controlled Shock:** Center, use it to subdue an animatronic when it's de-cloaked. Each shock has a short cooldown time and costs 10 percent of your battery. If you have less than 10 percent battery overall, the controlled shock becomes unusable.

♦ **Flashlight:** At right, the flashlight can make static more visible, but leaving it on drains a lot of battery. In fact, it costs 3 percent power just turning it on. If you can, it's best to avoid using it too often.

♦ **Buffs:** Before beginning an encounter, you can load buffs such as shield buff, attack boost, and more to help you in facing particularly tough animatronics.

SURVIVING AN ENCOUNTER

♦ **Cloaking:** In general, animatronics arrive cloaked in patented AnimStealth technology and will not be visible.

♦ **Static:** When static appears on your screen, it can help you locate the animatronic. You can use your flashlight to find static if necessary. Once you see it, the animatronic will either leave, charge, or go haywire. Certain characters' static might appear differently (Freddy Frostbear's static appears as frost).

> o **Interference:** Heavy static can sometimes appear to distract you. Shake your phone to dispel it.

> o **Sound:** Footsteps and voice lines often accompany an animatronic's approach. Turn in the direction of the sound to help you spot the animatronic sooner.

♦ **Rushing:** Don't shock until you can see the eyes of the animatronic. Sometimes an animatronic will rush at you but never fully appear. This trick can waste your battery—don't fall for it! Wait until the animatronic fully de-cloaks to shock. Failure to shock will result in a jump scare and loss.

♦ **Haywire:** If you see an animatronic go haywire, its eyes might be glowing, its movements might be erratic, and colored bands may appear across your screen. When this happens, look down as fast as possible and wait for it to stop. You may need to react faster to some animatronics than others. Do not shock an animatronic that's gone haywire!

REMEMBER TO SHOCK AN ANIMATRONIC UNTIL ITS HEALTH BAR IS DEPLETED. IT'S OFTEN NOT ENOUGH TO SHOCK IT ONCE!

WINNING . . . AND LOSING

Winning animatronic encounters have many benefits . . .

◆ **XP:** XP is granted at the end of each encounter, but you get significantly more by winning. Rewards are granted with each level up.

◆ **Buffs:** You may get buffs for winning, which give you an advantage in your next encounter.

◆ **Endoskeletons, CPUs, Mods, and Plush Suits:** Defeating animatronics will sometimes help you obtain their components.

◆ **Unlock Slots:** You might unlock slots in the workshop to help you upgrade animatronics.

◆ **Parts:** Parts are needed to repair, assemble, and upgrade your animatronics. Mods can open up new abilities for your animatronics.

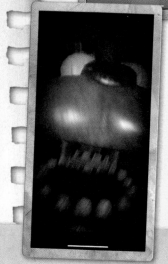

◆ **Faz-Coins:** Faz-Coins can be used to purchase helpful items from the store, including lures.

◆ **Remnant:** You can gain Remnant, which can make encounters easier and make your own animatronics stronger.

Losing an encounter leaves you with less power, and doesn't net you any rewards.

THE STORE
PURCHASABLE WITH PARTS

You can use the parts collected from encounters to buy helpful devices . . .

Transponder: Reveals the identity of an item on the map.

Salvage Scanner: Boosts your animatronics' salvaging efficiency.

EMF Meter: Increases the quality of collected remnant.

PURCHASABLE WITH FAZ-COINS

You can purchase Faz-Coins to spend on . . .

Extra Battery: Automatically activates if your battery goes to critical.

Lures: If you're unable to attract certain animatronics, purchase/place their corresponding lure and they'll come to you!

Plush Suits: If you're having trouble encountering a certain animatronic, you can purchase its corresponding plush suit to build your own.

Profile Icons: Purchase a new profile icon to appear on your map.

REMNANT

Remnant plays a special role in the game. Collecting a lot of it can help you reach Remnant Milestones, which provide helpful benefits, such as increasing the amount of time animatronics are vulnerable. Remnant can be obtained by winning encounters or by collecting it between encounters. Between encounters, use your flashlight to draw Remnant in, or you can tap to collect it.

When collecting Remnant, there are two types of Remnant to consider:

- **Bright Remnant:** Small, glowing orbs will appear in various colors. The orbs increase your Remnant count differently depending on their color.

- **Shadowy Remnant:** These dark orbs often appear circling Bright Remnant. Collecting too many of them will crowd your screen in shadow until you are attacked by RWQFSFASXC (Shadow Bonnie). Catch him in your flashlight to defeat him. Doing so will reward you with more Remnant.

BE CAREFUL,
RWQFSFASXC CAN
BE TOUGH TO BEAT.

WORKSHOP

This is where the magic happens. Here you can put the parts and components you received from animatronic encounters to good use.

♦ **Deploy/Send:** Send an animatronic to attack someone on your friend list. If your animatronic jump-scares your friend, you'll receive Parts. Your animatronic will likely need repairs when it returns.

♦ **Deploy/Salvage:** Send an animatronic to scavenge for Parts. Your animatronic will likely need repairs when it returns.

♦ **Recall:** Return a deployed animatronic to the Workshop.

♦ **Assemble:** Build an animatronic using Remnant and various components.

♦ **Repair:** After being deployed, an animatronic's condition will likely decrease. You can use Parts to repair it.

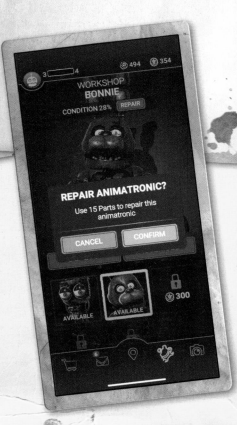

IT'S ALIVE!

Assembling a functioning animatronic isn't quite as complicated as one might think. All you need is . . .

 Endoskeleton: Similar to a skeleton, every animatronic needs an endoskeleton frame. You can acquire more endoskeletons by leveling up.

 CPU: Like the brain of an animatronic, the CPU determines the animatronic's behavior patterns and voice synthesizer.

 Plush Suits: Plush suits are like skin or clothes. They determine the animatronic's physical appearance on the map and in person.

 Mods: Special abilities you can add to an animatronic. Mods can increase an animatronic's static field, rushing speed, time haywire, etc. You can add up to four mods to each endoskeleton, and each mod is ranked with one to four stars depending on value.

Remnant: Improve your animatronic's salvaging or attacking abilities.

Codes, Glitches, and Secrets

Staff Advisory: Mail Server

04/18/2021

Staff Advisory: Mail Server

From: Fazbear Entertainment Office of Legal Affairs

To: All Staff

Due to technical complications, our mail server may be directing email to incorrect recipients.

If you receive an email that is not addressed to you, please forward it to the intended recipient and notify the IT department immediately.

As a friendly reminder, reading email that was not intended for your eyes is a violation of Fazbear Entertainment's company policy, and you may be subject to disciplinary action up to and including immediate termination. That policy remains in effect.

Please do not read email that is not your own. Thank you for your cooperation as we resolve this technical complication.

IMMEDIATE ACTION REQUIRED
Fazbear Entertainment Office of Legal Affairs

Dear Ms. Kwernto,

Please immediately cease all work on Fazbear Entertainment properties. Due to unforeseen circumstances, Fazbear Entertainment is ordering a halt to work on all existing contracts, especially in reference to any vintage hardware. We will be in touch regarding our future course of action; please contact our billing department regarding payment for completed work to-date action.

Sincerely,
Kayla Stringer
Associate General Counsel
Fazbear Entertainment

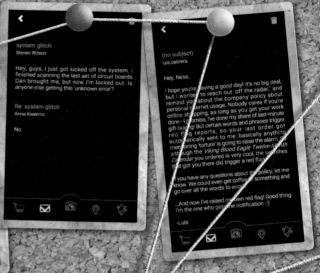

system glitch
Steven Wilson

Hey, guys, I just got kicked off the system. I finished scanning the last set of circuit boards Dan brought me, but now I'm locked out. Is anyone else getting this 'unknown error'?

Re: system glitch
Anna Kwernto

No.

(no subject)
luis.cabrera

Hey, Ness,

I hope you're having a good day! It's no big deal, but I wanted to reach out 'off the radar,' and remind you about the company policy about personal internet usage. Nobody cares if you're online shopping, as long as you get your work done—I promise, I've done my share of last-minute gift-buying! But certain words and phrases trigger red flag reports, so your last order got automatically sent to me; basically anything mentioning 'torture' is going to raise the alarm, although the *Viking Blood Eagle Twelve-Month Calendar* you ordered is very cool, the searches that got you there did trigger a red flag.

If you have any questions about the policy, let me know. We could even get coffee or something and go over all the words to avoid.

...And now I've raised my own red flag! Good thing I'm the one who gets the notification :-)

-Luis

EMAILS

Besides the store, map, workshop, and AR modes, there's another, less flashy component of *Special Delivery*: your inbox.

Most of the messages in your inbox come from a glitched Fazbear Entertainment account. These might be teasers for new animatronics, helpful tutorials, or notifications that your animatronics have finished salvaging or attacking. But early on, you get an interesting email from the Fazbear Entertainment Office of Legal Affairs. The office advises you that the mail server is malfunctioning, directing messages to the wrong recipients. You can read many of these emails in full on page 254, but three main threads emerge as the most troubling . . .

SHUTTING DOWN

PERSONS INVOLVED:
Anna Kwemto, Kayla Stringer, Steven Wilson

INCIDENT:
Fazbear Entertainment Office of Legal Affairs contacts Anna Kwemto to tell her to cease all work on Fazbear Entertainment properties, especially as it relates to "vintage hardware."

PERSONS INVOLVED:
James Campbell, Anna Kwemto, Daniel Rocha, Raha Salib, Steven Wilson

VIRUS

INCIDENT:
One of the Fazbear Entertainment circuit boards that was scanned unleashed a virus in the company's system, including the animatronics. Fazbear Entertainment was unresponsive.

PERSONS INVOLVED:
Luis Cabrero and nessie97 (Ness)

RED FLAGS

INCIDENT:
A representative from IT checks in on a coworker whose disturbing searches raised red flags.

(no subject)
luis.cabrera

Hey, Ness,

Just a quick FYI - I know I mentioned trigger words, but the AI is actually a little more sophisticated than that, and of course there are people like me watching the system, too.

So, the word *compliance* by itself isn't going to set off any red flags, but the sentence *how to induce compliance in human subjects*, and *how to induce self-compliance(?)* did actually get my attention. (I think the answer might involve chocolate chip cookies? Always works on me.)

I also thought it was strange that these were immediately followed by searches that couldn't possibly have any relevant answers for you. Did you search for 'help' by itself?

Anyway, my offer still stands if you want to go over the company policy. I'm free any day after work - we could grab dinner or coffee if you want. In the meantime you might want to do some of your more... interesting research at home.

-Luis

EMAILS

NESS AND TAPE GIRL

♦ The secret "merge" ending of *Help Wanted* seemed to indicate that Tape Girl met a similar fate—Glitchtrap found a way out of the game through her. And since the Reluctant Follower mask and tape cropped up in *Curse of Dreadbear*, fans quickly connected Tape Girl with Vanny.

♦ But with the release of *Special Delivery*, fans seemingly found another breadcrumb: The names "Vanny" and "Ness" could conceivably form a whole . . . "Vanessa."

♦ If Ness, Vanny, and Tape Girl are all one and the same, many pieces fall into place.

   o Ness's searches of "help" and "how to induce self-compliance" seem to indicate that Ness is fighting the digital consciousness transference.

   o Ness's experience with programming and QA testing also explains how she ended up in yet another job in a related field.

   o Her interest in IT and security via Luis would explain how she was able to slip the circuit board containing the Glitchtrap virus into the company's possession as well.

THE VIRUS

♦ *Help Wanted* introduced players to the Glitchtrap virus, and it was similarly uploaded to the Freddy Fazbear Virtual Experience via scanning old animatronic circuit boards.

♦ The cease work order from the Fazbear Entertainment Office of Legal Affairs seems to indicate that the company at some point becomes aware of the problem and tries to put a stop to it. That leaves one question . . . .just who is running the company?

REMNANT

Remnant has been referenced many times in the *FNAF* canon, but those who solely play the games may be only loosely familiar with it.

♦ Canonically, Remnant first popped up in *Sister Location*. The HRY223 blueprint for "SCUP" (found in *Pizzeria Simulator*) revealed that the Scooping Machine was actually built to extract Remnant, not animatronic endoskeletons, as was initially believed.

♦ Remnant was further expanded on in *The Fourth Closet* novel, where William Afton is shown combining the Remnant from the five original animatronics into one.

♦ The Fazbear Frights series further expanded on the concept, showing more scientists studying the properties of the material, and explaining it as . . .

04/18/2021
Using Remnant
From: Faz//...ar Ent##ain_Int
To: me

Greetings from Fazb//...ar Ent##_!ment!

You've been a busy little bee, haven't you? Collecting all that **Remnant** sure is funFUNFUNfun, though! Now that you've collected enough Remnant, why not put it back into your friendly animatronics?! They'll work even *better* than you can imagine.

Head to the **Workshop** and fill them up!

The Teeeeam at Fazb/////_ En.........

23:07:09

Remnant
13

"In nonscientific terms, it's like the metal is haunted. It's more complicated than that, of course, but it's similar to the way that water conducts electricity. Remnant is the mixing of the tangible with the intangible, of memory with the present. The people and things that are lost—it makes them almost real again."

♦ The Aftons seem to believe that Remnant is the key to power and eternal life, and they want as much of it as they can get.

REMNANT DEPOSIT

YOU FOUND REMNANT

COLLECT

REMNANT IN *SPECIAL DELIVERY*

♦ You've probably realized by now that one of the major goals in *Special Delivery* is to obtain Remnant, as much as you can. You find it in the animatronics you defeat, or scavenge it from the world around you. And the directive to obtain Remnant only appears after the virus takes over the Fazbear Funtime Service system.

♦ There are two kinds of Remnant—bright and shadowy—and when they spawn, the room is filled with ethereal whispering. If Remnant is a conductor of emotion, it's possible that bright Remnant forms from positive emotions, while shadowy Remnant is formed from negative ones.

♦ Why does RWQFSFASXC appear when you collect too much shadowy Remnant?

  o It's unclear. It's possible that RWQFSFASXC doesn't want you collecting this power . . . or it's possible that RWQFSFASXC wants to kill you to create more. Either way, seeing this character return in this capacity, many years after it first appeared in *FNAF2*, is sure to get fans talking.

Chapter 11
THE BOOKS

Following the overwhelming success of the video game series, *FNAF* creator Scott Cawthon worked to expand the lore and tell a bigger story through the eyes of a teenager affected by the events that took place at Freddy Fazbear's Pizza. *The Silver Eyes, The Twisted Ones,* and *The Fourth Closet,* all written by Scott Cawthon and Kira Breed-Wrisley, are a trilogy of novels set in the *FNAF* universe. The story follows Charlie, the daughter of Henry, founder of Fredbear's Family Diner and the engineer behind the original animatronics. Graphic novel adaptations were later released, which featured new insights and visual representations of the ideas first showcased in the novels.

Since the first book went into print, debates have raged among fans about how the books tie into the games, but one thing isn't in question: The books introduced many elements that later appeared in the game, from minor technology up to the name of the universe's central villain, William Afton.

FIVE NIGHTS AT FREDDY'S: SURVIVAL LOGBOOK

Released shortly after *Freddy Fazbear's Pizzeria Simulator*, the *Five Nights at Freddy's: Survival Logbook* offered a chance for *FNAF* fans to put themselves in the shoes of a new night guard at Freddy Fazbear's Pizza and reflect on their first week on the job. The book is divided into five sections, representing a guard's first five nights on the job, and is filled with interactive quizzes, activities, and "incident reports" to fill out. There are also a few secrets hiding in those pages that can help solve the many mysteries in *Freddy Fazbear's Pizzeria Simulator*!

Five Nights at Freddy's™

FREDDY FAZBEAR'S PIZZA

SURVIVAL

SECURITY LOGBOOK

All employees need to survive

Five Nights at Freddy's

THE SILVER EYES

SCOTT CAWTHON
IRA BREED-WRIS[...]

THE SILVER EYES

Ten years after the horrific murders at Freddy Fazbear's Pizza, the people of Hurricane, Utah, have mostly moved on. But Charlie and her childhood friends, who were directly affected by those events, can never forget. The old gang is thrown together again for a memorial service marking the anniversary of the children who were murdered—including their friend, Michael Brooks.

To face their tragic past, the group decides to visit the old pizza place one last time . . . When they arrive at the long-abandoned location, however, they're surprised to discover that the restaurant and its animatronics are very much intact. Little has changed for Freddy and his friends, and many of its nightmares have remained.

Hi.

...NNIE...

LET'S EAT!!!

...CHICA...

...AND FREDDY.

INSIGHTS FROM THE GRAPHIC NOVEL

The graphic novel is filled with fascinating visuals, many of which are firsts for the canon. For example, this is our first time seeing William Afton, who's previously only been glimpsed inside the Springtrap suit, or as his notorious purple sprite. His nasty scars from an accident with the spring lock suit are shown as well. Through Charlie's flashbacks we also get our first image of Henry, as well as the dark moment when he ended his life. This is also our first time seeing Fredbear's Family Diner, the origins of the Freddy's franchise, up close.

THE TWISTED ONES

The second book in the series takes place one year later and opens on Charlie, who is now in her freshman year of college in the neighboring town of New Harmony. Studying robotics like her father before her, Charlie has found herself connected to her past more than ever. After a tornado tears through Hurricane, a body is discovered, and it bears injuries that resemble those from a spring lock suit. Police chief Clay Burke reaches out to Charlie for help in solving the murder, but on their hunt for the killer, they unearth more sinister monsters long forgotten. And these monsters won't stop until they have what they want: Charlie.

DON'T TRUST YOUR EYES

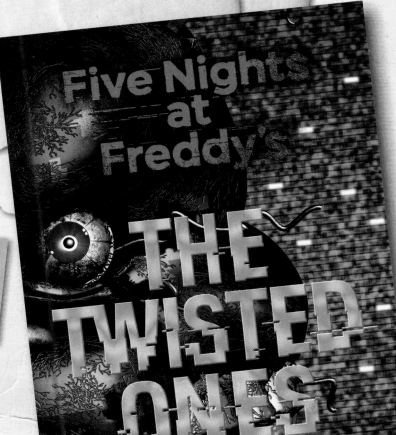

INSIGHTS FROM THE GRAPHIC NOVEL

The Twisted Ones introduced tons of fascinating new technology to the canon, from illusion discs to wearable earpieces that help people interact with animatronics. One of the best parts of the graphic novel is seeing all this technology come to life. But perhaps the most terrifying parts come from seeing how the illusion discs turn a normal animatronic into its twisted counterpart.

ONE OF THE MORE GRUESOME MOMENTS IN THE GRAPHIC NOVEL COMES FROM THE CLOSE-UPS OF THE NEWLY BORN SPRINGTRAP, AFTON'S BODY FUSED TO THE ANIMATRONIC.

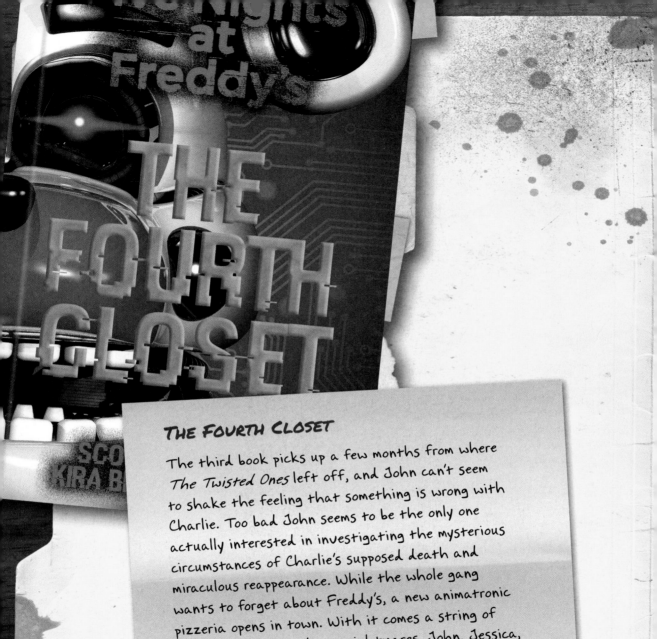

THE FOURTH CLOSET

The third book picks up a few months from where *The Twisted Ones* left off, and John can't seem to shake the feeling that something is wrong with Charlie. Too bad John seems to be the only one actually interested in investigating the mysterious circumstances of Charlie's supposed death and miraculous reappearance. While the whole gang wants to forget about Freddy's, a new animatronic pizzeria opens in town. With it comes a string of new kidnappings and new nightmares. John, Jessica, Marla, and Carlton join forces to figure out what's going on and try to stop more children from going missing. But the real mystery is what happened to Charlie . . . and the legacy her father's creations left behind.

"MY FIRST CAPTURE. MY FIRST KILL."

INSIGHTS FROM THE GRAPHIC NOVEL

The *Fourth Closet* puts all the pieces of the novel series together—from Remnant to the illusion discs to Charlie's childhood trauma. In an interesting first, the interior of an active Circus Baby's Pizzeria is shown in detail here. The scenes in Afton's laboratory give fans an interesting glimpse at the specific process behind using Remnant, and an idea of how Molten Freddy came to be. Also of note is a peek at the ghosts of the missing children.

OF COURSE IT IS. OF COURSE THEY ARE. RAISE IT TWO MORE DEGREES.

I DON'T CARE! D...

THEY'RE RAID. YOU'RE AT RISK OF DESTROYING THEM.

AND THEY CAN'T BE DESTROYED!

THEY CAN ONLY SER A GREATE PURPOSE

YOU DON'T HAVE TO DO THIS.

THE SMELL, SO FAMILIAR . . .

RUBBER, SWEAT, PIZZA . . .

...ING . . .

COMPLACENT PARENTS . . .

CHARACTER PROFILES

CHARLIE: Grew up in Hurricane, but left ten years earlier to live with her aunt Jen, who taught her to be fiercely independent and self-sufficient. Charlie becomes increasingly determined to find answers to the mysteries of her haunted past, clinging to the few childhood memories that have stuck with her.

JOHN: Charlie's childhood friend and crush, John is a writer and a keen observer of the world around him. He cares deeply for Charlie, always offering her support no matter how difficult or dangerous the situation.

JESSICA: One of Charlie's best friends, a sophisticated young woman with a love of fashion only surpassed by her love of forensics. Jessica frequently finds herself taking on the role of leader and strategist in the group.

CARLTON: A childhood friend of Charlie's who likes to goof around. His comedic nature helps to hide how the troubling events of his childhood affected him.

MARLA: Another childhood friend, a determined and strong-willed young woman training to be a nurse. Marla is extremely loyal to those she loves.

JASON: Marla's younger half brother, who sometimes fights to be taken seriously.

LAMAR: Smart and hardworking, Lamar is often the voice of reason among his friends.

AUNT JEN: Stepped in as Charlie's guardian after Henry's death. She taught Charlie to be ready for the harshness of the world, but believes painful memories are best forgotten.

CLAY BURKE: The police chief in Hurricane and father of Carlton. Clay is one of the few main characters who was directly involved in the case of the missing children.

"You know, I wasn't the chief back then. I was still a detective, and I was working on those disappearances. To this day, it was the worst thing I've ever had to see."
—from *The Silver Eyes*

WILLIAM AFTON: Business partner to Charlie's late father, Afton was also one of the prime suspects in the missing children case from ten years ago. Though he was never officially charged, he left town quickly and his current whereabouts are unknown.

"Before him stood someone who had spent so much of his life fighting like a cornered rat that he had taken on the mantle of bitter sadism as an integral part of himself. He would strike out against others and revel in their pain, feeling righteously that the world owed him his cruel pleasures."
—from *The Silver Eyes*

HENRY: The founder of Fredbear's Family Diner, Charlie's father was an engineer with a childlike sense of imagination. He personally built all the animatronics at the restaurant. Charlie remembers him as a good man, but he took many dark secrets to his grave.

THE MISSING CHILDREN:

Ten years prior to the events of the first novel, five children from Hurricane went missing—Susie; Cassidy; Fritz; an unnamed boy; and Michael Brooks, Charlie's childhood friend. Their disappearance is tied to Freddy Fazbear's Pizza, but their bodies have never been found, nor has their kidnapper been caught.

"*We* were the secret life. His real life was his work; it was what mattered. We were his guilty pleasure, the thing he got to love and sneak away to have time with, something he kept hidden away from the dangers of what he did in his *real* world. And when he was with us, there was always a part of him that was back in reality, whatever that was for him."
—from *The Silver Eyes*

Lore and Theories

CONNECTIONS BETWEEN THE BOOKS AND GAMES

While the books are set in a separate continuity from the games, they are considered canon. Many concepts first introduced in the novels later took hold in the games, while concepts introduced in the games were sometimes expanded on in the novels.

TECHNOLOGY: Several pieces of technology cross over between the books and games. Spring lock suits in particular feature heavily in both. We saw the idea of making someone or someplace invisible to an animatronic in both *FNAF3* and *The Fourth Closet*. The illusion discs in *The Twisted Ones* may have a place in the games as well, one possibility being the nightmare animatronics in *FNAF4*.

THE MISSING CHILDREN: While many fans have been quick to point out that Henry, William Afton, Charlie (Charlotte), and Elizabeth are all characters from the games and books, fans have also noted that two of the original victims in the books (Susie and Fritz) match the names etched on the tombstones in *Pizzeria Simulator*. One of the missing children in *The Fourth Closet* goes unnamed, though it is noted that he wears a striped shirt.

REMNANT: Remnant was initially mentioned in two of the hidden schematics in *Pizzeria Simulator*, but it wasn't until *The Fourth Closet* that this concept was seen in action. In Afton's lab, we see the superheating and injection of Remnant into an animatronic, and we see the spirits of the children haunting the animatronic. It seems Candy Cadet's secret stories of "five becoming one" were borne out after all.

THE CREATORS: The books offer a closer peek at Henry and William Afton, how their partnership flourished early on, and how their view of the animatronics evolved over time. Thoughtful fans might want to give these sections a closer look to determine how they impact the story of the games as well.

Chapter 12

FAZBEAR FRIGHTS

With the release of *The Fourth Closet*, it seemed as though the loose ends from the *FNAF* novel trilogy were all tied up . . . but that didn't mean Scott Cawthon was out of stories to tell.

Sometimes fiction—particularly short fiction—can provide a window into important concepts, characters, and technology. These elements can help resolve mysteries of the past or seed new things to come, while also serving as a genuinely terrifying read. The Fazbear Frights series offered all this and more, from time-traveling ball pits to framed kidnappers and everything in between.

But as the series went on, a meta story emerged in the post-story stingers, centering around one determined detective, a child trapped between worlds, and an evil that just won't die.

INTO THE PIT

Incident Report • Form 2530973 • *For Official Use Only*

Identities of Involved Persons	Occupation
	Student
Oswald	Cashier, Snack Space
Oswald's Dad	Owner, Jeff's Pizza
Jeff	Student
Chip	Student
Mike	

Description of Events

Oswald's best friend moved away, and he's having a tough time adjusting, especially as a boring, friendless summer vacation stretches out before him. That all changes when Oswald decides to chuck off his shoes and dive into the old, grody ball pit at Jeff's Pizza. Oswald emerges from the ball pit in Freddy Fazbear's Pizza, circa 1985. There he witnesses something truly horrific . . . and brings something terrible back with him.

Related Elements	Title
Freddy Fazbear's Pizza (remodeled/active): While the Fazbear Frights series features many iterations of Freddy's, this Freddy's is notable for being around in 1985, and for being the site of some of its infamous murders.	Various
Missing Children Incident: During one of his visits to 1985 Freddy's, Oswald follows a yellow rabbit animatronic back into the party room, where he finds six children murdered, still wearing their party hats.	Various
Yellow Rabbit: Oswald sees a man dressed as a yellow rabbit during his visits to 1985 Freddy's, and the rabbit is there when Oswald enters the horrific party room. The rabbit eventually follows him back through the ball pit. Could this be Springtrap, or Spring Bonnie, or something else entirely?	Various
Ball Pit: This isn't the first time something undesirable has been hiding inside a ball pit. In *Pizzeria Simulator*, Molten Freddy sneaks into your pizzeria if you buy the Discounted Ball Pit on Monday.	*Pizzeria Simulator*

New Leads

Time-Traveling Ball Pit: By diving into the pit and staying under for one hundred seconds, Oswald is able to travel back in time. Interestingly, things from the past are also able to switch places with something in the present.

TO BE BEAUTIFUL

Incident Report • Form 2530973 • *For Official Use Only*

Identities of Involved Persons	Occupation
Sarah	Student
Abby	Student
Lydia	Student
Mason Blair	Student
Sarah's Mom	Social Worker

Description of Events

If only Sarah were beautiful, her life would be easy: she'd be popular, she'd have cool friends, and she could date her crush. Passing a junkyard on her way home from school, Sarah finds Eleanor, a beautiful animatronic. For saving her, Eleanor says she'll grant Sarah any wish; Sarah wishes to be beautiful. Each night, Eleanor sings to her, and each morning Sarah wakes up a little more beautiful. But is Sarah truly becoming prettier, or is her appearance hiding a monstrous secret?

Related Elements

	Title
Illusion Discs: Eleanor gives Sarah a special necklace and tells her to never ever take it off. The end of the story reveals that this pendant seems to function similar to the illusion discs seen elsewhere in the canon.	The Twisted Ones, The Fourth Closet
Junkyard Animatronics: Sarah finds Eleanor in a junkyard, where we've seen many animatronics dumped throughout *FNAF* books and games.	The Fourth Closet, Pizzeria Simulator

New Leads

Eleanor: She seems to be a new animatronic, albeit with a familiar design. Her description and portrait closely matches that of Circus Baby, and her name, Eleanor, is oddly similar to Afton's daughter's name, Elizabeth.

Incident Report • Form 2530973 • *For Official Use O...*

Identities of Involved Persons	Occupation
Millie Fitzsimmons	Student
Dylan	Student
Millie's Grandfather	Retired

Description of Events

It seems like no one wants Millie around. Her parents abandoned her to live with her grandfather in his museum-like house of antiques and oddities. No one at school knows or cares that she exists. Millie spends most of her life romanticizing death, an end to her torment. But when Millie has the chance to get her wish, trapped inside the belly of an animatronic, why isn't she thrilled to die?

Related Elements	Title
Funtime Freddy: The animatronic Millie finds herself trapped in appears to be a Funtime Freddy, based on the description and large storage compartment in its belly.	*Sister Location*
Eaten Alive: Readers of *The Twisted Ones* graphic novel may recognize the similar illustration for this story.	*The Twisted Ones Graphic Novel*

New Leads

The Animatronics' Fate: We've seen several stories in which old animatronics are found in junkyards or abandoned in old pizzeria locations, but this is the first time we've seen an animatronic find its way into the hands of a random collector. It certainly won't be the last time, though.

FETCH

Incident Report • Form 2530973 • *For Official Use Only*

Identities of Involved Persons	Occupation
Greg	Student
Hadi	Student
Cyril	Student
Kimberly Bergstrom	Student
Uncle Dare (Darrin)	Inventor

Description of Events

Greg has become engrossed with the impact that thought and intention can have on random, real-world events. So one night, when he feels drawn to the old, run-down pizzeria in town, he doesn't hesitate before breaking in with his best friends. At the dusty prize counter, Greg finds a robotic dog called Fetch, the ultimate retrieval machine. Greg activates the animatronic but doesn't think much of it . . . until he starts getting strange texts from an unknown sender, and the answers to his darkest wishes.

Related Elements	Title
Freddy Fazbear's Pizza (abandoned): Greg finds Fetch at the prize counter of an abandoned Freddy Fazbear's Pizza. Though the place is dusty, it's largely intact. Cyril researches the location and the franchise on an online forum for people who explore abandoned places.	Various

New Leads

Fetch: This animatronic dog is designed to sync up with your phone in order to retrieve information and other things for you.

Animatronics Interacting with New Tech: From the story, it seems that the pizzeria has been closed for ten years or more. Fetch has been seemingly locked inside the pizzeria for just as long, but he's able to interact with Greg's smartphone. Could this point to the advanced technology of the robotics, or something else?

Random Event Generators (REGs): REGs are machines meant to generate a random response. Scientists designed them to test the power that a person's thought or intention might have over a random outcome. Greg is fascinated by this science, but as Kimberly points out, he's tangling with forces much larger than himself.

Incident Report • Form 2530973 • *For Official Use Only*

Identities of Involved Persons	Occupation
Alec	Student
Hazel	Student

Description of Events

Everything was great for Alec . . . until his spoiled sister, Hazel, came along. When their parents announce that Hazel is getting a birthday party at Freddy Fazbear's Pizza—the kind of party *he's* always wanted—it's the last straw. Alec is determined to ruin his sister's big day at any cost. While scoping out the pizzeria, Alec crosses paths with the "Lonely Freddys," a whole fleet of pint-size animatronics designed to hold conversations with lonely kids. Something about the Lonely Freddys feels creepy, but Alec has bigger priorities, especially when he hears his sister has a shot at winning a prized Yarg Foxy plush.

Related Elements	Title
Freddy Fazbear's Pizza (active): Hazel's birthday party is held at Freddy Fazbear's Pizza.	Various
Remnant: The soul-swapping abilities of the Lonely Freddy animatronics seem to imply some sort of Remnant-capturing technology, though how it works is unknown.	*Pizzeria Simulator, The Fourth Closet, Special Delivery*

New Leads

Lonely Freddy: A series of animatronics deployed at Freddy Fazbear's Pizza locations, designed to keep lonely kids company. In reality, these animatronics seemingly steal the souls of children.

Yarg Foxy: A variation of the Foxy animatronic, and a favorite of Alec and Hazel. The plush toy for Yarg Foxy is rare and can seemingly only be won by catching a prized Yarg Foxy ticket in the Wind Tunnel game.

Out of Stock

Identities of Involved Persons	Occupation
	Student
Oscar Avila	Student
Raj	Student
Isaac	

Description of Events

Oscar and his friends have been eagerly awaiting the release of the hottest new Freddy Fazbear toy, the Plushtrap Chaser. The friends pool their money and head to the store on release day, only to find out that the toy is sold out . . . although, not completely. One Plushtrap Chaser remains, though it looks a little too lifelike, and it's in a mangled box. Oscar is sick of missing out, so he slaps some money on the counter, grabs the toy, and runs. But is Oscar really bringing home the hottest new toy, or is he about to unwrap a nightmare?

Related Elements	Title
Plushtrap: The Plushtrap Chaser follows similar rules to the Plushtrap featured in *FNAF4*, in that it moves in the dark and freezes in the light.	*FNAF4, Help Wanted*

New Leads

Plushtrap Chaser: The Plushtrap Chaser is an animatronic toy that moves in the dark and freezes in the light. Oscar notes that Plushtrap is his favorite character from the Freddy Fazbear world, implying that Plushtrap is part of the Freddy Fazbear character canon, something that Fazbear Entertainment is marketing and profiting from, not trying to cover up.

Plushtrap Chaser: While Freddy-themed merchandise is available in the prize counter of Freddy's locations, this is the first time in the canon we've seen Freddy merch in an independent toy store.

Incident Report • Form 2530973 • F

Identities of Involved Persons	Occupation
Delilah	Waitress
Nate	Diner Owner
Harper	Actor

Description of Events

Delilah is a down-on-her-luck waitress, recently divorced and struggling to get by. While browsing a garage sale, she comes across Ella, an elaborate "helper doll" animatronic whose only working function is as an alarm clock. Delilah purchases Ella to help with her chronic lateness at work, and even sets the alarm when she gets home, but it doesn't go off. Thinking the doll is broken, Delilah throws Ella away, but Ella has a job to do, and nothing will stop her from doing it.

Related Elements

	Title
Ella: The design of Ella and some of her functions (serve drinks) seem to match the doll Henry created for Charlie in the novel series, though this Ella does seem to have more features and appears to have been mass-produced.	*The Silver Eyes, The Twisted Ones, The Fourth Closet*
Fazbear Entertainment: This is noted as the company that produced Ella, though Delilah says she's never heard of it.	Various

New Leads

Ella: She is an animatronic "helper doll" that can perform an exhaustive list of tasks, such as keep time, serve as an alarm clock, manage appointments, keep track of lists, take photos, read stories, sing songs, serve drinks, test the pH levels in water, and even do personality assessments based on a preprogrammed list of two hundred questions.

ROOM FOR ONE MORE

Incident Report • Form 2530973 • *For Official Use Only*

Identities of Involved Persons	Occupation
	Night Guard
Stanley	Courthouse Worker
Melissa	

Description of Events

Still reeling from a breakup with his long-term girlfriend, Stanley is feeling lonelier than ever. It doesn't help that Stanley works as the only night guard at an isolated, underground facility. Most nights, Stanley just falls asleep at his desk from sheer boredom. But that all changes when an alarm goes off in one of the vents, and a strange ballerina doll appears on his desk. The doll is whispering that it wants to go home with him . . .

Related Elements	Title
Minireenas: The dolls that made their first appearance in *Sister Location* appear here on Stanley's desk. The dolls speak with him and find a way to go home with Stanley each night.	*Sister Location, Ultimate Custom Night, Help Wanted*
Secretive Underground Facility: Stanley doesn't know the name of his employer, but the deep underground facility, cramped office, and vent monitors seem similar to the setting of *Sister Location*—Circus Baby's Entertainment and Rental.	*Sister Location, Help Wanted*

New Leads

Make Sure Nothing Gets Out: When you play as a *FNAF* security guard, your general mission is to ensure nothing gets into the office. This story seems to follow a thread similar to *Sister Location*, in which the animatronics are looking to escape.

Incident Report • Form 2530973

Identities of Involved Persons	
Devon Blaine Marks	**Occupation**
Mick Callahan	Student
Kelsey	Student
Heather	Student
	Student

Description of Events

Devon isn't the most popular kid in school, but he doesn't mind, so long as he can get his crush, Heather, to notice him. That all changes when Kelsey moves to town. The new kid is handsome and popular, and he even catches Heather's eye. Jealous, Devon invites Kelsey to an abandoned pizzeria out in the woods where an old animatronic costume—and revenge—waits.

Related Elements

	Title
Golden Freddy Spring Lock Suit: The old pizzeria contains a Golden Freddy spring lock suit that still functions. Kelsey notes that he's heard of more recent mascot costumes that are high-tech, allowing you to speak in the voice of the character. It is later noted that the animatronic does contain a dead body with curly black hair.	*FNAF4*
Freddy Fazbear's Pizza (abandoned): The old pizzeria is a bit moldy but largely intact, with most of its animatronics and furniture still inside.	Various

New Leads

Kelsey: There's something not right about Kelsey. He survives being trapped inside the spring lock suit, and seems to entrap multiple kids to similar fates. So who is he . . . and what does he want?

• Form 2530973 • *For Official Use Only*

Identities of Involved Persons	Occupation
	Student
Pete Dinglewood	Student
Chuck Dinglewood	

Description of Events

Pete was already having a hard enough time coping with his parents' divorce, but being saddled his younger brother, Chuck, has made things even worse. While babysitting Chuck at Freddy Fazbear's Pizza, Pete decides to play a prank on his younger brother. He takes him to the out-of-service Pirate Cove stage and activates Foxy. Chuck runs off, but Pete is suddenly entranced by the animatronic, which seems stuck on the same lyric: "You can be a pirate, but first you'll have to lose an eye and an arm! Yarg!" If only Pete knew how true those words would turn out to be. . . .

Related Elements	Title
Freddy Fazbear's Pizza (active): This location seems to be fairly active, with the usual out-of-service Pirate Cove.	Various
Foxy: Pete experiences an eerie feeling while watching the animatronic run through its performance, which seems to be due to the curse being placed. Chuck later returns to the animatronic for revenge, but feels nothing.	Various

New Leads

Curse: Pete's actions lead him to fall prey to a nasty curse, one that will stop at nothing to take his eye and arm. This is the first time such a curse has been noted in the canon.

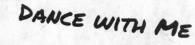

Incid...   ...cial Use Only

Identities of Involved Persons	Occupation
Kasey	Thief
Jack	Thief
AJ	Thief

Description of Events

Since her mom's boyfriend kicked her out, Kasey has had to fight to survive. When she discovered that stealing could get her much further, much faster than minimum wage, Kasey fell in with Jack and AJ, with whom she now steals for a living. But one night, Kasey steals from a family outside Circus Baby's Pizza World. The score isn't much, but it includes an interesting set of novelty glasses that show a animatronic ballerina dancing, slowly getting closer and closer . . .

Related Elements

	Title
Ballora: Ballora seems to appear only when the novelty glasses are worn, but some of Kasey's later interactions demonstrate that Ballora is physically present, regardless of whether the glasses are worn.	*Sister Location, Ultimate Custom Night*
Circus Baby's Pizza World: Kasey robs a family as they're leaving the pizzeria. The children can be overheard talking about some of the notable animatronics, including Circus Baby and Ballora.	*Sister Location, Help Wanted*

New Leads

Novelty Glasses: A pair of cardboard glasses with flimsy plastic lenses. A small slip of paper that comes with the glasses reads "Put on the glasses, and Ballora will dance for you." When worn, the glasses make Kasey dizzy, and she's able to see Ballora dancing in the distance. No one else can see the animatronic, except Kasey and the girl she stole the glasses from.

Incident Report • Form 25309

For Official Use Only

Identities of Involved Persons

Identities of Involved Persons	Occupation
Susie	Child
Samantha	Student
Patricia	Knitter

Description of Events

In a horrific tragedy, Susie was murdered at Freddy Fazbear's Pizza, and her family is still in the throes of grief. Susie has been trying to communicate with her sister for some time now, but no matter how hard she tries, Samantha isn't getting her messages. Susie's time with her family is almost up, but she's determined to show her mom and sister that she loves them, one last time.

Related Elements

Related Elements	Title
Missing Children Incident: The story explains that Susie was taken at Freddy Fazbear's Pizza, and her body was never recovered.	Various
Chica: Susie is shown here to be possessing the Chica animatronic.	Various

New Leads

Susie: She is noted as one of the missing children in both *The Fourth Closet* and on a tombstone in the secret ending of *Pizzeria Simulator*, but this is the first time fans have gotten to see a story dedicated to her and the aftermath of her disappearance.

Incident Report • Form 2530973 • *For Official Use Only*

Identities of Involved Persons

Identities of Involved Persons	Occupation
Bob Mackenzie	
Wanda Mackenzie	Unknown
Tyler Mackenzie	Unknown
Aaron Mackenzie	Student
Cindy Mackenzie	Student
	Child

Description of Events

Bob is an overworked, underappreciated dad who wishes he could catch a break. His family has dragged him to a summer vacation at Camp Etenia, which seems guaranteed to be the opposite of the restful break he so desperately needs. After a lengthy car ride and fraught check-in, Bob is told about the "Bunny Call," a traditional camp prank he can play on his family. Eager for some revenge, Bob quickly signs up, but he might later regret inviting the creepy Ralpho rabbit into their cabin . . .

Related Elements

	Title
Survive 'Til 6:00 a.m.: Ralpho may be a new animatronic, but the desperate defense Bob mounts until 6:00 a.m. will feel familiar to longtime *FNAF* players.	Various

New Leads

Ralpho: A massive rabbit suit worn by staff at Camp Etenia for conducting "Bunny Calls"—terrible prank wake-up calls with crashing symbols, loud screaming, and head spinning—that take place between 5:00 a.m. and 6:00 a.m.

How'd That Get Here?: A summer camp is certainly one of the more out-of-the-way places to find an animatronic, and it should be noted that no one in the story mentions Ralpho being affiliated with Fazbear Entertainment. The character's origins thus remain a mystery.

IN THE FLESH

• Form 2530973 • *For Official Use Only*

Identities of Involved Persons	Occupation
	Game Developer
Matt	Call Center Representative
Jason	Unemployed
Gene	

Description of Events

Matt is a game developer working on a new VR game for the popular *FNAF* series called *Springtrap's Revenge*. Matt redirects all the anger of his divorce and general dissatisfaction with life into the game, a maze in which players must avoid Springtrap. But when Matt hops in to quickly playtest the game, he's frustrated by the difficulty of the Springtrap AI. In a fit of rage, Matt programs the AI to torture itself to the point of corruption.

Related Elements	Title
FNAF (game): The game series of *FNAF* was mentioned in the introductory sequence of *Help Wanted*. Though Fazbear Entertainment initially claimed to be suing the developer, it was later revealed via Tape Girl that they were working with him.	*Help Wanted*
Springtrap/Glitchtrap: While it's unclear if the Springtrap seen here is related to Glitchtrap, many similar elements are present. This Springtrap is born of corrupted programming that makes its way into the real world by merging with a game developer.	*Help Wanted, The Curse of Dreadbear*

New Leads

Another VR Company?: Matt works for a VR game developer that was clearly in partnership with the indie developer of the in-world version of *FNAF*. So, what relationship—if any—does Matt's company have to Jeremiah's company from "The Prankster" or Tape Girl's company from *Help Wanted*?

Incident Report • Form 2530973 • *For Official Use Only*

Identities of Involved Persons	Occupation
Arthur Blythe	Priest
The Patient	Unknown
Mia Fremont	Nurse
Nurse Ackerman	Head Nurse
Nurse Colton	Nurse
Nurse Thomas	Nurse

Description of Events

Father Blythe is called to Room 1280 of Heracles Hospital to visit a patient in a dire state. The patient is horrifically burned, his organs exposed in places, and is largely unable to communicate. The nurses who tend to him have noted that there are two distinct electromagnetic signals in his brain. They take this to mean that there are two souls inside him, tormenting each other—it's the definition of evil. Father Blythe feels the nurses are biased against the man due to his gruesome appearance, so he sets out to help him. But the best-laid plans often have unintended consequences.

Related Elements	Title
The Stitchwraith: While several Fazbear Frights stories tie in to the series' larger meta story, "The Man in Room 1280" leads directly into the meta story—and the return of Afton.	Stitchwraith Stingers
William Afton: The events of the story seem to indicate that the man in Room 1280 is William Afton. This is backed up by the man's injuries (matching the ending of Pizzeria Simulator), the fact that he seems to be unkillable, the supernatural events that surround him, and the events of the stingers that follow the story.	Various

New Leads

Shadow Child: Throughout the story, various characters report seeing a little boy with curly black hair and a feral smile, wearing an alligator mask. The boy is believed by many to be a ghost and possesses some supernatural powers.

BLACKBIRD

Incident Report • Form 2530973 • *For Official Use Only*

Identities of Involved Persons	Occupation
	College Student
Nole Markman	College Student
Sam O'Neil	College Student
Amber	College Student
Christine Wilbur	

Description of Events

Nole and Sam are working on a short horror film for their filmography class when they decide to make a monster movie about a creepy animatronic-inspired creature called the Blackbird. They decide the Blackbird will punish guilty people, forcing them to admit to their past transgressions. But in talking about the Blackbird, Nole admits to having done some bullying in high school, which upsets Sam, who was himself the target of bullying. Nole doesn't see what the big deal is, but the Blackbird does.

Related Elements	Title
Freddy Fazbear's Pizza (past): Nole and Sam talk about how the characters at Freddy's used to freak them out as children.	Various

New Leads

The Blackbird: Nole is haunted by the Blackbird until he atones for the bullying he did. But when the haunting is over, Nole notes that Sam and the costume's location were accounted for during that time period, so what exactly was pursuing Nole?

Incident Report • Form 2530973 • *For Official Use Only*

Identities of Involved Persons	Occupation
Jake	Student
Evan	Soldier
Margie	Caretaker
Michael	Unknown

Description of Events

Nine-year-old Jake is growing weaker by the day, losing his battle with a rare brain tumor. His father, Evan, is with the military, stationed overseas, but he's left Jake in the care of Margie. Each night, Margie and Evan use a walkie-talkie to make it sound like a secret friend lives in the cupboard by Jake's bed. This friend, "Simon," asks Jake to pretend he isn't sick, and asks what his day was like—all the things he would've done if he had no limitations. When Jake is well enough, the idea is that he'll get out of bed, open the cabinet, and find a doll, the perfect replica of "The Real Jake"—one with baseball game tickets and grass stains on his knees, mementos of all the things he would've done. But will such a day ever arrive for Jake?

Related Elements

	Title
Michael: Some fans have called attention to the use of the name "Michael" for Jake's uncle, particularly around the fact that he's wealthy and is said to act "robotic." Could this be a reference to Michael Afton?	*Sister Location*

New Leads

The Real Jake Doll: The idea of a powerful spirit inhabiting something other than an animatronic is somewhat new for the canon.

The Stitchwraith: This story is highly significant to the meta story being told in the stingers, and the true identity of the Stitchwraith (see page 224).

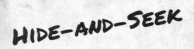

Incident Report • Form 2530973 • *For Official Use Only*

Identities of Involved Persons	Occupation
Toby	Student/Worker, Freddy Fazbear's Pizza and Games
Connor	Unknown
Tabitha	Student
Dan	Manager, Freddy Fazbear's Pizza and Games

Description of Events

Toby is sick of being in constant competition with Connor, his perfect older brother. Not only did Connor once work the same job as Toby at Freddy Fazbear's Pizza and Games, he also holds the high score on every game in the pizzeria. Fortunately, that is about to change: the pizzeria is installing a new game, called Hide-and-Seek. Toby is determined to get the high score and show his brother who's really the best, no matter the cost.

Related Elements	Title
Freddy Fazbear's Pizza and Games (active): Though named slightly different from other Freddy's locations, this restaurant and arcade seems to function the same.	Various
RWQFSFASXC (Shadow Bonnie): After destroying the game in a fit of anger, Shadow Bonnie attaches itself to Toby. Toby is able to see the animatronic behind him when he looks in the mirror, though no one else can.	*FNAF2, FNAF3, Ultimate Custom Night, Special Delivery*

New Leads

Hide-and-Seek Game: A new game/attraction that's set up in its own room. A Shadow Bonnie cutout travels on a track and is able to hide in one of three locations at each stop (the stops are painted to look like various parts of a town, including a police station, pizzeria, etc.). Players have three tries in three minutes to guess where Shadow Bonnie is hiding.

Incident Report • Form 2530973 • *For Official Use Only*

Identities of Involved Persons	Occupation
Robert Stanton	Graphic Designer
Tyler Stanton	Child
Jess	Copy Editor

Description of Events

Ever since his wife died in childbirth, Robert has been struggling to survive. Putting aside his insurmountable grief, Robert has devoted his life to raising their son, Tyler, a two-year-old ball of energy. Robert never stops worrying about his son and if he's doing a good enough job raising him, but some burden is lifted when his son picks out a new Tag-Along Freddy toy at the store. The toy purports to watch your child and send you live updates via a wristwatch that comes with the toy. Robert sees it as a win-win: Tyler gets a new playmate, and Robert gets some peace of mind. But when Tyler vanishes, Robert wonders if the toy was really "a kid's and parents' best pal" or something far more sinister.

Related Elements

	Title
Fredbear Plush/Monitor: Fans will recall a similar, albeit different Fredbear plush that monitored another child—the Bite Victim from *FNAF4*.	*FNAF4, Sister Location*
Merch: This is the second instance of a mass-produced toy being available outside of a Freddy's location (the first being the Plushtrap Chaser).	"Out of Stock"

New Leads

Tag-Along Freddy: A Freddy Fazbear plush toy that monitors children and sends a live update to a matching Tag-Along Time Wristwatch. The updates can get quite specific, even noting activities like finger painting, nap times, and meals.

Incident Report • Form 2530973 • *For Official Use Only*

Identities of Involved Persons	Occupation
Reed	Student
Julius	Student
Shelly Girard	Student
Pickle Girard	Student
Ory Girard	Student

Description of Events

Reed is tired of being bullied by Julius, a jock who's always had it in for Reed. While Reed is struggling through their robotics class with his action-figure-size endoskeleton, Julius has managed to create what he calls an "exosuit"—a life-size exoskeleton that can make him stronger and faster. After class one day, while wearing the suit, Julius threatens Reed yet again. But then Julius's exosuit malfunctions, and Reed locks the bully inside it. Reed sees this as Julius's just rewards and leaves him in the classroom, thinking he'll let him out in the morning. But is the exosuit really broken? Or is it just responding to a different set of commands?

Related Elements	Title
Robotics Class: Several Fazbear Frights short stories take place in classrooms, including some specifically dedicated to robotics. In these settings, animatronics provide an interesting avenue to study the field.	"Together Forever"

New Leads

Exosuit: For his class project, Julius creates an "exosuit"—a metal exoskeleton that a person can strap into and use to lift heavy objects, run faster, etc. It's pointed out in class that Julian's project uses the same frequency as Pickle's robot, making it follow any input from Pickle's remote.

IR and RF Remotes: Remotes that can control robots from afar. IR (infrared) remotes have a shorter range, and must be pointed directly at a receiver to transmit. RF (radio frequency) have a much longer range, with a signal that can penetrate doors, windows, walls, etc. Pickle's remote uses an extender to further the range of his remote.

Incident Report • Form 2530973 • *For Official Use Only*

Identities of Involved Persons

Identities of Involved Persons	Occupation
Chris Watson	Student
Dr. Little	High School Teacher

Description of Events

Chris is anxious to start high school, wanting to leave behind his working-class family and immature friends to make a better life for himself as a scientist. But the first step to becoming a scientist is acing Dr. Little's freshman science class and joining the exclusive Science Club, reserved for only the best and brightest. On the first day of class, Dr. Little announces the annual lock-in experiment, which is worth 500 points of extra credit and is all but required for those looking to join the Science Club. The lock-in seems like a life-changing experience, and Chris is all too eager to get in on the action.

Related Elements

Related Elements	Title
Biology-Altering Substances: The Fazbear Frights series contains several references to mystery substances, such as Faz-Goo, the Gumdrop Nose, and Sea Bonnies. These items, all produced by Fazbear Entertainment, seem to alter the biology of the people they come into contact with.	"Gumdrop Angel," "Sea Bonnies"

New Leads

Freddy Fazbear Mad Scientist Kit: A mass-produced "toy" science kit containing Faz-Goo. Interestingly, Dr. Little assures the class it is "most definitely not a toy, and if you treat it as one, it will be at your own peril."

Faz-Goo: A gooey pink substance seemingly capable of cloning when provided with DNA (such as a tooth) and a supply of living red blood cells. Organs seemed to be sucked out of the host's body until all that remains of the host is goo.

Dr. Little: He seems to know what the Faz-Goo does, and encourages its use among his students, so is he part of some larger conspiracy?

GUMDROP ANGEL

Incident Report • Form 2530973 • *For Official Use Only*

Identities of Involved Persons	Occupation
Angel	Student
Ophelia	Student
Dominic	Assistant Manager, Freddy Fazbear's Pizza

Description of Events

Angel is one month away from graduation, and it can't come fast enough. Ever since her mom married her new stepdad, Angel's life has been taken over by Ophelia, her spoiled younger stepsister. At Freddy Fazbear's Pizza, during Ophelia's extravagant birthday party, Ophelia is gifted with a Birthday Gummy, a life-size molded gummy treat. Angel is both mesmerized and disturbed by the gummy, especially after it starts to move on its own . . .

Related Elements	Title
Freddy Fazbear's Pizza (active): Ophelia has an extravagant birthday party at Freddy Fazbear's Pizza.	Various
Biology-Altering Substances: As noted, several Fazbear Frights stories are focused around biology-altering substances, including the Gumdrop Nose, Faz-Goo, and Sea Bonnies.	"He Told Me Everything," "Sea Bonnies"

New Leads

Birthday Gummy: A living gummy candy unlike any other. The treat is created when a person consumes the Gumdrop Nose, which changes the consumer's DNA into a gummy substance. Freddy Fazbear's Pizza offers them as a grand finale treat at birthday parties.

Complicit Fazbear Entertainment Employee: Dominic is noted to be the assistant manager at Freddy Fazbear's Pizza, and he seems to be fully aware of what's happening to Angel. While most Freddy's employees are unaware of the nefarious things that often happen at the pizzeria, Dominic seems fully complicit, if remorseful.

Incident Report • Form 2530973 • *For Official Use Only*

Identities of Involved Persons

	Occupation
Sergio	
Dale	Project Manager, Architectural Firm
Sophia Manchester	Senior Manager, Architectural Firm
	Unknown

Description of Events

Sergio is feeling pretty out of luck. The new promotion he received is too much work for too little pay, his SUV dies on the way home from the job, and he's stuck trudging through downtown in the rain looking for a phone . . . which is when he finds Lucky Boy. Lucky Boy is a small figurine who wants to make big changes in Sergio's life. But the more Sergio listens to Lucky Boy, the more he realizes he needs to take a more hands-on approach to happiness . . . even if it means taking a hacksaw to his life.

Related Elements

	Title
Balloon Boy: The Lucky Boy figurine bears resemblance to Balloon Boy and similar animatronics and even laughs in the same manner.	Various
Illusion Discs?: Sergio becomes more entranced by Lucky Boy—and more detached from reality—as the story goes on, even altering his body by himself. It's unclear if Lucky Boy contains some form of illusion technology, as seen in "To Be Beautiful," but others notice Sergio's at-home plastic surgery only after he leaves Lucky Boy in the hall.	*The Twisted Ones, The Fourth Closet,* "To Be Beautiful"

New Leads

Lucky Boy: A small electronic figurine, bearing some resemblance to Balloon Boy, except the sign in his hand says I'M A LUCKY BOY. Sergio finds the toy on the street. Lucky Boy gives Sergio vague advice on how he can change his life for the better, mainly by following his desires, no matter the consequences.

WHAT WE FOUND

Identities of Involved Persons	Occupation
Hudson	Security Guard
Barry	Military
Duane	Military

Description of Events

Hudson is grateful when he scores a well-paying job as a security guard at the Fazbear's Fright Horror Attraction in town. But that's about the beginning and end of Hudson's good fortune. Hudson is burdened with a dark past that seems to poison everything he touches in the present, a dark past he'll be forced to confront during his midnight shifts at Fazbear's Fright.

Related Elements	Title
Fazbear's Fright Horror Attraction: A haunted house of sorts, set up to look like an old Freddy Fazbear's Pizza. Real artifacts from the restaurant's history are being brought in to make the attraction feel authentic.	*FNAF3, Help Wanted*
Springtrap: Hudson faces off with Springtrap throughout the night, even noticing that there is a dead body within the animatronic.	*FNAF3, Help Wanted*

New Leads

Hudson: Is Hudson the night guard from *FNAF3*? In general, the events of the story seem to follow the events of *FNAF3* almost to the letter, right down to the ending. Hudson also experiences hallucinations throughout the night while dealing with Springtrap.

Incident Report • Form 2530973 • *For Official Use Only*

Identities of Involved Persons	Occupation
Jack	Owner, Pizza Playground
Porter	Handyman, Inventor
Sage Brantley	Custodian, Writer
Edwin	Cook
Angie	Waitress
Becky	Homemaker
Tyson	Student

Description of Events

Jack is a franchisee of the floundering Pizza Playground, an animatronic pizzeria. He employs Porter as handyman and animatronic technician, Sage as custodian, Edwin as cook, and Angie as waitress. Off the clock, Porter has invented a new machine, the Puppet Carver, that can carve low-cost animatronics for the restaurant out of a simple block of wood, but he hasn't quite worked out all the kinks yet. When a demonstration of the machine fails, Jack fires the staff in a fit of anger, determined to declare bankruptcy. Later that night, Jack hears a ticking coming from inside the machine. He enters the machine, trying to find a way to turn it off, and nearly dies when the machine turns on. But after his near-death experience, he feels like a changed man.

Related Elements

	Title
Mediocre Melodies: Pigpatch, or an animatronic much like him (a pig strumming a banjo) appears in Pizza Playground.	*Pizzeria Simulator*

New Leads

New Animatronics: Baron von Bear and an unknown bird animatronic are described in the story, and the bear is even recognized by one of the restaurant's young patrons.

Pizza Playground: An animatronic pizzeria franchise. It is unclear whether this franchise is related to Fazbear Entertainment or if it's a competitor.

The Puppet Carver: Peppered throughout the story are excerpts from Sage's novel, about a wooden puppet's journey to becoming human.

Incident Report • Form 2530973 • *For Official Use Only*

Identities of Involved Persons	Occupation
	Student
Colton	Student
Aidan	Mechanic
Mike	Shop Teacher
Mr. Harrison	Nurse
Colton's Mom	

Description of Events

Colton's mom doesn't make enough money to afford the newest gaming console, so Colton decides to earn the console himself by winning tickets at Freddy Fazbear's Pizza. The highest ticket-generating game in the arcade is the Ticket Pulverizer, but the game is rigged to favor little kids. Colton does some research into the game and makes a plan to break into Freddy's after hours to "fix" the Ticket Pulverizer for good.

Related Elements	Title
Freddy Fazbear's Pizza (active): This Freddy's location is an active hub for kids and teens.	Various
Arcade Games: References to other animatronics appear in some of the arcade games mentioned, such as "BB's Ball Drop" and "DeeDee's Fishing Game." DeeDee's game might be a reference to her fishing hole in *FNAF World*.	*FNAF2, FNAF World, Ultimate Custom Night*

New Leads

Coils the Birthday Clown: A clown animatronic with a gaping grin, googly eyes, spiral limbs, and a lanky body dressed in lemon-and-lime-colored stripes. It doesn't speak, but you can hear its jingly bells as it draws near. The animatronic seems to be sentient or to have some sort of child-monitoring capabilities, based on its actions in the story.

Ticket Pulverizer: An arcade game consisting of a sealed, transparent booth where players must jump as hard as they can within the time limit to generate tickets. Players may keep the tickets they catch. The game typically costs four tokens, but one visit is free on birthdays. The voice actor for Coils the Birthday Clown recorded a message that starts the game.

PIZZA KIT

Incident Report • Form 2530973 • *For Official Use Only*

Identities of Involved Persons

	Occupation
Payton Thompson	Student
Marley	Student
Abigail	Student
Mrs. Crutchfield	Home Economics Teacher
Payton's Mom	Unknown
Ms. Bryant	Freddy's Factory Manager

Description of Events

Payton has recently befriended Marley, one of the pretty popular girls in school. Marley can be a bit rebellious, and during a trip to the Freddy Fazbear's Pizza Kit Factory, she urges Payton to break away from the tour group. While separated from the group, Marley seemingly falls into a vat of boiling pizza sauce and doesn't return. Payton is afraid to get in trouble, so she doesn't tell anyone what happened. But her guilt might just eat her alive.

Related Elements

	Title
Freddy Fazbear's Pizza (past): Freddy Fazbear's Pizza is referenced as being nostalgic, though active locations aren't mentioned.	Various

New Leads

Freddy Fazbear's Pizza Kits: A popular kit of customizable components for kids to make their own single-serve Freddy Fazbear's pizzas.

Freddy Fazbear's Pizza Kit Factory: The factory where pizza kit components are made and shipped to stores and Freddy's locations. Kids can also tour the facility and make their own pizza kits.

FRIENDLY FACE

Incident Report • Form 2530973 • *For Official Use Only*

Identities of Involved Persons	Occupation
Edward	Student
Jack Weston	Student
Faraday	Cat
Edward's Mom	Unknown

Description of Events

Edward is a careless young man whose mind always seems to be somewhere else. He and his best friend, Jack, adopt a kitten they name Faraday, who quickly becomes the center of their world. But this happiness is shattered one afternoon when Faraday races out into a busy street, and Jack runs after him without thinking. Both of Edward's best friends are killed in the resulting accident. Drowning in grief, Edward sees a commercial for a new product — Fazbear Friendly Faces, and believes it could be the key to coping with the tragedy.

Related Elements	Title
Fazbear Entertainment: Fazbear Entertainment is mentioned in the commercial for Fazbear Friendly Faces. This seems to be the first time the company is seen marketing something mass-produced, outside of a toy, to an older demographic.	Various

New Leads

Fazbear Friendly Faces: An innovative new product from Fazbear Entertainment that uses a pet's DNA to craft an identical face, which is then integrated onto an animatronic body to create a loyal pet that will follow the consumer around forever.

Incident Report • Form 2530973 • *For Official Use Only*

Identities of Involved Persons	Occupation
Mott	Student
Rory	Student
Fritz	Goldfish
Dr. T (Ron Tabor)	Pediatrician

Description of Events

Mott's younger brother, Rory, wins a package of brand-new Sea Bonnies from the Freddy Fazbear's Pizza prize counter. Ever the dutiful big brother, Mott helps Rory set up the colony of disturbing creatures, but things quickly take a strange turn. The Sea Bonnies first attack Rory's goldfish, Fritz, and then they seemingly become the fish. Worried for his brother's safety, Mott flushes the Sea Bonnies down the toilet . . . but far from ending the nightmare, it seems Mott has simply given the monsters a bigger home.

Related Elements	Title
Freddy Fazbear's Pizza (active): Rory frequents Freddy Fazbear's Pizza, where Mott often babysits him.	Various
Biology-Altering Substances: As noted, several Fazbear Frights stories are focused around biology-altering substances, including the Gumdrop Nose, Faz-Goo, and Sea Bonnies.	"He Told Me Everything," "Gumdrop Angel"
Fritz: Rory's goldfish is named "Fritz," which matches one of the names of the Missing Children seen on a tombstone of the secret ending of *Pizzeria Simulator* and *The Fourth Closet* novel. They seem unrelated.	*Pizzeria Simulator, The Fourth Closet*

New Leads

Astounding Live Sea Bonnies: A prize at the Freddy Fazbear's Pizza prize counter that allows users to grow and nurture their own healthy colony of happy Sea Bonnies. Sea Bonnies are purplish-blue creatures genetically engineered to look like a cross between sea monkeys and rabbits, guaranteed to live for three years. The prize package contains two packets of Sea Bonnie live eggs, one packet of Sea Bonnie water purification powder, and one packet of Sea Bonnie super-duper growth food.

Incident Report • Form 2530973 • *For Official Use Only*

Identities of Involved Persons	Occupation
Jessica	Student
Brittany	Student
Mindy	Student
Cindy	Student
Mr. Thornton	Robotics Teacher

Description of Events

Sophomore best friends Jessica and Brittany are annoyed when eighth-grade gifted students Cindy and Mindy are invited to join their robotics class. The class is starting up a new assignment—reprogramming old animatronics—and Jessica and Brittany are assigned to Rosie Porkchop, a massive spring lock animatronic. As Jessica delves deeper into the assignment, she comes up with a genius plan to put the eighth graders in their place.

Related Elements	Title
Spring Lock Animatronics: As the girls read Rosie's operating manual, we learn that Rosie is a spring lock suit, capable of being switched into a human interface or "suit" mode.	Various
Animatronic Mechanisms: In working on the assignment, we come across several animatronic mechanisms we've heard of before (such as servos), as well as the problems that can plague different aspects of the machinery.	*The Twisted Ones, Help Wanted, Sister Location*
Robotics Class: Several Fazbear Frights short stories take place in classrooms, including some specifically dedicated to robotics. In these settings, animatronics provide an interesting avenue to study the field.	"The Breaking Wheel"

New Leads

Animatronic Remains: At the start of the assignment, Mr. Thornton wheels out a cartful of old animatronics: endoskeletons, aliens, dogs, cats, as well as a cow, horse, orangutan, black panther, flamingo, and pig.

Rosie Porkchop: Rosie is the only life-size animatronic on Mr. Thornton's cart, a massive pig dressed in a frilly dark pink waitress uniform. The pig animatronic is said to be old, with worn felt that can't fully hide its endoskeleton. Rosie is later revealed to be a spring lock animatronic, with a tank capable of fitting two people.

Incident Report • Form 2530973 • *For Official Use Only*

Identities of Involved Persons	Occupation
Jeremiah	Game Developer
Hope	Admin, Game Development
Parker	Game Developer
Unnamed Gamemaster	Unknown

Description of Events

Jeremiah, Hope, and Parker work at a small indie game developer that was recently bought out by Fazbear Entertainment. They're developing a Freddy VR game, but company downsizing has delayed the game and forced the three employees to work many late nights. Parker enjoys playing pranks on Jeremiah, some of which cross the line of professionalism. But on Jeremiah's birthday, he's invited to play a sinister game, one that might not be a prank at all.

Related Elements	Title
Secret Tapes: Jeremiah is working for Fazbear Entertainment on a VR game, and his name is misspelled "Jeremy" on his birthday cake. Could he be the "Jeremy" referred to in the secret tapes in *Help Wanted*?	*Help Wanted*
***FNAF* VR:** Matt from "In the Flesh" is also developing a VR game for Fazbear Entertainment.	"In the Flesh"

New Leads

Unnamed Gamemaster: This character's voice is described as sounding deep and electronic, as though it had gone through a filter of some kind.

Meta Story Clues: Some of the puzzle clues, such as "STINGER MOOT" and "EVEN MORE FRIGHTS" may have implications beyond the plot. Careful readers may want to give these scenes a second look.

...ident Report • Form 2530973 • *For Official Use Only*

Identities of Involved Persons	Occupation
Joel D'Agostino	Student/Gardener
Steve D'Agostino	Owner, D'Agostino's Nursery and Garden Center
Mrs. D'Agostino	Author of Knitting Patterns
Caleb Bell	Student
Chief Montgomery	Police Chief

Description of Events

Joel is set to graduate high school soon, and all he wants is to escape his small town to become a musician and model. His parents are often on his case about working harder, taking life more seriously, and being careful, but Joel finds them uptight and overbearing. One night, Joel is driving recklessly and hits a child. Rather than confront his misdeed, Joel chooses to pretend it never happened. In the days that follow, he is haunted by plastic "Kids at Play" figures, part of a public safety initiative, as he grapples with what to do next.

Related Elements	Title
Fazbear Entertainment: There are a few Freddy's branded things in Joel's world, though a specific Freddy Fazbear's Pizza location isn't mentioned.	Various

New Leads

Kids at Play Figures: These three-foot-tall plastic figures hold a flag that reads KIDS AT PLAY, and are meant to alert drivers to children in the area. The figures seem to be part of a Fazbear Entertainment–sponsored public safety initiative, as Joel finds one in his Fazcrunch cereal box.

Fazbear Fazcrunch Cereal: A Freddy Fazbear–themed cereal that Joel has been eating for a number of years.

FIND PLAYER TWO!

Incident Report • Form 2530973 • *For Official Use Only*

Identities of Involved Persons	Occupation
Aimee	Student
Mary Jo	Student
Emmett Tucker	Unknown
Gretta	Student

Description of Events

Bookish Aimee and outspoken Mary Jo have been best friends since they were small. As eleven-year-olds, they spend most of their time at the local Freddy Fazbear's Pizza, playing in the Hiding Maze, a game that's no longer in active use, but is still playable. One day, a strange man follows the girls into the maze, and Aimee flees the pizzeria. That's the last time she ever sees Mary Jo, but ten years later, Aimee is determined to find out what happened to her friend.

Related Elements

	Title
Missing Children Incident: Though Mary Jo's disappearance seems unrelated to the Missing Children Incident, there seems to be a lot of attention on kidnappings at Freddy Fazbear's Pizza locations in the media around this time.	Various
Freddy Fazbear's Pizza (remodeled): This story details the events that preceded the closing of a Freddy's location, and later shows how the building was repurposed.	Various

New Leads

Freddy's Hiding Maze Hide-and-Seek Game: A timed, themed maze game for two players. Player two chooses one of the many cubbyholes throughout the maze to hide in. The cubbyholes are sealed with hatch-like doors. Player one must navigate the rain forest–themed maze to find their companion.

Emmett Tucker: A man arrested for a kidnapping, who was seen by Aimee and Mary Jo at the Freddy Fazbear's Pizza location they frequented.

Incident Report • Form 2530973 • *For Official Use Only*

Identities of Involved Persons	Occupation
Everett Larson	Detective
Jake	N/A
Andrew	N/A
Dr. Phineas Taggart	Scientist
The Agony	N/A
Renelle	Student
Dr. Talbert	Scientist
Eleanor	N/A

Description of Events

Larson: Detective Larson is given the unfortunate task of investigating the "Stitchwraith," a strange case that seems part serial tragedy, part urban legend. A number of strange incidents are tracked in the case file, but all are connected by sightings of animatronics . . . and by a terrifying hooded figure lugging around piles of garbage.

Jake: Years after his death, Jake finds himself possessing an animatronic endoskeleton, which he can control with the help of Andrew, another lost and angry child whose soul is tethered to the animatronic's battery pack. Jake is able to "move on" if he focuses hard enough on a happy memory, but he can't bear the thought of leaving Andrew behind. Plus, Andrew's anger has infected a lot of objects—animatronics, toys, dolls . . . Someone has to destroy them before they hurt someone.

Related Elements	Title
Freddy Fazbear's Pizza: The franchise is mentioned several times, and remnants of the pizzeria (such as a Foxy animatronic) appear.	Various
Missing Children Incident: Larson mentions the "Freddy's murders" and seems aware that William Afton was responsible.	Various
The Fire: The incident shown in *Pizzeria Simulator* and its aftermath are revisited via police evidence . . . It seems that Cassette Man's plan did not work exactly as intended.	*Pizzeria Simulator*
The Puppet: Larson pulls the Puppet from an evidence locker, where evidence from the *Pizzeria Simulator* fire is housed.	Various

Continued on next page (page 1 of 2)

Related Elements	Title
William Afton: He makes a terrifying return after the events in "The Man in Room 1280."	"The Man in Room 1280"
Remnant: Experiments on and technology developed around Remnant take center stage in the Stitchwraith story.	Various
Ball Pit: The famous time-traveling ball pit makes a comeback in later stingers.	"Into the Pit"
Eleanor: The animatronic Eleanor makes a reappearance later in the Stitchwraith's story.	"To Be Beautiful"
Witness Reports: Sarah's case is part of the Stitchwraith case file that Larson receives from Chief Monahan.	"To Be Beautiful"
Millie Fitzsimmons: Millie's fate is revealed in the final stinger.	"Count the Ways"
Andrew's Origins: Andrew's spirit possessed the battery pack that powered Fetch.	"Fetch"
REG: Dr. Taggart has an REG and practices visualization and intention-setting, similar to Greg.	"Fetch"
Plushtrap Chaser: The Stitchwraith reclaims the Plushtrap Chaser.	"Out of Stock"
Ella: The Stitchwraith reclaims the Ella doll.	"1:35 A.M."
Step Closer: Larson gains insight into the events of this story, and the Stitchwraith is seen destroying a Foxy animatronic.	"Step Closer"
Blackbird: Larson gains insight into and affects the outcome of this story.	"Blackbird"
Jake: Chronicles the end of Jake's life.	"The Real Jake"
Hide-and-Seek: Larson gains insight into the events of this story.	"Hide-and-Seek"

ANDREW HAS SOMETHING INTERESTING TO SAY ABOUT HIS ANGER, AND THE REASON HE'S TETHERED TO FETCH'S BATTERY PACK: "I DO REMEMBER WANTING TO GET BACK AT SOMEONE WHO HURT ME. I THINK I ATTACHED MYSELF TO HIM. I GOT INTO HIS SOUL, MADE SURE HE COULDN'T MOVE ON WHEN HE SHOULDA DIED.

I REMEMBER I WANTED HIM TO SUFFER, THE WAY HE MADE ME SUFFER. BUT I DON'T REMEMBER WHAT HE DID. I JUST KNOW I HUNG ON, NO MATTER WHAT THEY DID TO HIM TO TRY AND SAVE HIM. I WANTED HIM TO HURT!"

STITCHING IT TOGETHER

THE REAL JAKE

Takes place three years prior to the stingers.

Jake is the Stitchwraith, focused on cleaning up the "haunted" Remnant-containing objects that are causing chaos.

FETCH

Andrew had possessed Fetch via its battery pack, he seems to have been one of Afton's victims.

THE MAN IN ROOM 1280

The burned man described in the story is William Afton.

Andrew may be somewhat responsible for Afton's soul remaining tethered to this world, as he insists he couldn't let him go.

INTO THE PIT

After being stabbed by The Agony, Larson experiences strange visions where he seems to travel through time via a ball pit. He tracks down the ball pit and takes thirty samples, scraped off the balls. When the results come in, they show that the same person has been bleeding in the ball pit over thirty years.

Several elements from this story later return in the Stitchwraith stingers—Eleanor, the heart-shaped pendant, and witness reports of Sarah's story.

TO BE BEAUTIFUL

Eleanor's pendant is shown to have unique properties, including the ability to change the appearance of the wearer.

REMNANT

Dr. Taggart and Dr. Talbert are both scientists studying Remnant and metal as a conductor of powerful emotion.

When the Stitchwraith is initially created, he kills anyone he touches, causing them to wither away and cry black tears.

Chapter 13

FAZBEAR ENTERTAINMENT, INC. ARCHIVES

Over the years, Fazbear Entertainment and its associated enterprises have accumulated an archive of documents as winding and varied as the company itself. From recipes to soap opera scripts, blueprints and schematics to training tape transcripts, pore over this treasure trove of documents straight from the source!

FAZBEAR ENTERTAINMENT RECIPES

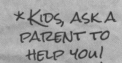

Fazbear's Twisted Pizza

Ingredients:

- Two 1-lb. loaves Fazbear Entertainment Brand Frozen Bread (roll) Dough
- Tomato sauce
- Shredded mozzarella cheese
- Mini pepperonis
- Parmesan cheese
- Italian seasoning
- Flour

Directions:

1. Thaw the bread dough and roll it onto flour covered boards. Shape into half-inch thick rectangles.
2. Spread the pizza sauce lightly on one rectangle, then sprinkle with the mozzarella cheese and pepperonis. Place the second dough rectangle on top of the first one and press it together before slicing into one-inch wide strips.
3. Twist these strips, sprinkle with Parmesan cheese and Italian seasoning (optional), and place them onto a baking sheet.
4. Bake at 400 degrees for 15 to 20 minutes, or until the sticks are golden brown. Plate with extra tomato sauce for dipping.

Chica's Golden Cupcake Pizzas

Ingredients:

- 1 can (8 oz) Fazbear Entertainment Brand Triangle Dinner Rolls
- Pizza sauce
- Mini pepperonis
- Shredded mozzarella cheese
- Italian sausage, precooked

*KIDS, ASK A PARENT TO HELP YOU!

Directions:

1. Spray a cupcake pan with cooking spray. Separate the eight triangle dinner rolls and press each one into a cup.
2. In a separate bowl, mix about a half cup of pizza sauce with mini pepperonis, shredded mozzarella cheese, and precooked Italian sausage. Spoon the mixture into each cup, then top with additional mozzarella cheese.
3. Bake at 350 degrees for 16 to 18 minutes or until the edges are lightly browned.

Eggs Benedict

Ingredients:

- Fazbear Entertainment Brand English muffins
- Butter
- Sliced Canadian bacon or ham
- Distilled white vinegar
- 4 eggs
- Hollandaise sauce
- Paprika

Directions:

1. Split and toast English muffins, then spread with butter. Brown Canadian bacon or ham in skillet using melted butter over medium heat.
2. Fill another skillet with 2-3 inches of water, and add four teaspoons of vinegar. Bring to a boil, then reduce to simmer. Break a cold egg into a separate dish, then slip carefully into water. Cook 3-5 minutes until whites and yolks are firm.
3. Place slices of Canadian bacon on each muffin half. Add poached egg. Spoon hollandaise sauce over eggs. Sprinkle paprika if desired.

Foxy Cove Cooler

Ingredients:

- 3 cups pineapple juice
- 2 cups lemon-lime soda
- 3/4 cup lemonade concentrate
- 3/4 cup orange juice concentrate
- 2 tbsp grenadine

Directions:

1. Combine all ingredients in a punch bowl or pitcher with ice.*

*Fazbear Entertainment reminds employees that this recipe should stretch to fill two pitchers, provided employees follow proper ice protocols.

*KIDS, ASK A PARENT TO HELP YOU!

Pirate Plunderbar

Ingredients:

- 12 tbsp unsalted butter
- 16 oz mini marshmallows
- 1/2 teaspoon cinnamon
- 1/2 teaspoon salt
- 1/4 teaspoon vanilla extract
- 8 cups toasted rice cereal
- 8 oz semisweet chocolate chips

Directions:

1. Melt butter over medium heat in a large pot, then add marshmallows. Stir until fully melted.

2. Add cinnamon, salt, and vanilla extract and stir until evenly mixed.

3. Remove from heat and add rice cereal. Stir until roughly even.

4. Line a 9-by-13-in. pan with parchment or wax paper. Empty marshmallow-rice mixture into the pan and shape so the surface is even. Do not compress the mixture too hard.

5. Once cool, slice into rectangular bars and remove from pan.

6. In a medium pot, melt the chocolate chips.

7. Once melted, cover marshmallow-rice bars. Place in the refrigerator for 30 minutes, until chocolate hardens.

Official Fazbear Entertainment Birthday Cake

Ingredients:

- 2 cups sugar
- 8 tbsp butter
- 4 eggs
- 1 tbsp vanilla extract
- 3 cups flour
- 3 tsp baking powder
- 1/2 tsp salt
- 1 cup whole milk
- Fazbear Entertainment Brand Frosting (chocolate or vanilla, per order sheet)

Directions:

1. Preheat the oven to 350 degrees. Butter the sides and bottom of two 9-inch round cake pans. Set aside.

2. In a large bowl, mix sugar and butter evenly. Whisk together with eggs and vanilla.

3. In a separate bowl, combine flour, baking powder, and salt. Add to your mixture from step two along with milk. Mix until all are combined.

4. Divide the batter in half, one for each pan. Bake for 20-30 minutes, checking at the 15-minute mark. Remove when a knife comes out with only crumbs.

5. Allow to cool, then top with Fazbear Entertainment Brand chocolate or vanilla icing, per order sheet, on each layer. Pipe edges and birthday message. Garnish with rainbow sprinkles.

Night 1: Hello, hello? Hello? Uh, I wanted to record a message for you to help you get settled in on your first night. Um, I actually worked in that office before you. I'm finishing up my last week now, as a matter of fact. So, I know it can be a bit overwhelming, but I'm here to tell you there's nothing to worry about. Uh, you'll do fine. So, let's just focus on getting you through your first week. Okay? Uh, let's see, first there's an introductory greeting from the company that I'm supposed to read. Uh, it-it's kind of a legal thing, you know. Um, "Welcome to Freddy Fazbear's Pizza. A magical place for kids and grown-ups alike, where fantasy and fun come to life. Fazbear Entertainment is not responsible for damage to property or person. Upon discovering that damage or death has occurred, a missing person report will be filed within 90 days, or as soon as property and premises have been thoroughly cleaned and bleached, and the carpets have been replaced." Blah blah blah, now that might sound bad, I know, but there's really nothing to worry about. Uh, the animatronic characters here do get a bit quirky at night, but do I blame them? No. If I were forced to sing those same stupid songs for twenty years and I never got a bath? I'd probably be a bit irritable at night, too. So, remember, these characters hold a special place in the hearts of children and we need to show them a little respect, right? Okay. So, just be aware, the characters do tend to wander a bit. Uh, they're left in some kind of free roaming mode at night. Uh, something about their servos locking up if they get turned off for too long. Uh, they used to be allowed to walk around during the day, too. But then there was The Bite of '87. Yeah. I-it's amazing that the human body can live without the frontal lobe, you know? Uh, now concerning your safety, the only real risk to you as a night watchman here, if any, is the fact that these characters, uh, if they happen to see you after hours, probably won't recognize you as a person. They'll p-most likely see you as a metal endoskeleton without its costume on. Now since that's against the rules here at Freddy Fazbear's Pizza, they'll probably try to . . . forcefully stuff you inside a Freddy Fazbear suit. Um, now, that wouldn't be so bad if the suits themselves weren't filled with crossbeams, wires, and animatronic devices, especially around the facial area. So, you could imagine how having your head forcefully pressed inside one of those could cause a bit of discomfort . . . and death. Uh, the only parts of you that would likely see the light of day again would be your eyeballs and teeth when they pop out the front of the mask, heh.

Y-yeah, they don't tell you these things when you sign up. But hey, first day should be a breeze. I'll chat with you tomorrow. Uh, check those cameras, and remember to close the doors only if absolutely necessary. Gotta conserve power. All right, good night.

Night 2: Uh, Hello? Hello? Uh, well, if you're hearing this and you made it to day two, uh, congrats! I-I-I won't talk quite as long this time since Freddy and his friends tend to become more active as the week progresses. Uh, it might be a good idea to peek at those cameras while I talk just to make sure everyone's in their proper place. You know. Uh, interestingly enough, Freddy himself doesn't come off stage very often. I heard he becomes a lot more active in the dark, though, so, hey, I guess that's one more reason not to run out of power, right? I-I also want to emphasize the importance of using your door lights. Uh, there are blind spots in your camera views, and those blind spots happen to be right outside of your doors. So if-if you can't find something, or someone, on your cameras, uh, be sure to check the door lights. Uh, you might only have a few seconds to react . . . Uh, not that you would be in any danger, of course. Uh, I'm not implying that. Uh, also, uh check on the curtain in Pirate Cove from time to time. The character in there seems unique in that he becomes more active if the cameras remain off for long periods of time. I guess he doesn't like being watched. I don't know. Uh, anyway, I'm sure you have everything under control! Uh, talk to you soon.

Night 3: Hello, hello? Hey you're doing great! Uh, most people don't last this long. I mean, you know, they usually move on to other things by now. Uh, I'm not implying that they died. Th-th-that's not what I meant. Uh, anyway I better not take up too much of your time. Uh, things start getting real tonight. Uh, hey, listen, I had an idea: if you happen to get caught and want to avoid getting stuffed into a Freddy suit, uh, try playing dead. You know, go limp. Then there's a chance that, uh, maybe they'll think that you're an empty costume instead. Then again if they think you're an empty costume, they might try to . . . stuff a metal skeleton into you. I wonder how that would work. Yeah, never mind, scratch that. It's best just not to get caught.
Um . . . Okay, I'll leave you to it. See you on the flip side.

Night 4: Hello, hello? Hey! Hey, wow, day four. I knew you could do it. Uh, hey, listen, I may not be around to send you a message tomorrow. *banging* It's-it's been a bad night here for me. Um, I-I'm kinda glad that I recorded my messages for you *clears throat* uh, when I did. Uh, hey, do me a favor. *banging* Maybe sometime, uh, you could check inside those suits, uh, in the back room? *banging* I'm gonna try to hold out until someone checks. Maybe it won't be so bad. *banging* Uh, I-I-I-I always wondered what was in all those empty heads back there. *Torreador March plays*. You know . . . *moan* oh, no— *animatronic scream* *static*

Night 1: Uh, hello? Hello, hello? Uh, hello and welcome to your new summer job at the new and improved Freddy Fazbear's Pizza. Uh, I'm here to talk you through some of the things you can expect to see during your first week here and to help you get started down this new and exciting career path. Uh, now, I want you to forget anything you may have heard about the old location, you know. Uh, some people still have a somewhat negative impression of the company. Uh, that old restaurant was kind of left to rot for quite a while, but I want to reassure you, Fazbear Entertainment is committed to family fun and, above all, safety. They've spent a small fortune on these new animatronics, uh, facial recognition, advanced mobility, they even let them walk around during the day. Isn't that neat? *clears throat* But most importantly, they're all tied into some kind of criminal database so they can detect a predator a mile away. Heck, we should be paying them to guard you. Uh, now that being said, no new system is without its . . . kinks. Uh, you're only the second guard to work at that location. Uh, the first guy finished his week, but complained about . . . conditions. Uh, we switched him over to the day shift, so hey, lucky you, right? Uh mainly he expressed concern that certain characters seemed to move around at night and even attempted to get into his office. Now, from what we know, that should be impossible. Uh, that restaurant should be the safest place on earth. So while our engineers don't really have an explanation for this, the working theory is that . . . the robots were never given a proper "night mode." So when it gets quiet, they think they're in the wrong room, so then they go try to find where the people are, and in this case, that's your office. So, our temporary solution is this: there's a music box over by the prize counter, and it's rigged to be wound up remotely. So just, every once in a while, switch over to the prize counter video feed and wind it up for a few seconds. It doesn't seem to affect all the animatronics, but it does affect . . . one of them. *clears throat* Uh, and as for the rest of them, we have an even easier solution. You see, there may be a minor glitch in the system, something about robots seeing you as an endoskeleton without its costume on, and wanting to stuff you in a suit, so hey, we've given you an empty Freddy Fazbear head. Problem solved! You can put it on anytime and leave it on for as long as you want. Eventually anything that wandered in will wander back out. Uh, something else worth mentioning is kind of the quirky modern design of the building. You may have noticed there are no doors for you to close, heh. Uh, but hey, you have a light! And even though your flashlight can run out of power, the building cannot. So, don't worry about the place going dark. Well, I think that's it. Uh, you should be golden. Uh, check the lights, put on the Freddy head if you need to, uh, keep the music box wound up, piece of cake. Have a good night, and I'll talk to you tomorrow.

Night 2: Uh, hello, hello? Uh, see, I told you your first night wouldn't be a problem. You're a natural! Uh, by now I'm sure you've noticed the older models sitting in the back room. Uh, those are from the previous location, and we just use them for parts now. The idea at first was to repair them . . . uh, they even started retrofitting them with some of the newer technology, but they were just so ugly, you know? And the smell . . . uh, uh, so the company decided to just go in a whole new direction and make them super kid-friendly. Uh, those older ones shouldn't be able to walk around, but if they do, the whole Freddy head trick should work on them, too, so, whatever.

Uh, heh . . . I love those old characters. Uh, did you ever see Foxy the pirate? Oh wait, Foxy . . . oh yeah, Foxy! Uh, hey, listen, uh, that one was always a bit twitchy, uh, I'm not sure the Freddy head trick will work on Foxy, uh. If for some reason he activates during the night and you see him standing at the far end of the hall, uh, just flash your light at him from time to time. Those older models would always get disoriented with bright lights. It would cause a system restart, or something. Uh, come to think of it, you might want to try that on any room where something undesirable might be. It might hold them in place for a few seconds. That glitch might've carried over to the newer models, too. One more thing—don't forget the music box. I'll be honest, I never liked that puppet thing. It's always . . . thinking, and it can go anywhere . . . uh, I don't think a Freddy mask will fool it, so just don't forget the music box. Um, anyway, I'm sure it won't be a problem. Uh, have a good night, and talk to you tomorrow.

Night 3: Uh, hello, hello! See? I told ya you wouldn't have any problems! Did, uh, did Foxy ever appear in the hallway? Probably not. I was just curious. Like I said, he was always my favorite. They tried to remake Foxy, ya know? Uh, they thought the first one was too scary, so they redesigned him to be more kid-friendly and put him in Kid's Cove. To keep the toddlers entertained, you know . . . But kids these days just can't keep their hands to themselves. The staff literally had to put Foxy back together at the end of every shift. Eventually they stopped trying and left him as some "take apart and put back together" attraction. Now he's just a mess of parts. I think the employees refer to him as just "The Mangle." Uh, oh, hey, before I go, uh, I wanted to ease your mind about any rumors you might have heard lately. Uh, you know how these local stories come and go and seldom mean anything. I can personally assure you that, whatever is going on out there, and however tragic it may be, has nothing to do with our establishment. It's just all rumor and speculation . . . People trying to make a buck. You know . . . Uh, our guard during the day has reported nothing unusual. And he's on watch from opening 'til close. Okay, well anyway, hang in there and I'll talk with you tomorrow.

Night 4: Hello, hello? Uh, hey there, night four! I told you you'd get the hang of it! Okay, so uh, just to update you, uh, there's been somewhat of an investigation going on. Uh, we may end up having to close for a few days . . . I don't know. Uh, I want to emphasize, though, that it's really just a precaution. Uh, Fazbear Entertainment denies any wrongdoing. These things happen sometimes. Um . . . it'll all get sorted out in a few days. Just keep an eye on things, and I'll keep you posted. Uh, just as a side note, though, try to avoid eye contact with any of the animatronics tonight if you can. Uh, someone may have tampered with their facial recognition systems—we're not sure. But the characters have been acting very unusual, almost aggressive toward the staff. They interact with the kids just fine, but when they encounter an adult, they just . . . stare. Uh, anyways, hang tight. It'll all pass. Good night!

Night 5: Hello, hello? Hey, good job, night five! Um, hey, uh, keep a close eye on things tonight, okay? Uh, from what I understand, the building is on *lockdown*, uh, no one is allowed in or out, y'know, especially concerning any . . . *previous employees*. Um, when we get it all sorted out, we may move you to the day shift. A position just became . . . available. Uh, we don't have a replacement for your shift yet, but we're working on it. Uh, we're going to try to contact the original restaurant owner. Uh, I think the name of the place was . . . "Fredbear's Family Diner" or something like that. It's been closed for years, though, I doubt we'll be able to track anybody down. Uh, so just get through one more night! Uh, hang in there! Good night!

Night 6: Hello, hello, uh, what on earth are you doing there? Uh didn't you get the memo? Uh, the place is closed down, a-at least for a while. Someone used one of the suits. We had a spare in the back, a yellow one, someone used it . . . now none of them are acting right. Listen, j-just finish your shift, it's safer than trying to leave in the middle of the night. Uh, we have one more event scheduled for tomorrow, a-a birthday. You'll be on day shift. Wear your uniform, stay close to the animatronics, and make sure they don't hurt anyone, okay? Uh, for now just make it through the night, uh, when the place eventually opens again, I'll probably take the night shift myself. Okay, good night and good luck.

Night 1:

Phone Dude: Hey, hey! Glad you came back for another night! I promise it'll be a lot more interesting this time. We found some-some great new relics over the weekend. And we're out tracking down a new lead, right now. So, uh, lemme just update you real quick, then you can get to work. Like, the attraction opens in, like, a week, so we had to make sure everything works, and nothing catches on fire! Uh, when the place opens, people will come in at the opposite end of the building and work their way toward you, then past you and out the exit. Uh, yeah. You've officially become a part of the attraction. Uh, you'll be starring as . . . the security guard! So not only will you be monitoring the people on the camera as they pass through, y'know, to make sure no one steals anything or makes out in the corner, but you'll also be a part of the show. It'll make it feel really authentic, I think. Uh, now let me tell you about what's new. We found another set of drawings, always nice, and a Foxy head! Which we think could be authentic . . . then again it might just be another crappy cosplay, and we found a desk fan, very old-school metal, though, so watch the fingers. Uh-heh, uh, right now the place is basically just, you know, flashing lights and spooky props. Uh, I honestly thought we'd have more by now, uh, if we don't have something really cool by next week, then we may have to suit you up in a furry suit and make you walk around saying, "Boo" . . . he-he, uh, but, you know, like I said, we're trying to track down a good lead right now. Uh, some guy who helped design one of the buildings says there was, like, an extra room that got boarded up or, uh, something like that. So, we're gonna take a peek and see what we can find. Uh, for now just get comfortable with the new setup, um . . . You can check the security cameras over to your right with a click of that blue button. Uh, you can toggle between the hall cams and the vent cams . . . Uh, then over to your far left, uh, you can flip up your maintenance panel. Y'know, use this to reboot any systems that may go offline. Heh. So, in trying to make the place feel vintage we may have overdone it a bit, he-he . . . Some of this equipment is barely functional. Yeah, I wasn't joking about the fire. Tha-tha-that's a real risk. Uh, the most important thing you want to watch for is the ventilation. Look, this place will give you the spooks, man, and if you let that ventilation go offline, then you'll start seeing some crazy stuff, man. Keep that air a flowin'. Okay, keep an eye on things, and we'll try to have something new for ya tomorrow night.

Night 2:

Phone Dude: Hey, man. Okay, I have some awesome news for you! First of all, we found some vintage audio training cassettes! Dude, these are, like, *prehistoric!* I think they were, like, training tapes for, like, other employees or something like that. So, I thought we could, like, have them playing, like, over the speakers as people walk through the attraction. Dude, that makes this feel legit, man. But I have an even better surprise for you, and you're not gonna believe this. We found one. A *real* one. Uh-uh-oh, gotta go man. Uh, well-well, look, i-it's in there somewhere, I'm-I'm sure you'll see it. Okay, I'll leave you with some of this great audio that I found! Talk to you later, man!

Phone Guy: Uh, hello! Hello, hello! Uh, welcome to your new career as a performer/entertainer for Freddy Fazbear's Pizza. Uh, these tapes will provide you with much needed information on how to handle/climb into/climb out of mascot costumes. Right now, we have two specially designed suits that double as both animatronic and suit. So please pay close attention while learning how to operate these suits, as accidents/injuries/death/irreparable and grotesque maiming can occur. First, we'll discuss how to operate the mascots when in animatronic form. For ease of operation, the animatronics are set to turn and walk toward sounds they hear, which is an easy and hands-free approach to making sure the animatronics stay where the children are for maximum entertainment/crowd-pleasing value. To change the animatronics to suit mode, insert and turn firmly the hand crank provided by the manufacturer. Turning the crank will recoil and compress the animatronic parts around the sides of the suit, providing room to climb inside. Please make sure the spring locks are fastened tight to ensure the animatronic devices remain safe. We will cover this in more detail in tomorrow's session. Remember to smile; you are the face of Freddy Fazbear's Pizza.

Night 3:

Phone Guy: Uh, hello, hello. Uh, for today's lesson, we will be continuing our training on proper suit-handling techniques. When using an animatronic as a suit, please ensure that the animatronic parts are tightly compressed and fastened by the spring locks located around the inside of the suit. It may take a few moments to position your head and torso between these parts in a manner where you can move and speak. Try not to nudge or press against any of the spring locks inside the suit. Do not touch the spring locks at any time. Do not breathe on the spring locks, as moisture may loosen them and cause them to break loose. In the case of the spring locks come loose while you are wearing the suit, please try to maneuver away from populated areas before bleeding out, as to not ruin the customers' experience. As always, if there is ever an emergency, please go to the designated safe room. Every location is built with one extra room that is not included in the digital map layouts programmed in the animatronics or the security system. This room is hidden to customers, invisible to animatronics, and is always off-camera. As always, remember to smile; you are the face of Freddy Fazbear's Pizza.

Night 4:

Phone Guy: Uh, hello? Hello, hello! Uh, there's been a slight change of company policy concerning use of the suits. Um, *don't*. After learning of an unfortunate incident at the sister location, involving multiple and simultaneous spring lock failures, the company has deemed the suits temporarily unfit for employees. Safety is top priority at Freddy Fazbear's Pizza, which is why the classic suits are being retired to an appropriate location, while being looked at by our technician. Until replacements arrive, you'll be expected to wear the temporary costumes provided to you. Keep in mind that they were found on very short notice, so questions about appropriateness/relevance should be deflected. I repeat, the classic suits are not to be touched, activated, or worn. That being said, we are free of liability, do as you wish. As always, remember to smile; you are the face of Freddy Fazbear's Pizza.

Night 5:

Phone Guy: Hello? Hello? Um, this is just a reminder of company policy concerning the safe room. The safe room is reserved for equipment and/or other property not being currently used and as a backup safety location for employees only. This is not a break room, and should not be considered a place for employees to hide and/or congregate, and under no circumstance should a customer ever be taken into this room and out of the main show area. Management has also been made aware that the Spring Bonnie animatronic has been noticeably moved. We would like to remind employees that this costume is not safe to wear under any circumstances. Thank you and remember to smile; you are the face of Freddy Fazbear's Pizza.

Nightmare:

Phone Guy: Uh, hello? Hello? Uh, this is just to inform all employees that due to budget restrictions, the previously mentioned safe rooms are being sealed at most locations, including this one. Work crews will be here most of the day today, constructing a false wall over the old door base. Nothing is being taken out beforehand, so if you've left anything inside, then it's your own fault. Management also requests that this room not be mentioned to family, friends, or insurance representatives. Thanks again, and remember to smile; you are the face of Freddy Fazbear's Pizza.

The Immortal and the Restless [Episode 1]

Narrator: Another day, another dramatic entry in the lives of Vlad and his distressed mistress! Where will they go? What will they do? All of that and more . . . happening now!

Vlad: Clara, I tell you, the baby isn't mine!

Clara: Count, I tell you that it is! You're the only vampire I've ever loved! And the baby turns his bottles into powdered milk.

Vlad: That doesn't mean anything.

Clara: He sleeps on the ceiling fan!

Vlad: Upright, or upside down?

Clara: What does it matter? You *need* to be part of your son's life!

Vlad: I'm an old man, Clara! I can't be a father!

Clara: Well, then, at least pay your child support, you deadbeat!

Narrator: Will Vlad and his distressed mistress find common ground? Tune in next time!

The Immortal and the Restless [Episode 2]

Narrator: As the sun sets, so also does another chapter in the saga of love lost between Vlad and his distressed mistress. Can they be reconciled? Can their love rise again? That and more . . . happening now!

Vlad: Clara, the baby isn't mine!

Clara: It is, Vlad! They had trouble catching him in the nursery today!

Vlad: So what? Lots of kids get hyper and run around and stuff.

Clara: They had to knock him out of the air with a broom!

Vlad: I have to go.

Clara: They're going to dock your paychecks.

Vlad: They can't do that! I'm a vampire, I don't get paychecks!

Clara: You work the graveyard shift at the Friny Taco. Don't lie to me!

Narrator: Oh, the humanity! When will the heartbreak end? When will these two ships passing in the night rekindle their long-lost love? Tune in tomorrow to find out.

The Immortal and the Restless [Episode 3]

Narrator: As the moon rises, so also rises the tension between sworn lovers.

Vlad: Clara, it's not my baby.

Clara: Vlad, you suck.

Vlad: Wait, was that a vampire joke? That was so lame, Clara, like I've never heard that a million times.

Clara: Okay, well how's this: I'm taking the car!

Vlad: The joke's on you! It's a rental.

Clara: Well, the joke's on you. I set the thermostat to ninety before I left.

Vlad: Good, I like it warm.

Clara: Good! Because I also set the house on fire!

Narrator: How will it all end? The passion! The tension! The intrigue! Tune in tomorrow for the exciting conclusion.

The Immortal and the Restless [Episode 4]

Narrator: As the trees sway in the wind, so also do emotions sway between star-crossed lovers!

Vlad: You burned down my house?!

Clara: You call that a house? It was like a morgue in there.

Vlad: I may be undead, but you're heartless.

Clara: You need to see your son!

Vlad: The baby isn't mine!

Clara: He ate the cat!

Vlad: Sounds like something he got from your side of the family!

Clara: Well, how's this? I'm keeping the diamond ring.

Vlad: The joke's on you! I found it in a kid's meal!

Clara: You bought a kid's meal? Oh, Vlad!

Vlad: Clara!

Narrator: As the hair on the back of the cat stands up straight, so also does the love between Vlad and Clara stand up against all obstacles. But what about the baby? What about the back child support? Stay tuned next season for those answers, and more.

To be continued . . .

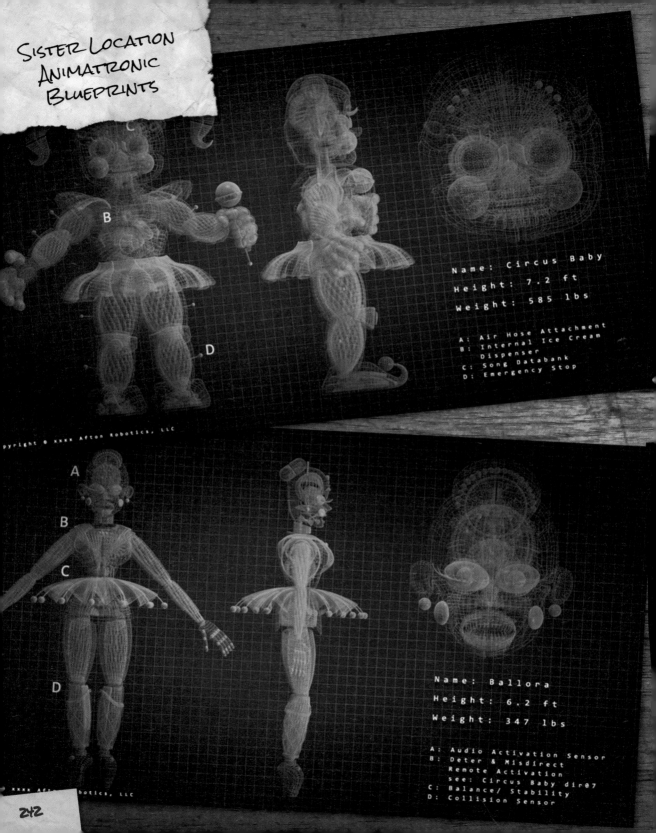

Name: Circus Baby
Height: 7.2 ft
Weight: 585 lbs

A: Air Hose Attachment
B: Internal Ice Cream
   Dispenser
C: Song Databank
D: Emergency Stop

pyright © xxxx Afton Robotics, LLC

Name: Ballora
Height: 6.2 ft
Weight: 347 lbs

A: Audio Activation Sensor
B: Deter & Misdirect
   Remote Activation
   see: Circus Baby dir87
C: Balance/ Stability
D: Collision Sensor

xxxx Af   botics, LLC

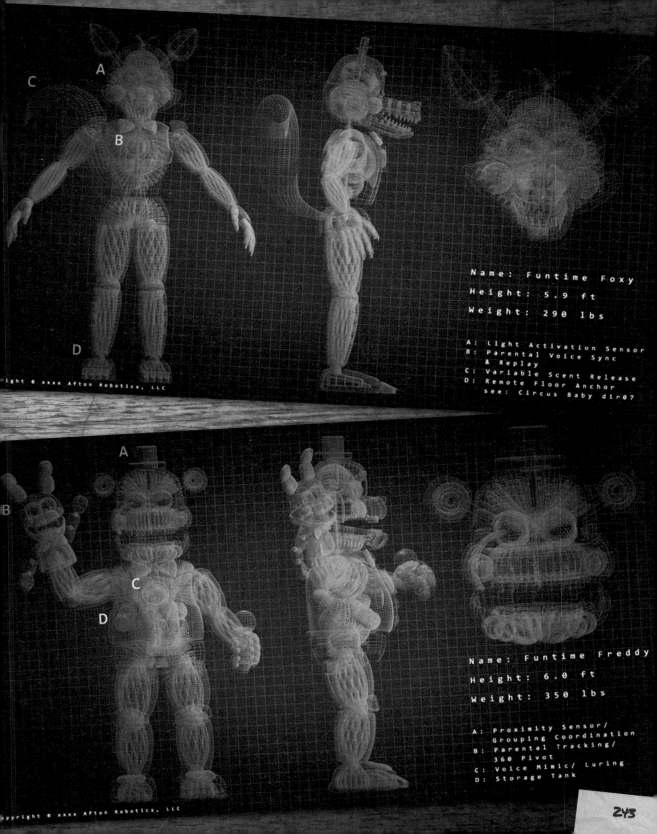

Name: Funtime Foxy
Height: 5.9 ft
Weight: 290 lbs

A: Light Activation Sensor
B: Parental Voice Sync
   & Replay
C: Variable Scent Release
D: Remote Floor Anchor
   see: Circus Baby dir07

Name: Funtime Freddy
Height: 6.0 ft
Weight: 350 lbs

A: Proximity Sensor/
   Grouping Coordination
B: Parental Tracking/
   360 Pivot
C: Voice Mimic/ Luring
D: Storage Tank

L.ure E.ncapsulate F.use T.ransport & E.xtract

A: Navigational Sensors

B: False Sensory Output

NOTES: Bracelet code 93401233. Emit for security receiver frequency FZ554.

C: "Dream Wand"/ Soother

NOTES: Use lullaby index 01. Upon suit-seal, provide steady voltage throughout. Behavior upon suit-seal not guaranteed.

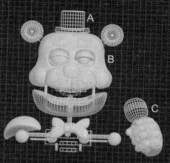

Fazbear Entertainment, Inc

Facial Recognition File 0072

Security Tags Active:

001 "Funtime Freddy"
002 "Funtime Foxy"
003 "Ballora"

Priority One

With the most amount of remnant collectively in its structure, this amalgamation of Afton's constructs is a necessary element of Paragraph 4.

R.emote A.ctivated S.imulated C.

A: Navigational Sensors

B: Heat Uplink/ Sensor Override

NOTES: Must remain connected to central server at all times or risk duplicate signature. Variable Alpha to remain at 98.6.

C: Individual Emitter

NOTES: Must remain connected to central server at all times or risk inaccurate represented population. Audio controlled by central server.

Fazbear Entertainment, Inc

S.calable C.reation of U.lterior P.resence

A: Excavating Arm

B: Remnant Injector

NOTES: Leave trace line amount on interior. Over-usage/ Over-exposure negates effect.

C: Arm Base and Balance

D: Remnant Reservoir

NOTES: When heated, no observable motion. Keep in heated tank at sustained temperature. Substance should be malleable, but not more.

There is a possibility that overheating might neutralize the effects permanently.

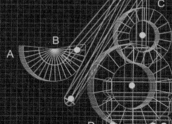

Afton Robotics, LLC

Help Wanted: Full Legal Disclaimer

Welcome to the Fazbear quality assurance team. Before we can officially congratulate you on your fabulous lifetime career choice, you must first agree to this simple waiver. Our lawyers have come up with a way to save you time by bypassing all the legal terms, and pages and pages of law-related verbiage by creating this simple in-game app. The important points have been condensed to a single page. Consider precious moments of your life saved.

The auto-scroll feature was designed to protect you from potential repetitive stress injuries. It's just another way that Fazbear Entertainment cares for its employees. You should also take care not to overexert your eyes while looking at such small text on a highly contrasting document screen. Therefore, it is recommended that you rest your eyes while accepting these terms. Please close them now, for safety purposes. Are they closed? Good. If you agree to the terms presented, you may press the button in front of you to confirm. Or, if you would like to further reduce the risk of repetitive stress injury, you may allow the ACCEPT "button" to remain untouched for ten seconds. The ten-second mark will let us know that you intend to press the ACCEPT "button", but are a health-conscious individual.

Tape One:

Hello? Can you hear me? Don't exit this room, okay? This isn't a mistake. This *room* isn't a mistake. I had to hide these logs away from the core gameplay files, in a place that only a beta tester would look and in a place where the files could be protected. I just really, really hope that the next development team finds this before the game is released to the public. This game has some kind of malicious code in it that we haven't been able to fully contain or even understand for that matter. We're over budget and out of time. But that's not the reason that we're shutting down. Listen, I have to keep this short so the file size will be small enough to fly under the radar. There are more. They may not be in order.

Tape Two:

I saw it for the first time today. There was a character, I couldn't make out who it was, standing at the end of the hall.
I thought it was just bugged out, so I made a note of it and kept playing. But then it was looking in the window . . . and not like Chica or Bonnie would. It was like it was actually looking in the window, seeing what I was doing.

Tape Three:

I heard a pretty heated conversation this morning between Dale, our manager, and someone else on the line. It really feels like this project is in trouble, in no small part because of the lawsuit, I'm sure. There has to be a lawsuit. There's no way there isn't. It happened in this building just a few doors down from me. I think it's made worse by the fact that Jeremy tried to tell us something was wrong. But as a dev team, we all just saw it as a challenge to find what the problem was and fix it. Who could have known that—I have to go.

Tape Four:

Have you ever heard of a guillotine paper slicer? It sounds made up, but it's an actual piece of office equipment. I didn't even know we had one in the supply room. I guess they're more common at businesses that do a lot of graphic design work. I remember seeing one when I was still in school, and even then, I knew how dangerous it looked. I was always afraid of losing a finger. That seems so silly now. Jeremy used to do design work. I guess that's how he knew it was there.

Tape Five:

The drawers have been emptied out. Someone was here. I don't think it was spring cleaning, either. No. There was plastic on the floor. Someone was definitely here during the night—it had to have been the client. I mean, they sent us that stuff in the first place with no explanation, told us to scan it, said it would expedite the process so we wouldn't need to program any pathfinding ourselves. It was a budget thing, I guess. It was just junk—circuit boards and things like that. Looked pretty old. Somehow, though, there was usable code on some of it. It seemed to take hold by itself. Things started changing. But then he started appearing . . . At least that's what Jeremy said.

Tape Six:

I came in early that morning. No one else was there. At least, that's what I thought. The supply room was lit. I didn't even notice Jeremy standing in the testing room as I walked past. The supply room was so bright, glowing from all the way down the hall.

Tape Seven:

Jeremy complained of nightmares when he came in this morning. He wasn't talking about it like someone telling a friend about his dreams, though. He was pale. Looked like he hadn't eaten in days. He spent an hour talking in Dale's office, but it didn't look like he was given much sympathy. When he came out, he went directly back to the testing room. He doesn't even jump anymore—nothing scares him. He just stands there like he's talking to someone. Sometimes he rocks from side to side. We were told to leave him alone. I knew I was in line to do the testing next. They'd been prepping me for it. I guess they knew that Jeremy would need to be replaced soon.

Tape Eight:

You can always tell when a company is getting ready to fire someone. They start giving out written warnings for silly things, making sure to build a paper trail and make a case for a firing. Things that normally no one would care about suddenly become grave offenses, all worthy of being written and documented. I guess it works two ways, because it also encourages a person to quit rather than be scrutinized so heavily. I think Jeremy was too far gone to consider that option, though. The thing about it is, that I don't think they were going to fire him because of anything he was doing wrong. They just *knew* he'd seen something. They *needed* to discredit him.

Tape Nine:

There was something that looked like a Halloween mask laying on the floor. I didn't understand. Ink must have spilled. It was only then that I heard a shuffle from the testing room and realized Jeremy must be there. I went back and peered in the window. I couldn't see his face. He had the visor covering his head. He had ink spilled on himself as well. The front of his shirt looked black in the dark room. He turned his head in my direction, but I don't think he *knew* I was there.

Tape Ten:

I was told I had three days to finish Jeremy's work, but I know it's just passing the time. They don't really expect me to do anything. It's just to keep up appearances until the buyout is complete. We have to *look* like we have things under control. There's another potential development studio that wants to pick up from here, but who knows what kind of lies they're being fed to convince them to do it. Against my better judgment, I'm going to do my best to see what's here, make notes of it, and try to isolate where this thing is hiding. At least then the next person that tests this will have a chance of getting rid of it.

Tape Eleven:

Today was the last day of beta testing and the anomaly that I've been seeing is nowhere to be found. But after inspecting some of the files, it seems that it's attached itself to these logs. *My logs.* That *can't* be an accident. So now I have to make a choice. Do I leave these logs here for you to find, or do I try to purge this thing myself by destroying the logs? I've chosen the latter.

Tape Twelve:

I can't delete them. By creating a protected area to store these logs apart from the game, I effectively gave this thing a safe place to hide itself. It's *in* here now. I may not be able to delete it, but I might be able to do something else now that it's attached itself. I have an idea.

Tape Thirteen:

They lied to us. They lied to all of us. They told us that the whole point of this VR game was to undo the bad PR done by a rogue indie game developer, who supposedly made up a bunch of crazy stories that tarnished the brand. But that's not true at all. In their haste to develop this VR game and clear their name, they sent us some things I don't think they intended us to see, such as a hard drive containing emails between Fazbear Entertainment and a certain indie developer. Fazbear Entertainment *hired* the game developer. Those indie games were designed to conceal and make light of what happened. This isn't just an attempt to rebrand—it's an elaborate cover-up, a campaign to discredit everything.

Tape Fourteen:

I ran a fragmentation program on the area of memory that was storing these logs for you. I effectively broke the files into pieces and broke the anomaly along with it. That means that you won't have my warnings to guide you. But hopefully, it also means that this anomaly—this virus, or whatever it is—will remain broken and unable to do more damage.

Tape Fifteen:

Hello. You don't know me. I'd created a series of logs for you documenting the troubled development of this VR game that you're now testing, in hopes that you, whoever you are, and whatever team you are with, will abandon development. Now I fear that those logs are being used as a trojan horse. If you're unable to abandon development, hide all traces of these logs that I've created. I fear that finding them and reassembling them will also reassemble the very thing I've tried so desperately to destroy.

Tape Sixteen:

There is a way to kill it. It wants to escape. To escape through someone. Someone plugged into this game. That's *you* now. You have to let it begin the process of leaving through you, then use the disconnect switch that I've embedded by the main stage. Let it approach you. Let it begin to merge with you. Play the music and flip the switch. That will cause a hard restart of the game and flush the memory, effectively killing it . . . I hope. I don't know when it will come for you.

Staff Advisory: Mail Server

From: Fazbear Entertainment Office of Legal Affairs

Due to technical complications, our mail server may be directing email to incorrect recipients.

If you receive an email that is not addressed to you, please forward it to the intended recipient and notify the IT department immediately.

As a friendly reminder, reading an email that was not intended for your eyes is a violation of Fazbear Entertainment's company policy, and you may be subject to disciplinary action up to and including immediate termination. That policy remains in effect.

Please do not read an email that is not your own. Thank you for your cooperation as we resolve this technical complication.

11/28/2019
(no subject)
From: luis.cabrera
To: nessie97

Hey, Ness,

I hope you're having a good day! It's no big deal, but I wanted to reach out "off the radar," and remind you about the company policy about personal internet usage. Nobody cares if you're online shopping, as long as you get your work done—I promise—I've done my share of last-minute gift-buying! But certain words and phrases trigger red flag reports, so your last order got automatically sent to me: basically anything mentioning "torture" is going to raise the alarm. So although the *Viking Blood Eagle Twelve-Month Calendar* you ordered is very cool, the searches that got you there did trigger a red flag.

If you have any questions about the policy, let me know. We could even get coffee or something and go over all the words to avoid.

. . . And now I've raised my own red flag! Good thing I'm the one who gets the notification :-)

-Luis

11/28/2019
Re: (no subject)
From: Mark Cho

These things are creeping me out.

Re: (no subject)
From: Raha Salib

Seriously. We don't have room for them, I don't know why Anna agreed to take this job.

Re: (no subject)
From: Mark Cho

$$$$$

Re: (no subject)
From: Raha Salib

More like $

Re: (no subject)
From: Mark Cho

lol

11/29/2019
Can I use power tools?
From: Daniel Rocha
To: Anna Kwemto

Hey, Anna,

The casings on the animatronics are really hard to get off. Can you approve me to use the power drill?

Best,
Dan

Re: Can I use power tools?
From: Anna Kwemto
To: Daniel Rocha

No.

Re: Can I use power tools?
From: Daniel Rocha
To: Anna Kwemto

Please? I'm serious, I can't get the casing off without it.

Re: Can I use power tools?
From: Anna Kwemto
To: Daniel Rocha

Raha is the only one certified. Quit asking.

11/29/2019
Come drill for me?
From: Daniel Rocha
To: Raha Salib

Need to get the circuit boards out. Anna says you're the only one who can use the power drill.

Re: Come drill for me?
From: Raha Salib
To: Daniel Rocha

15 min.

11/30/2019
System glitch
From: Steven Wilson

Hey, guys, I just got kicked off the system. I finished scanning the last set of circuit boards Dan brought me, but now I'm locked out. Is anyone else getting this "unknown error"?

Re: System glitch
From: Anna Kwemto

No.

12/01/2019
IMMEDIATE ACTION REQUIRED
From: Fazbear Entertainment Office of Legal Affairs
To: Anna Kwemto

Dear Ms. Kwemto,

Please immediately cease all work on Fazbear Entertainment properties. Due to unforeseen circumstances, Fazbear Entertainment is ordering a halt to work on all existing contracts, especially in reference to any vintage hardware. We will be in touch regarding our future course of action; please contact our billing department regarding payment for completed work-to-date action.

Sincerely,

Kayla Stringer

Associate General Counsel

Fazbear Entertainment

12/01/2019
Fwd: IMMEDIATE ACTION REQUIRED
From: Anna Kwemto

Fazbear just ordered us to stop working. It sounds like they're halting work with all their contractors, not just us. They said they'll be in touch about "our future course of action."

Re: Fwd: IMMEDIATE ACTION REQUIRED
From: Steven Wilson

Anna, are we still getting paid for this?

Re: Fwd: IMMEDIATE ACTION REQUIRED
From: Anna Kwemto

For work-to-date only. Make sure
you have everything logged.

12/02/2019
(no subject)
From: luis.cabrera
To: nessie97

Hey, Ness,

Just a quick FYI—I know I mentioned trigger
words, but the AI is actually a little more
sophisticated than that, and of course there
are people like me watching the system, too.

So, the word *compliance* by itself isn't going
to set off any red flags, but the sentence *how
to induce compliance in human subjects and
how to include self-compliance(?)* did actually
get my attention. (I think the answer might
involve chocolate chip cookies? Always works
on me.)

I also thought it was strange that these
were immediately followed by searches that
couldn't possibly have any relevant answers
for you. Did you search for "help" by itself?

Anyway, my offer still stands if you want to go
over the company policy. I'm free any day after
work—we could grab dinner or coffee
if you want. In the meantime you might want
to do some of your more . . . interesting
research at home.

-Luis

12/03/2019
(no subject)
Form: Mark Cho
To: Raha Salib

It'll be ok. We have other contracts.

Re: (no subject)
From: Raha Salib
To: Mark Cho

Yeah, but this was a big job.

Re: (no subject)
From: Mark Cho
To: Raha Salib

:-(

12/03/2019
Re: System glitch
From: Raha Salib

Steve, which circuit board did you scan?

Re: System glitch
From: Steven Wilson

Whatever Dan brought me.

12/04/2019
(no subject)
From: luis.cabrera
To: nessie97

Hey, Ness,

I wanted to see if you're doing ok. I appreciate your taking my advice about red flag search terms, if I thought I'd have to file an incident report on you, I think I'd just have to quit instead. So, my student loans thank you!

I do have to keep checking online activity periodically after getting a red flag report, and I was a little worried maybe something is going on with you? One day you're researching flowers and the migration patterns of bees (fascinating, right?) and the next day you type in "How far can a human being be cut in half before losing consciousness."

I figured, maybe you're writing a screenplay or something? But it was a little startling to see it written out. I hope you know I'm always here if you need me.

-Luis

12/05/2019
Virus detected
From: Daniel Rocha

Turns out that wasn't just a glitch, we released a virus when we scanned that last circuit board. It's spreading really fast, we're going to need all hands on deck.

12/06/2019
(no subject)
From: luis.cabrera
To: nessie97

Hey, Ness,

I hope things are good! I saw you ordered three "lifelike, human male rubber masks" and I was dying to ask what they're for—was my screenplay guess right? Are you making a movie, or putting together some kind of performance?

Everything's the same as usual with me—but I guess you know that, you see me every day at work! Maybe one day soon we can get that coffee.

-Luis

12/07/2019
URGENT: Virus caused by FE circuit board upload
To: James Campbell
From: Steven Wilson

Hey, Jim,

We have a virus spreading through our system, and we've traced it back to one of the circuit board scans we performed for Fazbear Entertainment. Are you aware of this issue? Can you send any guidance?

Best,

Steve

12/08/2019
(no subject)
To: nessie97
From: luis.cabrera

Hey, Ness,

It was really great talking to you today. I think that might be the first time we've actually had an in-person conversation, lol. It's weird, I feel like I know you so well, but I guess you don't know so much about me. We're just going to have to fix that!

I had no idea you were into IT stuff. I always think my job sounds so boring, but you were so interested it made me start thinking, hey, maybe IT is cool after all. Or maybe you're just a good listener. Anyway, it was nice to have some in-person time. Maybe we can do it again soon. I still owe you that coffee I keep saying we should get.

-Luis

12/09/2019
(no subject)
To: nessie97
From: luis.cabrera

Hey, Ness,

Is everything OK? I came by your desk to say hi today and I don't think you even heard me. You had your face so close to the screen, that can't be good for your eyes (I know, I know, I sound like somebody's grandma). I waited for a second to see if you would turn around, but it was like you were in another world. It must be useful to be able to shut out the world and focus like that, I wish I could do it. I thought you were on a conference call at first because I heard voices.

Ness, if you ever want to talk about anything, I'm always here for you. I thought your hair looked nice today, the rainbow streaks brightened up the office—and the office is always in desperate need of some brightening!

-Luis

12/10/2019

URGENT: Virus

To: James Campbell, Anna Kwemto

From: Steven Wilson

Just checking in. I emailed you earlier this week about a virus caused by one of your circuit boards, which is currently spreading throughout our systems and causing serious problems. Please contact me ASAP. Thanks.

Best,

Steve.

12/17/2019
Might need more time
To: Compliance Team
From: Nora (R&D)

Okay, we got the new one up and running, like you guys wanted. Gotta say, though . . . the facial recognition upgrades aren't taking the exact effect we expected. We've got our best looking at it, now.

I would suggest getting an extension, if possible. Would hate for these to go out before they're ready.

Thanks, Nora

P.S. Still waiting to hear back about the other ones. Did anyone even see that request?

Re: Might need more time

To: Nora (R&D)

From: Tristan (Compliance Team)

That's a no-go on an extension. You mentioned the other day in the sync meeting that your guys found a work-around, right?

Just go with that and hit the original ideas.

Tristan

Oh and I saw the earlier request, nothing I can say about them yet. (You know how it is . . .)

1/16/2020
Still can't reproduce the issue
From: Charles (QA)
To: Nora (R&D)

We've tried everything we can think of here to reproduce the issue you were seeing with the new toy model, but can't seem to get it to happen here.

Are you sure about the eyes changing color before the behavioral matrix went haywire?

CD

1/17/2020
Re: Still can't reproduce the issue
From: Nora (R&D)
To: Charles (QA)

It was only the once, and only one of the guys reported it. I've caught him sleeping on the job twice this week, too, so he's probably just imagining things.

Honestly, what's the worst that could happen?

Just note it in the log as "Cannot Reproduce" and move on to the rest, or we're never going to meet the new deadline.

Nora

1/31/2020
Not cool
From: Tristan (Compliance Team)
To: Nora (R&D)

Nora,

I heard about you trying to go over my head to my boss about the Toy Freddy issue. While I appreciate you are trying to do what you feel is your job, defining compliance and safety standards is my department, not yours.

Our product analysts have determined that the Toy Freddy issue is negligible. We'll just slap a note at the bottom of the outgoing customer outreach emails—it's not like any of the users even read those, and we'll be covered legally.

Tristan

P.S. Next time you feel like going over my head, come talk to me, or you'll force me to bring this up with Human Resources. Sorry to be the bad guy about this, but you're really not leaving me with any other choice.

2/04/2020
Re: Not cool
From: Nora (R&D)
To: Tristan (Compliance Team)

Fine. But I want it noted in writing what my department reported.

Toy Freddy is not safe to go out to the public. The interference happening with the upgraded facial recognition suite risks rendering all the safety functions on the users' handsets useless.

Nora

2/11/2020
Couple of weird customer reports
From: Isolde (Customer Service)
To: Tristan (Compliance Team)

Hey, Tristan,

We've been getting some weird reports here in Customer Service that I don't really know how to respond to.

A handful of our more hardcore users of the service have been reporting service calls from an animatronic that isn't appearing anywhere in our database. Some kind of vintage Bonnie model. A couple of people have mentioned a really bad smell from it as well.

Is it possible some old secondhand model somehow made it into the deployment rotation?

Izzy

3/03/2020
New Multarticulus Model Delays
From: Tristan (Compliance Team)
To: Nora (R&D)

Nora,

I've been looking over those reports on the motility tests for the new model, and I gotta say I'm a little disturbed by the lack of progress. The original was purportedly able to move along the ceiling, and from what I'm seeing here, we're having issues getting our rebuilds to even move on level ground properly.

What kind of shop are you guys running down there? The marketing guys are lighting fires under me to promise we'll hit the launch date for this, and what I'm seeing is not filling me with confidence.

Tristan

3/05/2020

Re: New Multarticulus Model Delays
From: Nora (R&D)
To: Tristan (Compliance Team)

First, tell the marketing people to go jump off a bridge. They just have to write some fancy copy while we're down here trying to make their crazy promises work in reality on unrealistic budgets and completely insane timelines. We're doing the best we can.

Second, there's a *huge* difference between a new model based on the same bipedal chassis and one based on a . . . whatever you want to call this thing. A quadruped? A spider? A tripod? The locomotion is *completely* different, which means the power needs are different, the hydraulic calibrations have to be completely redone, and the CPU has to be switched out for a newer one with a faster baud rate. And then on top of all that, we have to put together this "Controlled Disassembly" feature? The marketing people are crazy.

Third, GET OFF MY BACK!!! I *warned* management that reproducing the more exotic endoskeletons would be a problem, and they decided to go ahead and put them on the schedule anyway. They're just going to have to live with the limitations of, you know, *basic physics*.

Nora

3/11/2020
Circuit board changes?
From: Charles (QA)
To: Tristan (Compliance Team)

Hey Tristan,

Sorry to bother you, but wanted to confirm that there were no changes on the circuit board side of things?

The documentation says it's just external changes to the plush suit, but some of the testers here are swearing the behavioral matrix is kinda, well, aggressive.

CD

3/12/2020
Re: Circuit board changes?
From: Charles (QA)
To: Tristan (Compliance Team)

The documentation is accurate. The only adjustments are the external alterations to the plush suit—R&D hasn't even touched the holiday release.

What do your people think, a computer-controlled animatronic can somehow get into the holiday spirit and reprogram itself? It's just a machine controlled by a circuit board. It has to do what we tell it to and nothing more.

Tristan

4/08/2020
Are we doing this again?
From: Nora (R&D)
To: Charles (QA)

I'm heading this off at the pass **before** you get any ideas.

R&D HAS NOT TOUCHED THE ANIMATRONICS.

You have any other questions, go send them to Tristan. I'm sure he'd love to hear from you.

Nora

Chapter 14
ANIMATRONICS INVENTORY

Withered, twisted, rockstar, mediocre, shadow, nightmare, phantom . . . is your head spinning yet? *FNAF*'s roster of animatronics has grown beyond 150+ since the series first reached gamers. The original five animatronics were reimagined through countless lenses all while entirely new animatronics were released. Explore the animatronics from every game, story, or book here, from the main attractions to the smallest side character.

8-BIT BABY: An arcade-themed animatronic, with a design similar to Circus Baby's mini game in *Sister Location*. 8-Bit Baby is manufactured and delivered by Fazbear Funtime Service.

Appearances: *Sister Location, Special Delivery*

ARCTIC BALLORA: A winter skin used to customize the Ballora plush suit in *Special Delivery*.

Appearances: *Special Delivery*

BALLOON BOY (BB): A humanoid animatronic that wears a red-and-blue-striped shirt and a propeller beanie. He carries a balloon as well as a sign that reads BALLOONS! He often calls out "Hello?" and "Hi!" and sometimes giggles. In several games, Balloon Boy doesn't kill you, but he does disable your defenses, which can leave you completely helpless.

Appearances: *FNAF2, FNAF3, Ultimate Custom Night, Help Wanted, Curse of Dreadbear, Special Delivery, The Twisted Ones*

BALLORA: A sound-activated ballerina animatronic with painted white skin, rosy cheeks, blue hair, and a purple tutu. She occupies Ballora Gallery in *Sister Location*, and sings a creepy song on Night 2 if you listen closely. Ballora is often accompanied by minireenas (see page 275), and has several unique capabilities mentioned in her blueprint (see page 242).

Appearances: *Sister Location, Ultimate Custom Night, Help Wanted, Special Delivery,* "Dance with Me"

BIDYBABS: Small, baby doll-like animatronics that typically perform alongside Circus Baby. They appear in Circus Gallery in *Sister Location*; players must fend them off once in the secret compartment and again in the Private Room.

Appearances: *Sister Location, Ultimate Custom Night, Help Wanted*

BLACK HEART BONNIE: A holiday-themed animatronic skin for the Bonnie plush suit in *Special Delivery*.

Appearances: *Special Delivery*

BLACK ICE FREDDY FROSTBEAR: A winter-themed animatronic skin for the Freddy Frostbear plush suit in *Special Delivery*.

Appearances: *Special Delivery*

BLIZZARD BALLOON BOY: A winter-themed animatronic skin for the Balloon Boy plush suit in *Special Delivery*.

Appearances: *Special Delivery*

BON-BON (BONNIE HAND PUPPET): An animatronic hand puppet with a Bonnie design that typically appears on the right arm of Funtime Freddy. He seems to have a calming effect on the Funtime Freddy animatronic. Bon-Bon has a female counterpart named Bonnet.

Appearances: *Sister Location, Ultimate Custom Night, Help Wanted*

BONNET: A pink animatronic hand puppet with a Bonnie design, seemingly built to go with Funtime Freddy. Bonnet first appears in the Private Room in *Sister Location*, but in *Help Wanted*, she appears alongside Funtime Freddy and Bonnet's male counterpart, Bon-Bon.

Appearances: *Sister Location, Ultimate Custom Night, Help Wanted*

BONNIE: A bluish-purple animatronic rabbit with a red bow tie, plays guitar in the animatronic band. Typically approaches from the left, but it should be noted that Bonnie doesn't seem to abide by the laws of physics.

Appearances: *FNAF, FNAF2* (mini game/hallucinations), *FNAF3* (mini game), *FNAF4* (mini game), *Ultimate Custom Night, Help Wanted, Curse of Dreadbear, Special Delivery, The Silver Eyes, The Twisted Ones, The Fourth Closet,* "The New Kid," "Hide-and-Seek," "Sea Bonnies," "Find Player Two!," *Stitchwraith Stingers*

BOULDER TOY BONNIE: A forest-themed animatronic skin for the Toy Bonnie plush suit in *Special Delivery*.

Appearances: *Special Delivery*

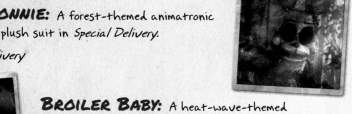

BROILER BABY: A heat-wave-themed animatronic skin for the Circus Baby plush suit in *Special Delivery*.

Appearances: *Special Delivery*

CANDY CADET: A robot animatronic that will tell the player stories if play tested. Candy Cadet tells three stories, each about five things merging into one.

Appearances: *Pizzeria Simulator, Ultimate Custom Night* (deactivated)

CAPTAIN FOXY: A fox animatronic dressed in a pirate coat and hat, with a model nearly identical to Foxy. Captain Foxy presides over Captain Foxy's Pirate Adventure, a classic dark ride in *Curse of Dreadbear.*

Appearances: *Curse of Dreadbear*

CATRINA TOY CHICA: A holiday-themed animatronic skin for the Toy Chica plush suit in *Special Delivery.*

Appearances: *Special Delivery*

CHARLIE: (Spoilers) A highly complex humanoid animatronic crafted by Henry, the original inventor of the animatronics, to fill the void left by the murder of his beloved daughter, Charlotte. It's stated that Charlie is actually four animatronics—each built to allow Charlie to grow up. Her "youngest" incarnation was the Ella doll, while her "oldest" was unfinished, completed by William Afton, and ultimately possessed by Elizabeth Afton.

Appearances: *The Silver Eyes, The Twisted Ones, The Fourth Closet*

CHICA: A yellow animatronic chicken, wears a bib that says LET'S EAT! Chica carries a plate with an anthropomorphic pink cupcake that seems to have a life of its own. Chica can often be found in the kitchen in various games, and generally approaches players from the right. Chica was confirmed to be possessed by Susie in the Fazbear Frights story "Coming Home."

Appearances: *FNAF, FNAF2* (mini game/hallucinations), *FNAF3* (mini game), *FNAF4* (mini game), *Ultimate Custom Night, Help Wanted, Curse of Dreadbear, Special Delivery, The Silver Eyes, The Twisted Ones, The Fourth Closet,* "Coming Home," "The New Kid," "What We Found," "Pizza Kit," "Sea Bonnies," "Find Player Two!"

CHOCOLATE BONNIE:

A holiday-themed animatronic skin for the Bonnie plush suit in *Special Delivery.*

Appearances: *Special Delivery*

CIRCUS BABY (BABY): A humanoid animatronic and the mascot of Circus Baby's Pizza World. Circus Baby is possessed by the spirit of Elizabeth Afton, William Afton's daughter, who was snatched by the animatronic after being told to stay away from her. After the possession, Circus Baby's eyes turned green. Circus Baby assists in her father's plans, particularly in *The Fourth Closet*. In *Sister Location*, she orchestrates the escape of the animatronics from Circus Baby Entertainment and Rental.

Appearances: *Sister Location, Ultimate Custom Night, Help Wanted, Special Delivery, The Fourth Closet,* "Dance with Me"

CLOWN SPRINGTRAP: A circus-themed animatronic skin for the Springtrap plush suit in *Special Delivery*.

Appearances: *Special Delivery*

COILS THE BIRTHDAY CLOWN: A clown animatronic with a lanky body and coiled arms, dressed in a lemon-and-lime striped costume with bells. The animatronic seems to have some sort of awareness or safety features, since it tries to rescue Colton in "Jump for Tickets."

Appearances: "Jump for Tickets"

THE CURSE: An Aztec-themed animatronic skin for the Springtrap plush suit in *Special Delivery*.

Appearances: *Special Delivery*

DEEDEE: A humanoid animatronic with a similar design to BB and JJ. She complicates *Ultimate Custom Night* by triggering a whole new set of animatronics at random. She also seems to have her own arcade game (DeeDee's Fishing Game), as seen in "Jump for Tickets."

Appearances: *Ultimate Custom Night,* "Jump for Tickets" (referenced)

DREADBEAR (FRANKEN FREDDY):
An animatronic Frankensteined with stitching and neck bolts in the likeness of Freddy Fazbear. His feet have three toes (matching the toy animatronics), while his hands have five fingers (matching the nightmare animatronics). Dreadbear appears as part of a research and development game, where players must program his brain.

Appearances: *Curse of Dreadbear*

EASTER BONNIE:
A holiday-themed animatronic skin for the Bonnie plush suit in *Special Delivery*.

Appearances: *Special Delivery*

EGG BABY:
An animatronic featuring a data archive. It's key to unlocking some of the secrets in *Pizzeria Simulator*.

Appearances: *Pizzeria Simulator, Ultimate Custom Night*

EL CHIP:
A beaver animatronic that wears a sombrero and plays a mandolin. El Chip is purchasable as an animatronic in *Pizzeria Simulator*, but appears in *Ultimate Custom Night* as the mascot for a restaurant, El Chip's Fiesta Buffet. In *Help Wanted*, he has his own branded tortilla chips.

Appearances: *Pizzeria Simulator, Ultimate Custom Night* (referenced), *Help Wanted* (referenced)

ELEANOR:
A humanoid animatronic resembling Circus Baby, found deactivated in a junkyard. Eleanor possesses a special heart-shaped pendant that seemingly allows her to change form at will, whether her own form or that of another.

Appearances: "1:35 A.M.," Stitchwraith Stingers

ELECTROBAB:
An electrified variation of the BidyBab, capable of draining power. Appears in the Private Room in *Sister Location*.

Appearances: *Sister Location*

ELLA: (Spoilers) A highly complex humanoid animatronic, the youngest incarnation meant to house Charlie's consciousness. After Charlie "grew out" of Ella's size, Henry reprogrammed her as a plaything for Charlie. She occupied a closet, and would exit it on a track to serve tea. It seems the doll was later mass-produced by Fazbear Entertainment as a "helper" doll with a variety of functions. The doll in "1:35 A.M." is later confirmed to contain Remnant.

Appearances: *The Silver Eyes, The Twisted Ones, The Fourth Closet,* "1:35 A.M.," *Stitchwraith Stingers*

ENDO-01 (BARE ENDO): A simple animatronic endoskeleton that appears rarely in *FNAF* and *Help Wanted.* In *Special Delivery,* Endo-01 is referred to as "Bare Endo" and can be customized with different plush suits and CPUs.

Appearances: *FNAF, Help Wanted, Special Delivery*

ENDO-02: A sturdier animatronic endoskeleton, judging by its articulated joints, bulkier framing, and more complex electronics.

Appearances: *FNAF2, Help Wanted*

ENNARD:

A terrifying amalgamation formed from the "scooped" Sister Location animatronics (Ballora, Bon-Bon, Circus Baby, Funtime Foxy, Funtime Freddy). Ennard does not wear a typical plush suit, instead entering the body of Michael Afton. After abandoning Michael, Ennard was mainly controlled by Circus Baby. When the other animatronics kicked Baby out, Ennard was split into Scrap Baby and Molten Freddy.

Appearances: *Sister Location, Ultimate Custom Night, Help Wanted*

FETCH: A dog animatronic programmed to sync up with the user's phone and retrieve whatever the user needs. The animatronic was the "Top Prize" at an abandoned Freddy Fazbear's Pizza location. It's noted that the animatronic looks as though it was created before smartphone technology.

Appearances: "Fetch," *Stitchwraith Stingers*

FIREWORK FREDDY: A holiday-themed animatronic skin for the Freddy Fazbear plush suit in *Special Delivery*.

Appearances: *Special Delivery*

FLAMETHROWER BARE ENDO: A heat-wave-themed animatronic skin for Bare Endo (Endo-Ø1) in *Special Delivery*.

Appearances: *Special Delivery*

FLAMING SPRINGTRAP: A heat-wave-themed animatronic skin for the Springtrap plush suit in *Special Delivery*.

Appearances: *Special Delivery*

FOXY: An animatronic pirate fox with an eye patch over his right eye and a hook for his right hand. Foxy is housed on his own stage, Pirate Cove, separate from the other animatronics. The stage notes that Foxy is out of order, and his plush suit is damaged in places. He operates differently from the other animatronics, advancing in phases before attacking.

Appearances: *FNAF, FNAF2* (mini game), *FNAF3* (mini game), *FNAF4* (mini game), *Ultimate Custom Night, Help Wanted, Curse of Dreadbear, Special Delivery, The Silver Eyes, The Twisted Ones, The Fourth Closet,* "Lonely Freddy," "Step Closer," "The New Kid," "What We Found," "Sea Bonnies," *Stitchwraith Stingers*

FREDBEAR: A yellow bear spring lock animatronic with a purple bow tie and top hat, the first known animatronic Henry made, and the mascot of Fredbear's Family Diner. Fredbear is mentioned or shown in 8-bit from across several games, but only appears physically in *Ultimately Custom Night*. In *The Silver Eyes*, Henry is known to have worn the Fredbear suit.

Appearances: *FNF2* (mention), *FNAF3* (mini game), *FNAF4* (plush, mini game), *Ultimate Custom Night, The Silver Eyes* (mention), "The New Kid"

FREDDLES: Small nightmare animatronics similar in design to Nightmare Freddy. Freddles sometimes hang off Nightmare Freddy, and other times sprout from the bed behind you in *FNAF4*. They flee from your flashlight, similar to plush animatronics.

Appearances: *FNAF4, Ultimate Custom Night, Curse of Dreadbear*

FREDDY FAZBEAR: A light brown bear animatronic with a black bow tie and top hat, singer in the animatronic band, and the mascot of Freddy Fazbear's Pizza. When his face is enhanced, it reveals a handprint on his right eye and another across his lower jaw. His eyes change color from brown to blue when he appears outside the office door.

Appearances: *FNAF, FNAF2* (mini game/hallucinations), *FNAF3* (mini game), *FNAF4* (mini game), *Ultimate Custom Night, Help Wanted, Curse of Dreadbear, Special Delivery, The Silver Eyes, The Twisted Ones, The Fourth Closet,* "Into the Pit," "To Be Beautiful," "Lonely Freddy," "Out of Stock," "The New Kid," "Step Closer," "Blackbird," "Hide-and-Seek," "The Cliffs," "He Told Me Everything," "Gumdrop Angel," "What We Found," "Jump for Tickets," "Pizza Kit," "Friendly Face," "Sea Bonnies," "The Prankster," "Kids at Play," "Find Player Two!"

FROST PLUSHTRAP: A winter-themed animatronic skin for the Plushtrap plush suit in *Special Delivery*.

Appearances: *Special Delivery*

FUNTIME CHICA: A funtime animatronic with Chica's design. Funtime Chica debuted later than the other funtime animatronics; she first appears in *Pizzeria Simulator*.

Appearances: *Pizzeria Simulator, Ultimate Custom Night*

FUNTIME FOXY: A funtime animatronic with Foxy's design. Funtime Foxy is motion activated and lives in the Funtime Auditorium. The animatronic has several unique capabilities, as seen in its blueprint (see page 243).

Appearances: *Sister Location, Ultimate Custom Night, Help Wanted, The Fourth Closet*

FUNTIME FREDDY: A funtime animatronic with Freddy Fazbear's design. Funtime Freddy contains a special arm that can be removed and replaced with a hand puppet animatronic like Bon-Bon or Bonnet. He has several other special features noted in his blueprint (see page 243), including a massive storage tank, as seen in "Count the Ways."

Appearances: *Sister Location, Ultimate Custom Night, Help Wanted, The Fourth Closet,* "Count the Ways"

GLITCHTRAP (THE ANOMALY): A virus replicating within *The Freddy Fazbear Virtual Experience* game. The virus appears as a man inside a Spring Bonnie animatronic, starting out as green, glitching code with purple eyes, and slowly becoming more solid. Glitchtrap seems capable of digital consciousness transference.

Appearances: *Help Wanted, Curse of Dreadbear, Special Delivery,* "In the Flesh," "The Prankster"

GOLDEN FREDDY: A yellow bear animatronic that appears to be nonfunctioning. Golden Freddy appears at random in the office and causes the game to crash. Though it holds some resemblance to the Fredbear animatronic, its true origins are unknown.

Appearances: *FNAF, FNAF2, FNAF3, Ultimate Custom Night, Special Delivery*

GRIMM FOXY: A flaming animatronic that uses Foxy's design, but replaces his hook with a scythe.

Appearances: *Curse of Dreadbear*

HANDUNIT/TUTORIAL UNIT: A monitor at various Fazbear Entertainment locations that's designed to help guide workers through their nightly duties.

Appearances: *Sister Location, Pizzeria Simulator, Help Wanted, Curse of Dreadbear, Special Delivery*

HAPPY FROG: A frog animatronic, part of the Mediocre Melodies. It's unconfirmed, but a child in the *FNAF3 Happiest Day* mini game appears to be wearing a Happy Frog mask.

Appearances: *Pizzeria Simulator, Ultimate Custom Night*

HEARTSICK BABY: A holiday-themed animatronic skin for the Circus Baby plush suit in *Special Delivery*.

Appearances: *Special Delivery*

HIGHSCORE TOY CHICA: An arcade-themed animatronic skin for the Toy Chica plush suit in *Special Delivery*.

Appearances: *Special Delivery*

JACK-O-BONNIE: A nightmare animatronic designed after Bonnie, with a jack-o'-lantern twist.

Appearances: *FNAF4 (Halloween DLC), Ultimate Custom Night, Curse of Dreadbear*

JACK-O-CHICA: A nightmare animatronic designed after Chica, with a jack-o'-lantern twist.

Appearances: *FNAF4 (Halloween DLC), Ultimate Custom Night, Curse of Dreadbear*

JJ (BALLOON GIRL): A humanoid animatronic similar to Balloon Boy, but with a different color scheme.

Appearances: *FNAF2, Ultimate Custom Night*

LEFTY: A rockstar animatronic with a bear design and microphone similar to Freddy, though his left eye seems to be broken. Lefty gets his name from an acronym—Lure Encapsulate Fuse Transport Extract—and has several special features according to his blueprint. Lefty is later shown to have the Puppet inside him.

Appearances: *Pizzeria Simulator, Ultimate Custom Night*

LIBERTY CHICA: A holiday-themed animatronic skin for the Chica plush suit in *Special Delivery*.

Appearances: *Special Delivery*

LITTLE JOE: A humanoid figure that appears hanging from the wall in Circus Control. It's unconfirmed if Little Joe is a functioning animatronic, but he does appear in the Lally's Lollies advertisement in *Pizzeria Simulator*.

Appearances: *Sister Location, Pizzeria Simulator*

LOLBIT: A Funtime, fox-themed animatronic with purple, orange, and white coloring.

Appearances: *Sister Location, Ultimate Custom Night, Help Wanted*

LONELY FREDDY: A series of smaller Freddy animatronics dispatched to various Freddy Fazbear's Pizza locations. The animatronics use patented technology to befriend misfit children and ultimately swap bodies.

Appearances: "Lonely Freddy"

LUCKY BOY: A small, ten-inch figurine roughly matching the design of Balloon Boy. Instead of a sign saying BALLOONS!, Lucky Boy's sign says I'M A LUCKY BOY. Lucky Boy can speak and give advice. He's found on the street, near a Dumpster.

Appearances: "Sergio's Lucky Day"

MAGICIAN: A humanoid figure that appears on the dashboard in Circus Control. It's unconfirmed if Magician is just a toy or a functioning animatronic.

Appearances: *Sister Location*

MAGICIAN MANGLE: A circus-themed animatronic skin for the Mangle plush suit in *Special Delivery*.

Appearances: *Special Delivery*

MANGLE: He was previously a Foxy animatronic, but now she's an amalgamation of various animatronics—part of a "take apart, put back together" attraction in Kid's Cove. Mangle features in his own game, "Build-A-Mangle," in *Curse of Dreadbear*, in which players can create their own Mangle from various animatronic parts.

Appearances: *FNAF2, FNAF3, FNAF4, Ultimate Custom Night, Help Wanted, Curse of Dreadbear, Special Delivery, The Fourth Closet*

MELTED CHOCOLATE BONNIE: A holiday-themed animatronic skin for the Bonnie plush suit in *Special Delivery*.

Appearances: *Special Delivery*

MINIREENAS: Small, puppetlike dolls with tutus and white face masks. Minireenas typically accompany Ballora, and are stored with her in the Ballora Gallery. They're capable of speech and of organizing to achieve their goals, as seen in "Room for One More."

Appearances: *Sister Location, Ultimate Custom Night, Help Wanted, Special Delivery,* "Room for One More"

MOLTEN FREDDY: A crumbling amalgamation of animatronics (Ballora, Bon-Bon, Funtime Foxy, Funtime Freddy) formed after Circus Baby was ejected from Ennard. Eyeballs from the various animatronics can be seen poking out at random.

Appearances: *Pizzeria Simulator, Ultimate Custom Night*

MR. HIPPO: A hippo animatronic, part of the Mediocre Melodies. Mr. Hippo is quite long-winded; he loves to talk about his good friend, Orville Elephant. It's unconfirmed, but a child in the *FNAF3 Happiest Day* mini game appears to be wearing a Mr. Hippo mask.

Appearances: *Pizzeria Simulator, Ultimate Custom Night*

MUSIC MAN: A sound sensitive animatronic that appears to be a spider in the same family as the funtime animatronics. Music Man will smash his cymbals together when agitated.

Appearances: *Pizzeria Simulator, Ultimate Custom Night*

NEDD BEAR: A bear animatronic, part of the Mediocre Melodies.

Appearances: *Pizzeria Simulator, Ultimate Custom Night*

NIGHTMARE: A nightmare animatronic with inverted Fredbear coloring (black fur, yellow bow tie/top hat).

Appearances: *FNAF4, Ultimate Custom Night*

NIGHTMARE BALLOON BOY: A nightmare animatronic with a Balloon Boy design; he's notably missing his balloon and sign, and possesses fingers. He pauses in the light, per his mini game "Fun with Balloon Boy."

Appearances: *FNAF4* (Halloween DLC), *Ultimate Custom Night, Help Wanted*

NIGHTMARE BONNIE: A nightmare animatronic with a Bonnie design.

Appearances: *FNAF4, Ultimate Custom Night, Help Wanted, Curse of Dreadbear*

NIGHTMARE CHICA: A nightmare animatronic with a Chica design. Notably, Chica's cupcake can enter the bedroom and attack players there.

Appearances: *FNAF4, Ultimate Custom Night, Help Wanted, Curse of Dreadbear*

NIGHTMARE ENDO: A bare endoskeleton outfitted for the nightmare animatronics.

Appearances: *Help Wanted*

NIGHTMARE FOXY:

A nightmare animatronic with a Foxy design, notably missing his eye patch. In lieu of the Pirate Cove stage, Nightmare Foxy cycles through various poses via the bedroom closet.

Appearances: *FNAF4, Ultimate Custom Night, Curse of Dreadbear*

NIGHTMARE FREDBEAR: A nightmare animatronic with a Fredbear design; notably has a large slit across his stomach and bloodstained teeth. You can hear his now-infamous laughter as he approaches.

Appearances: *FNAF4, Ultimate Custom Night, Help Wanted*

NIGHTMARE FREDDY: A nightmare animatronic with a Freddy Fazbear design; three miniature animatronics, called "Freddles," are attached to his body.

Appearances: *FNAF4, Ultimate Custom Night, Curse of Dreadbear*

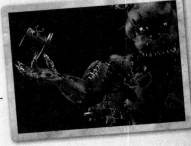

NIGHTMARE MANGLE: A nightmare animatronic with a Mangle design; notably possesses a bulkier endoskeleton with three legs

Appearances: *FNAF4 (Halloween DLC), Ultimate Custom Night*

NIGHTMARIONNE: A nightmare animatronic with a Puppet design. The Puppet's music box plays while Nightmarionne is active, but there is no mechanic (such as keeping the box wound) that can prevent its attack.

Appearances: *FNAF 4 (Halloween DLC), Ultimate Custom Night, Help Wanted, Special Delivery*

OLD MAN CONSEQUENCES:
An 8-bit sprite who sits fishing at a pond and urges players to rest and avoid digging too deep.

Appearances: *Ultimate Custom Night*

ORVILLE ELEPHANT:
An elephant magician animatronic, part of the Mediocre Melodies. Orville is good friends with Mr. Hippo. It's unconfirmed, but a child in the FNAF3 Happiest Day mini game appears to be wearing an Orville Elephant mask.

Appearances: *Pizzeria Simulator, Ultimate Custom Night*

PHANTOM BALLOON BOY:
A phantom animatronic, hallucinated with a Balloon Boy design; notably missing his balloon and sign.

Appearances: *FNAF3, Ultimate Custom Night, Help Wanted*

PHANTOM CHICA:
A phantom animatronic, hallucinated with a Chica design. Phantom Chica does not carry a cupcake.

Appearances: *FNAF3, Ultimate Custom Night*

PHANTOM FOXY:
A phantom animatronic, hallucinated with a Foxy design.

Appearances: *FNAF3, Help Wanted*

PHANTOM FREDDY:
A phantom animatronic, hallucinated with a Freddy design.

Appearances: *FNAF3, Ultimate Custom Night, Help Wanted*

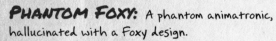

PHANTOM MANGLE: A phantom animatronic, hallucinated with a Mangle design.

Appearances: *FNAF3, Ultimate Custom Night, Help Wanted*

PHANTOM PUPPET: A phantom animatronic, hallucinated with a Puppet design.

Appearances: *FNAF3*

PHONE GUY: A former night guard at Freddy Fazbear's Pizza, responsible for training the new night guard. His lessons can be heard via the answering machine and can sometimes be a challenging distraction for players.

Appearances: *FNAF, FNAF2, FNAF3, Ultimate Custom Night, Help Wanted*

PIGPATCH: A pig animatronic that plays the banjo, part of the Mediocre Melodies. It's unconfirmed, but a child in the FNAF3 Happiest Day mini game appears to be wearing a Pigpatch mask.

Appearances: *Pizzeria Simulator, Ultimate Custom Night, "The Puppet Carver"*

PLUSHBABIES: Small plush doll animatronics, made with Circus Baby's design. The classic PlushBaby comes in red, yellow, and blue dress colors. There's also a variation that's modeled after Scrap Baby. A third variation, the Plushkin, dons a BB, Chica, Foxy, or Freddy mask. Much like other plush animatronics, they flee from light.

Appearances: *Help Wanted, Curse of Dreadbear*

PLUSHTRAP: A smaller plush animatronic, made with Springtrap's design. Like other plush animatronics, it flees or freezes in light. A variation of Plushtrap, called the Plushtrap Chaser, was mass-produced and distributed by Fazbear Entertainment.

Appearances: *FNAF4, Ultimate Custom Night, Help Wanted, Special Delivery, "Out of Stock"*

THE PUPPET (THE MARIONETTE): A puppet animatronic with a lanky black body, white stripes on his arms and legs, and a white face with painted cheeks and lips. The Puppet usually stays inside its gift box so long as its music box is wound. Henry's daughter, Charlotte, is confirmed to possess the Puppet. After her death, she helped William Afton's murder victims find new life—and a chance for revenge—in possessing the other animatronics.

Appearances: *FNAF2, FNAF3, Pizzeria Simulator, Ultimate Custom Night, Help Wanted*

RADIOACTIVE FOXY: A wasteland-themed animatronic skin for the Foxy plush suit in *Special Delivery*.

Appearances: *Special Delivery*

RALPHO: A rabbit mascot costume, or possibly animatronic, owned by Camp Etenia. Ralpho conducts "bunny calls" as a prank to unsuspecting campers between the hours of 5:00 a.m. and 6:00 a.m. Reportedly, he bursts into the cabin screaming, crashing his cymbals, and spinning his head.

Appearances: "Bunny Call"

RINGMASTER FOXY: A circus-themed animatronic skin for the Foxy plush suit in *Special Delivery*.

Appearances: *Special Delivery*

ROCKSTAR BONNIE: A rockstar animatronic with a Bonnie design.

Appearances: *Pizzeria Simulator, Ultimate Custom Night*

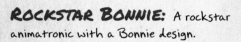

ROCKSTAR CHICA: A rockstar animatronic with a Chica design. Rockstar Chica is the only incarnation of Chica to not have a cupcake. Instead she holds maracas, and her bib reads LET'S ROCK!

Appearances: *Pizzeria Simulator, Ultimate Custom Night*

ROCKSTAR FOXY: A rockstar animatronic with a Foxy design. Rockstar Foxy has a peg leg, plays the accordion, and has a companion parrot that sits on his left shoulder.

Appearances: *Pizzeria Simulator, Ultimate Custom Night*

ROCKSTAR FREDDY: A rockstar animatronic with a Freddy design.

Appearances: Pizzeria Simulator, Ultimate Custom Night

RWQFSFASXC (SHADOW BONNIE): A shadow version of Toy Bonnie. Similar to Golden Freddy, doesn't appear to follow normal laws of physics, appearing and disappearing at will, phasing through various mini games in *FNAF3*, etc. In *Special Delivery*, Shadow Bonnie appears when the player collects too much dark Remnant.

Appearances: *FNAF2, FNAF3* (mini game), *Ultimate Custom Night, Curse of Dreadbear* (Easter egg), *Special Delivery*

SCORCHING CHICA: A heat-wave-themed animatronic skin for the Chica plush suit in *Special Delivery*.

Appearances: *Special Delivery*

SCRAP BABY: A humanoid animatronic, re-formed in the likeness of Circus Baby after she was ejected from Ennard.

Appearances: *Pizzeria Simulator, Ultimate Custom Night*

SCRAPTRAP: A tattered spring lock animatronic, a more worn version of Springtrap. Scraptrap sports a severed forearm, no ears, and some rotting, human-looking parts beneath his fur.

Appearances: *Pizzeria Simulator, Ultimate Custom Night*

SECURITY PUPPET: A puppet animatronic with security functions. Play-testing the Security Puppet in *Pizzeria Simulator* takes players to a mini game with lore implications for the Puppet.

Appearances: *Pizzeria Simulator, Ultimate Custom Night*

SERPENT MANGLE: An Aztec-themed animatronic skin for the Mangle plush suit in *Special Delivery*.

Appearances: *Special Delivery*

SHADOW FREDDY: A shadow bear animatronic. Similar to RWQFSFASXC, Shadow Freddy moves mysteriously, seemingly appearing/disappearing at random. Shadow Freddy also appears in 8-bit form in several mini games, guiding players through all the night-end mini games in *FNAF3*.

Appearances: *FNAF2, FNAF3, Pizzeria Simulator*

SHADOW MANGLE (BLACKLIGHT MANGLE): A shadow animatronic that looks similar to Mangle, but with different colored eyes. Attacks alongside Mangle in the blacklight level of Vent Repair: Mangle.

Appearances: *Help Wanted*

SHAMROCK FREDDY: A holiday-themed animatronic skin for the Freddy Fazbear plush suit in *Special Delivery*.

Appearances: *Special Delivery*

SPRING BONNIE: A yellow rabbit spring lock animatronic, one of the first created by Henry. Spring Bonnie was often worn by William Afton, who prided himself on effortlessly performing in the suit. He used the costume to gain the trust of, and ultimately murder, numerous children.

Appearances: *FNAF3* (mini game), *FNAF4* (mini game), *Pizzeria Simulator, Ultimate Custom Night* (Easter egg), *The Silver Eyes,* "Into the Pit"

SPRINGTRAP: A tarnished Spring Bonnie spring lock animatronic, fused with the corpse of William Afton, who continues to possess the animatronic.

Appearances: *FNAF3*, *Sister Location* (secret ending), *Ultimate Custom Night*, *Help Wanted*, *Curse of Dreadbear*, *Special Delivery*, *The Silver Eyes*, *The Twisted Ones*, *The Fourth Closet*, "*In the Flesh*," *Stitchwraith Stingers*

STANLEY: A white unicorn animatronic created by Henry for Charlie. Stanley travels on a track around Charlie's room.

Appearances: *The Silver Eyes*, *The Twisted Ones*, *The Fourth Closet*

STITCHWRAITH: An animatronic created by Dr. Phineas Taggart in his studies of emotion. It was formed from an endoskeleton, the doll from "*The Real Jake*," and the battery pack from the Fetch animatronic.

Appearances: *Stitchwraith Stingers*

SWAMP BALLOON BOY:

A forest-themed animatronic skin for the Balloon Boy plush suit in *Special Delivery*.

Appearances: *Special Delivery*

SYSTEM ERROR TOY BONNIE:

An arcade-themed animatronic skin for the Bonnie plush suit in *Special Delivery*.

Appearances: *Special Delivery*

TAG-ALONG FREDDY:

A stuffed bear that monitors a child's actions and reports them back to a parent via an accompanying wristwatch. The toy was mass-produced by Fazbear Entertainment and sold in stores.

Appearances: "*The Cliffs*"

THEODORE: A small purple rabbit animatronic created by Henry for Charlie. It could wave, tilt its head, and repeat a recording from Henry saying, "I love you, Charlie." Charlie later takes Theodore apart for her robotics project.

Appearances: *The Silver Eyes, The Twisted Ones, The Fourth Closet*

TOY BONNIE: A toy animatronic with a Bonnie design, featuring glossy green eyes and buck teeth.

Appearances: *FNAF2, FNAF3, FNAF4* (mini game), *Ultimate Custom Night, Help Wanted, Special Delivery*

TOY CHICA: A toy animatronic with a Chica design; her bib reads LET'S PARTY! After leaving the Show Stage in *FNAF2*, her eyes and bill are missing. Toy Chica stars in "Toy Chica: The High School Years" in *Ultimate Custom Night*, where she romantically pursues various animatronics.

Appearances: *FNAF2, FNAF3, FNAF4* (mini game), *Ultimate Custom Night, Help Wanted, Special Delivery*

TOY FREDDY: A toy animatronic with a Freddy design. In Ultimate Custom Night, he plays his own version of FNAF, *Five Nights with Mr. Hugs.*

Appearances: *FNAF2, FNAF3, FNAF4* (mini game), *Ultimate Custom Night, Help Wanted, Special Delivery*

TOXIC SPRINGTRAP: A wasteland-themed animatronic skin for the Springtrap plush suit in *Special Delivery.*

Appearances: *Special Delivery*

TRASH AND THE GANG: The cheapest "animatronics" to purchase in *Pizzeria Simulator*, this set is made up of Bucket Bob, Mr. Can-Do, Mr. Hugs, No. 1 Crate, and Pan Stan. In *Pizzeria Simulator*, Pan Stan can be seen sitting when a salvage animatronic entered the pizzeria through other means. In *Ultimate Custom Night*, Mr. Hugs plays a FNAF-like game with Toy Freddy.

Appearances: *Pizzeria Simulator, Ultimate Custom Night*

TWISTED BONNIE: A twisted animatronic with Bonnie's design; illusion disc technology makes him appear biological, with boils, spikes, and multiple rows of teeth.

Appearances: *The Twisted Ones*

TWISTED CHICA: A twisted animatronic with Chica's design; illusion disc technology makes her appear biological, with warts and a second mouth in her stomach. Although Twisted Chica was never seen in the book series, her existence is implied, and she appears in other media.

Appearances: *The Twisted Ones* (implied)

TWISTED FOXY: A twisted animatronic with Foxy's design; illusion disc technology makes him appear biological, with rotting flesh, barnacle-like growths, and too many teeth.

Appearances: *The Twisted Ones*

TWISTED FREDDY: A twisted animatronic with Freddy's design; illusion disc technology makes him appear biological, with lengthy talons and bubbling blisters eating his face.

Appearances: *The Twisted Ones*

TWISTED WOLF: A twisted animatronic of a gray wolf. A long mane runs over its back, turning into spikes when illusion disc technology is activated. Though Twisted Wolf debuted without a name, there is speculation that it could be a twisted version of Roxanne Wolf.

Appearances: *Pizzeria Simulator* (Easter egg), *Ultimate Custom Night* (Easter egg), *The Twisted Ones*

VR TOY FREDDY: An arcade-themed animatronic skin for the Toy Freddy plush suit in *Special Delivery*.

Appearances: *Special Delivery*

WITHERED BONNIE: A withered animatronic with a Bonnie design, notably missing his face.

Appearances: *FNAF2, Ultimate Custom Night, Help Wanted*

WITHERED CHICA: A withered animatronic with a Chica design, notably missing her arms and cupcake. Her design—less rounded frame, all-yellow legs, and three toes—also differs substantially from *FNAF*'s Chica.

Appearances: *FNAF2, Ultimate Custom Night, Help Wanted*

WITHERED FOXY: A withered animatronic with a Foxy design.

Appearances: *FNAF2, Help Wanted*

WITHERED FREDDY: A withered animatronic with a Freddy design.

Appearances: *FNAF2, Help Wanted*

WITHERED GOLDEN FREDDY: A withered animatronic with a Golden Freddy design.

Appearances: *FNAF2, Ultimate Custom Night*

WOODLAND TOY FREDDY:
A forest-themed animatronic skin for the Toy Freddy plush suit in *Special Delivery*.

Appearances: *Special Delivery*

XOR (SHADOW DEEDEE): A shadow animatronic of DeeDee, who appears to complicate your night in *Ultimate Custom Night*.

Appearances: *Ultimate Custom Night*

YARG FOXY: A pirate-themed animatronic with a Foxy design. This animatronic appears to really sell the pirate theme with a hook, peg leg, and eye patch.

Appearances: "Lonely Freddy"

YENNDO: A burly endoskeleton capable of supporting the funtime animatronics.

Appearances: *Sister Location*

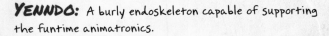

COLLECT THEM ALL!

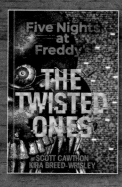

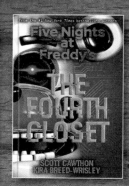

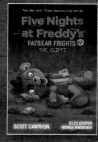